Georgine Kalil, Frances Kregler, Alan McElroy, Roisin Sweeny

Education For You

English for Jobs in Education

2. Auflage

Bestellnummer 30331

Bildungsverlag EINS
westermann

Die in diesem Produkt gemachten Angaben zu Unternehmen (Namen, Internet- und E-Mail-Adressen, Handelsregistereintragungen, Bankverbindungen, Steuer-, Telefon- und Faxnummern und alle weiteren Angaben) sind i. d. R. fiktiv, d. h., sie stehen in keinem Zusammenhang mit einem real existierenden Unternehmen in der dargestellten oder einer ähnlichen Form. Dies gilt auch für alle Kunden, Lieferanten und sonstigen Geschäftspartner der Unternehmen wie z. B. Kreditinstitute, Versicherungsunternehmen und andere Dienstleistungsunternehmen. Ausschließlich zum Zwecke der Authentizität werden die Namen real existierender Unternehmen und z. B. im Fall von Kreditinstituten auch deren IBANs und BICs verwendet.

Die in diesem Werk aufgeführten Internetadressen sind auf dem Stand zum Zeitpunkt der Drucklegung. Die ständige Aktualität der Adressen kann vonseiten des Verlages nicht gewährleistet werden. Darüber hinaus übernimmt der Verlag keine Verantwortung für die Inhalte dieser Seiten.

service@bv-1.de
www.bildungsverlag1.de

Bildungsverlag EINS GmbH
Ettore-Bugatti-Straße 6-14, 51149 Köln

ISBN 978-3-427-**30331**-2

westermann *GRUPPE*

Vorwort

Das Lehrwerk **Education For You** richtet sich an Lehrende, vor allem aber an junge Menschen, die sich in der Ausbildung zur Erzieherin und zum Erzieher befinden, sowie an Studierende der Sozialpädagogik beziehungsweise der Fachrichtung Erziehung und Bildung im Kindesalter. Es eignet sich für den fachsprachlichen Unterricht an Berufsschulen, Fachoberschulen und Hochschulen.

Das Buch ist für Lernende konzipiert, die über Vorkenntnisse auf der Mittelstufe verfügen. Seine Inhalte entsprechen den curricularen Vorgaben für das B2-Niveau des gemeinsamen europäischen Referenzrahmens.

In 13 Units werden Themenschwerpunkte aus verschiedenen Bereichen der frühkindlichen Bildung, der Sozialpädagogik und der Heilerziehung behandelt. Jede Unit umfasst drei Module, die jeweils unterschiedliche Aspekte des Hauptthemas behandeln. Die Module sind in sich abgeschlossen und können einzeln durchgearbeitet werden.

Education For You bietet sprachliche Übungen an, die ein abwechslungsreiches und handlungsorientiertes Lernen ermöglichen. Die Aufgaben sind sowohl für eine individuelle als auch für eine kooperative Bearbeitung konzipiert. In praxisnahen Texten, Case Studies und Aufgaben wie z. B. Activity-Tasks werden die Lernenden mit beruflichen Situationen des Alltags konfrontiert, welche die kommunikativen Fähigkeiten durch situationsgebundene Sprech- und Schreibanlässe fördern. Die Situationen haben die pädagogische Arbeit mit Krippenkindern, Jugendlichen und Menschen mit besonderen Bedürfnissen zum Gegenstand. Der allgemeinsprachliche Wortschatz wird durch die Arbeit mit dem Lehrbuch gefestigt und zu einem fachspezifischen Wortschatz ausgebaut.

Die Listening-Übungen sind zum Download zu finden
unter www.bildungsverlag1.de/audio-portal

Das Autorenteam wünscht viel Freude beim Lernen und viel Erfolg im Beruf!
Georgine Kalil, Frances Kregler, Alan McElroy und Roisin Sweeny

Contents

STARTER:
Getting to know each other

Who am I?

If you are planning to work with children and adolescents, now is a good time to reflect upon your childhood and all of the things that made you the person you are today. Naturally, parents, siblings, friends and teachers have all left lasting impressions on you, but significant and small experiences have shaped your personality as well. Have you ever thought about why you do things the way you do? Or, where your opinions and preferences come from?
You may already know the people in your class by name, but how well do you *really* know them? Before you get to know each other better, think about who you are first.

Activity

Task 1

Bring in a picture of yourself as a child and share it with a partner. Where and when was the picture taken? Is there anybody else in the picture? Do you remember the occasion? What were you doing? Ask each other questions to learn more about your childhood memories.

Task 2

Draw a picture of yourself. Don't worry – it doesn't have to be a work of art; it can be a simple figure. Designate each part of your body to an interesting fact about yourself. See the example on the next page.

Who am I?

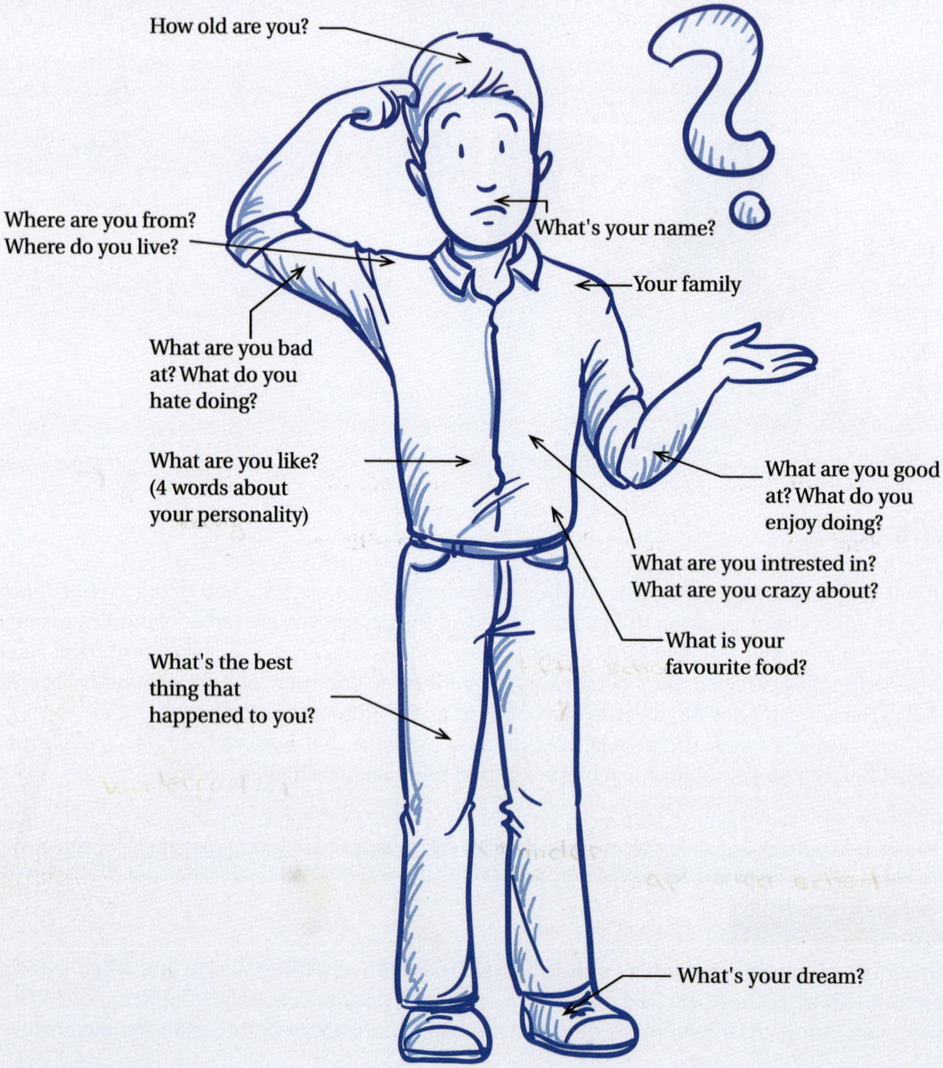

Task 3

Exchange drawings with a partner. Talk about the significance of the information in your picture. Ask questions to find out more about each other.

Activity

Task 4

Find out what you have in common with the other students in your class.

a. First, think of five interesting things about yourself, for example, “I was born in June”, “My favourite colour is yellow” etc.
b. Then, think of how you would ask someone to get similar information about themselves, i.e. “What month were you born in?”, “What’s your favourite colour?”.
c. Next, circulate around the class and ask each other questions. If you find somebody you have something in common with, write it down.
d. When you’ve finished interviewing each other, tell the class who you have things in common with.

Task 5

Look at the pictures below and choose a door that looks most inviting to you. It is the door to your future. Write a short piece about why you chose that door and what or where you think it leads to. Where do you think your future will take you? Write no more than 200 words. Exchange compositions with a partner and talk about your future plans.

UNIT 1:
Working with children – working in institutions of childcare

Module 1: The childcare professional – practitioners and their work settings

Little did Friedrich Fröbel know when he founded the first play and activity institute in Bad Blankenburg in 1837, that his concept of "kindergarten" would become so influential that the German word he coined would still be commonly used around the world today.
In fact, much more of Fröbel's work has become the foundation of early education in English-speaking countries.

Although the term "kindergarten" is used in many countries, it isn't always used to mean the same thing. Because the development of the educational system is historically different in each country, the words for some concepts and professionals are often culturally unique and thus difficult to translate into other languages.

The German word "Erzieher", for example, could be a *kindergarten* or *nursery school teacher*, an *educator*, a *childminder*, a *nanny*, or an *early childhood practitioner* largely depending on the setting the professional works in and the country.

The provision of childcare outside the home emerged contemporaneously with the Industrial Revolution when mothers of young children were increasingly drawn into the labour market. *Infant schools*, as they were called in Great Britain, or *salles d'asile*, literally "rooms of the asylum" in France were merely daytime refuges for children who were still too young to attend school, or work themselves. The minding of the children was left to young women who generally had no training and earned meagre wages for their work.

It became apparent rather quickly that these young children in the absence of their parents required specialised care and rearing. By the turn of the twentieth century the ideas of pedagogues like Pestalozzi, McMillan and Montessori had helped shape the education and training of childcarers throughout Europe, greatly improving the quality of care they provide and lending the occupation a professional profile.

Today childcare professionals work in a number of different settings. In Germany, roughly two-thirds of all childcare professionals work in preschool settings, including nursery schools, crèches and kindergartens, and after-school care clubs. In most anglophone countries, "kindergarten" denotes the year of education in a primary or elementary school prior to the first grade. However, in England this year is commonly referred to as "reception".

Childcare professionals are also employed in institutions of social welfare, such as approved or reform schools for delinquent juveniles, children's homes, youth centres, recreation programmes, welfare agencies for children and youth, and children's wards in hospitals. Additionally, childcare professionals may work in institutions for the care, occupation and integration of people with mental and physical disabilities.

Comprehension

Task 1

The different names of childcare professionals and their work settings can be confusing. Try to match the term with its description. Use a dictionary to help you.

after-school care club	approved school	childminder	educator
kindergarten	nanny	nursery	reception

a. a general word for a teacher or an instructor, particularly in a school or university
b. the first year of compulsory schooling in England
c. a place school-aged children can go after school
d. a preschool setting for children 0–3 years
e. a person, usually a woman, who is privately employed to rear children in their homes
f. a non-compulsory year of education for children before they enter first grade in the United States
g. a registered professional day carer who works in their own home and provides care for up to three children under the age of five
h. an institution which educates and disciplines errant youths

Task 2

Not everybody is suited to become a childcare professional. There are certain qualities a person should naturally have or develop to be able to work with children competently. Look at the words in the box and decide which of these personal attributes a childcare professional should have. Discuss your choices.

affectionate	alert	boring	calm	caring
cheerful	cold	conceited	considerate	cooperative
creative	dishonest	enthusiastic	friendly	honest
immature	impatient	inattentive	inconsiderate	indifferent
interested	interesting	intolerant	irresponsible	mature
observant	open-minded	organised	patient	polite
prejudiced	punctual	relaxed	respectful	responsible
sympathetic	tolerant	trusting	unimaginative	untrustworthy

Task 3

a. Using the adjectives from the box in Task 2, find as many antonym pairs as you can. Some words have more than one possible antonym. Use a dictionary to help you. A first pair has been done for you.

alert ≠ inattentive

b. Now, see how many noun forms correspond to the adjectives in the box and add them to the list. A first pair has been done for you.

honest	honesty

Task 4

What about you? Which of these attributes would you use to describe yourself? Now, choose a partner you know well and see how similar you are.

Grammar

Simple present tense

We usually use the simple present when we talk about:

- permanent conditions and states, including possession, relationships, illness and characteristics,
- facts and opinions,
- actions that happen all the time or on a regular basis,
- habitual actions.

Affirmative	Negative	Question Negated Question
I work at a kindergarten.	*I do not work at a kindergarten.* *I don't work at a kindergarten.*	*Do I work at a kindergarten?* *Don't I work at a kindergarten?*
You work at a kindergarten.	*You do not work at a kindergarten.* *You don't work at a kindergarten.*	*Do you work at a kindergarten?* *Don't you work at a kindergarten?*
Ann works at a kindergarten. *She works at a kindergarten.*	*She does not work at a kindergarten.* *She doesn't work at a kindergarten.*	*Does Ann work at a kindergarten?* *Doesn't she work at a kindergarten?*
We work at a kindergarten.	*We do not work at a kindergarten.* *We don't work at a kindergarten.*	*Do we work at a kindergarten?* *Don't we work at a kindergarten?*
They work at a kindergarten.	*They do not work at a kindergarten.* *They don't work at a kindergarten.*	*Do they work at a kindergarten?* *Don't they work at a kindergarten?*

Take a look at these examples:

permanent conditions and states	*St. Mary's Nursery School accepts children under the age of three.*
possession	*The mittens don't belong to Elena.*
illness	*Jacob has a hearing impairment.*
characteristics	*Cole doesn't like cabbage.*
fact	*Grace is five years old.*
opinion	*I think she is ill.*
actions that happen on a regular basis, habitual actions	*The children brush their teeth after breakfast.*

Task 5

What do the children do all week? Look at the schedule and write down the group's weekly activities using appropriate verbs in the simple present tense. A couple of examples have been done for you.

On Monday mornings the Busy Bees sing songs.
The Busy Bees sing songs on Monday mornings.

	Busy Bees' Weekly Activities	
	Morning	Afternoon
Monday	singing	playground
Tuesday	art	yoga
Wednesday	storytime	science
Thursday	outing	music
Friday	free play	playground

Task 6

You are a childcare practitioner in a preschool and you and your colleague are responsible for planning the group's daily activities for children age four and five. What would your typical day look like? Use the simple present to prepare an activity schedule from 8 a.m. to 4 p.m.

Task 7

Early years teachers have a demanding job and a multitude of responsibilities. Use these verbs in the left column with one of the activity descriptions in the right column to form meaningful sentences about their typical tasks. The first one has been done for you.

Early years teachers ... ***assist the children with the development of basic skills.***

assist	... a curriculum with a wide-range of activities that promote children's curiosity and knowledge.
devise	... a positive and supportive working relationship with children, staff members and parents.
encourage	... care and support to children in a secure environment.
ensure	... children's creative development through stories, arts and imaginative play.
maintain	... each child on an individual basis and record their progress.
observe	... the children with the development of basic skills.
provide	... the children's learning abilities through the access to new experiences.
stimulate	... that the health and safety of children is maintained during activities, both inside and outside.

Task 8

What kind of day-to-day difficulties could you expect to have as a childcare practitioner? Write a short paragraph about what you see in the cartoon. Discuss your ideas as a group.

Module 2: A day in the life of a childcare professional

20-year-old Vivien Young works as an early years preschool assistant in Birmingham. She has a diploma in Health and Social Care, but is currently studying Children's Care, Learning and Development at a local college.

Vivien's day begins at half past eight in the morning when she signs in. First she liaises with the other staff members and starts to organise the morning's activities. Vivien greets the children and their parents as they start arriving at a quarter to nine. By quarter past nine, all of the children have arrived and they can begin "Circle Time". Vivien takes the register and talks to the children about the weekly theme, the weather and the types of clothes that are appropriate for that day. She usually reads the children a story that is relevant to the weekly theme.

They go outside until half past ten, and when they come back in, Vivien helps the children wash their hands and prepares a fruit snack for them. At quarter to eleven the children get to choose which activity they'd like to do: crafts, construction toys, or dramatic play. While they're occupied with their activities, Vivien goes around playing with the children and noting any important observations.

Shortly before noon, she supervises the children with the tidying up. Once they have put everything away, Vivien helps the children take out their lunch boxes and makes sure that any children with food allergies do not eat foods they do not tolerate.

After lunch Vivien takes some of the children with developmental difficulties to the local education authority setting, where they will receive special attention. There she talks to the staff and reports any information.

She's back at the preschool by one o'clock to start setting up the afternoon activities using their planning sheets. While the children get dressed to go outside, Vivien checks the playground and makes sure the equipment is safe and in working order.

At around two o'clock they all have a snack and some juice. The children have time for free play until their parents come to collect them at three o'clock. Vivien signs the children out as they are picked up and passes on any important information to the parents and answers their questions. If a child has had an accident, Vivien asks the parents to sign the accident record book.

Before Vivien can go home, there are a few more things that need to be done. She clears the setting and checks to see if everything is safe and in order. She looks to see whether any belongings were left behind and puts them in the lost property bin. Then she makes sure the heating is off and all the windows and doors have been secured. When her colleagues have completed their tasks, they exchange ideas about the next day and finish up. Vivien goes home at four o'clock after a long and exhausting day.

Comprehension

Task 1

What is Vivien Young's typical day like? Complete an activity schedule using the simple present tense. Write the schedule on a separate piece of paper or in your notebook. An example has been done for you.

8:30 a.m.	Vivien signs in at 8:30 in the morning.
9:15 a.m.	At 9:15 a.m. Vivien…

Task 2

Vivien Young's job is demanding and multifaceted. Not only is she responsible for the health and safety of the children, but also for their emotional and physical development and the acquisition of social skills. Together with a partner, find the tasks and activities in the text that correspond to these responsibilities and complete the table below. Can you think of any more?

Health	Safety	Physical Development	Emotional Development	Social Skills
			greets the children	

Grammar

Present progressive tense

We usually use the present progressive when we talk about:

- actions that are happening at the moment of speaking,
- actions that are temporary,
- repeated actions,
- developments and changes,
- things that are about to happen.

Affirmative	Negative	Question Negated Question
I am taking a break. *I'm taking a break.*	*I am not taking a break.* *I'm not taking a break.*	*Am I taking a break?* *Aren't I taking a break?*
You are taking a break. *You're taking a break.*	*You are not taking a break.* *Your're not / You aren't taking a break.*	*Are you taking a break?* *Aren't you taking a break?*
Ann is taking a break. *Ann's taking a break.*	*She is not taking a break.* *She's not / She isn't taking a break.*	*Is Ann taking a break?* *Isn't she taking a break?*
We are taking a break. *We're taking a break.*	*We are not taking a break.* *We're not / We aren't taking a break.*	*Are we taking a break?* *Aren't we taking a break?*
They are taking a break. *They're taking a break.*	*They are not taking a break.* *They're not / They aren't taking a break.*	*Are they taking a break?* *Aren't they taking a break?*

Take a look at these examples:

actions that are happening at the moment of speaking	*The children are listening to a story in the book corner.*
actions that are temporary	*The light isn't working.*
repeated actions	*Leah is having difficulty saying goodbye to her mum in the morning.*
developments and changes	*Emil's language skills are improving every day.*
things that are about to happen	*The children are going home in a few minutes.*

Task 3

Complete the sentences in the present progressive using the verbs and phrases in the box. Do the exercise on a separate piece of paper or in your notebook. The first one has been done for you.

a. Ssshh! The children are *having a nap.*
b. I'm afraid she cannot come to the phone at the moment. She ...
c. Quick! Matthew ...
d. It looks like we won't be going outside to play. It ...
e. What happened to Carla? Why ... she ...?
f. We have to go home now. It ...
g. I haven't seen the children for a long time. My goodness, they ...!

to cry – to change a baby's nappy – to get big – to get dark outside – to have a nap – to rain – to run away

Task 4

Tense discrimination is the ability to recognise and use the two different aspects of a tense. Can you discriminate between the simple and progressive aspects of the present tense? Read the following text and complete the sentences with the verbs from the box in the appropriate form. Place the adverbs in brackets in the correct positions. Not all of the verbs will be used. Do the exercise on a separate piece of paper or in your notebook.

draw – prepare – try – seem – flush – come – put – hit – care – have – seem – get – cry – get – undress – take

Miss Madeleine's mischief-makers

Miss Madeleine ...(1)... for five children; she is a live-in nanny. She ...(2)... to keep her tots occupied, but it ...(3)... they ...(4)... (constantly) themselves into mischief. In the morning, while she is getting one child dressed, the other one ...(5)... (already) himself again. And while she ...(6)... a meal for lunch in the kitchen, there's havoc in the nursery: James ...(7)... on the walls with markers. Sarah ...(8)... marbles in her mouth. Jude ...(9)... Asher and Asher simply ...(10)... Where's Peter? Oh no! He ...(11)... wax crayons down the toilet. Who ...(12)... to the rescue? Miss Madeleine, of course! She finally ...(13)... her break while the little darlings ...(14)... a nap.

Environment matters

The childcare environment can have a profound effect on the overall well-being of the children and the staff. Colour, lighting, sound and layout of a setting all influence a child's responsiveness as well as their ability to concentrate and learn.

Although nursery-aged children are particularly responsive to warm bright colours, too many primary colours can be over-stimulating or unsettling. Softer shades have a calming effect, and children are in fact less likely to show hyperactivity.

Likewise, sound levels in rooms have an impact on children's sensitivity. Carpeting, drapes and the height of a ceiling can help reduce excessive noise, producing an environment which is conducive to concentrated learning.

Both children and adults find a friendly and comfortable setting most inviting. For lack of space, rooms are usually used for more than one purpose. Therefore, the layout of the room should be flexible and the equipment and materials well-organised.

Spaces for children are full of toys and learning materials to provide ample opportunity for different types of play and activities. Dividing the space into separate areas for different kinds of learning can help children orient themselves in their setting, but also help the childcare provider monitor the children.

Comprehension

Task 5

a. Make a list of the words in the text that are unfamiliar to you. Try to understand their meanings from the context.

b. Now, find the words in the text which mean:

1. make smaller or less in amount
2. cause to feel anxious or uneasy
3. maintain regular surveillance over
4. the necessary items for a particular purpose
5. making a certain situation or outcome likely or possible
6. find one's position in a surrounding
7. long curtains
8. very great or intense
9. responding readily and with interest or enthusiasm
10. enough or more than enough of something

Grammar

Prepositions of place

Prepositions of place show someone's or something's position or location. Sometimes there's more than one possible choice. This can be confusing.

When do we use *at*?

- to talk about the position of something at a point, particularly at larger places, destinations, like airports, and meeting points or social institutions
- before the names of places or buildings, especially when we are thinking of the activity inside the place
- in front of proper nouns, like the names of institutions and addresses containing a house number
- to talk about being at someone's house or business

When do we use *in*?

- to talk about a dimensional position within a large area, like geographical location
- to talk about a position inside a three-dimensional space, including vehicles
- to talk about being within the surrounding environment
- to talk about being covered with or by a material

When do we use *on*?

- to talk about being at a dimensional position or on the surface of something
- to show that something is attached to something else
- to talk about a position by a lake or sea
- to talk about being inside some types of transport, e.g. on flight 587

We can use both *in* and *on* before nouns denoting enclosed open spaces, such as a field or on a surface, such as a window. However, *on* is used when the space is considered a surface, and in when the space is considered an area.

When do we use *over* and *above*?

- to show that something is higher than a particular point, but not touching it

When do we use *under*, *underneath*, *beneath* and *below*?

- to show that something is lower than a particular point

When do we use *near*, *by*, *next to*, *between*, *among and opposite*?

- to show that something is close to a particular point

Task 6

Which prepositions are used with these places? Choose an appropriate preposition and write a sentence for each of the words in the box. Use a dictionary if you need help.

bus	cot	cubby	door	first floor	fish tank	lavatory	
library	playground	row	shade	swing	table	tree	tricycle

Activity

Task 7

Imagine you had to design a preschool room. What would it look like? Which age group would it serve? What would you put in it? Work with a partner and design your own preschool room. Use the area words in the box to help you. Share your designs with the other groups. There's an example below to help you.

arts and crafts	baby hygiene	construction	cookery	domestic play
dramatic play	growing and living things interest table		listening	make-believe play
making music	manipulatives	natural materials	naptime area	puzzles and games
quiet time	sand and water	technology	sensory development	
small-world toys	workshop	writing and graphics		

Conversation with René Dietrich, 29, preschool teacher in Berlin

How did you become a preschool teacher?

René: Well, after I finished my secondary education, I got my vocational training in business for wholesale and foreign trade. I worked at a car dealership. Thereafter I knew I wanted to go to college, but I didn't know what I wanted to study. But before I could apply for college, I needed to earn my diploma first. So, I went to a vocational school for economics and got my vocational diploma. Then I decided to study social pedagogy in Berlin. My focus was actually in education – primarily in early childhood education and social politics. And now I'm here with the Friedenau Rascals, where I've been working for about a year now.

Did you have any practical experience?

René: Yes, I did a three-month internship at a youth club. I organised a hip-hop project for kids. I also worked at another youth recreation facility awhile which provided programmes and rooms music education. We helped organise lessons for youths who wanted to learn an instrument, or music rehearsals for teens who wanted to play in a band together. We would also help the kids set up concerts and stages for their performances.

Why did you decide to study social pedagogy?

René: Well, after having worked in business and trade so intensively, which was my personal area of expertise, I knew I wasn't going to learn much more that would truly interest me. I was more interested in working with people, the way people live together. And so, I thought about social pedagogy because it leads to many different professions which all have to do with psychology, education and social politics.

Had you ever considered working in a preschool?

René: No, I had never really considered this. I was indeed interested in early childhood education in my course of studies, but I didn't think that I would actually go into it professionally. In fact, I didn't even know during my course of studies that I would be able to work as a preschool teacher with my qualifications.

After you graduated from college you applied for jobs.

René: Yeah, then I finally made the decision! By then I knew I was interested in education because from experience I knew that working in social work projects often didn't lead anywhere. However, I did have my problems with school. I had thought about becoming a school social worker, but because I had had problems in school myself, I really didn't want to "go back to school". Since I really enjoyed working with young kids, I thought I'd try applying to preschools. I did apply to other jobs, too, because my primary goal was to find employment. But then, I was glad that I got a job at a preschool after all.

So, after a year, you can probably judge whether this profession is one you'd like to stay in, or not.

René: I can't say yet whether it will be my profession for life, but I can say that I am quite satisfied with where I am at the moment and the fact that I am learning new things every day. As long as I can learn new things, I have fun with what I do. My interests may change as I get older; but at the moment I can see myself working here for at least the next five or six years.

What kinds of things have you learned from your practical experience with children that you never learned in college? It's probably a very stressful job, isn't it?

René: It can be quite stressful at times. That's something they don't write in textbooks. Someone once said child-rearing is war, but is also very rewarding. Of course you always have to deal with power struggles with some kids. And it can be more difficult than anyone can imagine.

What are some of the positive things you experience in your preschool workaday life?

René: It's definitely being greeted in the morning. When I come to work in the morning there are always so many cheerful faces smiling at me. Kids come up and hug me. That's what I like about my job. I find it fascinating the way children can smile all the time. I'm also fascinated by the way they learn. They're under a constant inebriation of feelings of happiness because they are learning. I have to admit that I'm often envious of them. It's unfortunate that we gradually lose this ability. What I also like about my job is being a part of the whole, and being privileged to accompany these children in the first stage of their lives.

Comprehension

Task 8

Answer the following questions. Discuss your answers in a group.

a. What influenced René to become a preschool teacher?
b. What does René enjoy about being a preschool teacher?
c. In your opinion, what kind of personality should an early years practitioner have?

Task 9

What are some of the social benefits of having men as early childhood educators? How can children profit by this?

Module 3: Career opportunities – applying for a job

Finding a job

Listen to Sandra, Geoffrey, Julia and Claire talk about their qualifications. Use the table below to help you take notes. Copy the table onto a separate piece of paper. The transcription of the audio can be found on page 200 at the back of the book.

Name	Sandra	Geoffrey	Julia	Claire
Age				
Education				
Experience				
Skills / Interests				

Comprehension

Task 1

Once you have listened to all four people, find the job advert below that is best suited for each of them. Then explain your choice.

Job Advertisements

Title: Childminding Assistant
Terms of employment: permanent part-time
Working schedule: 22 hrs/week, Mon., Wed., Thurs. 8 AM–5.30 PM
Employer: Little Acorns Childminding Services
Salary: minimal wage
Experience: Previous experience would be an advantage but not essential as training will be provided.
Job description: Duties will involve assisting the childminder in the day to day care and supervision of children aged 6 months up to 5 years providing a fun, playful and stimulating environment. Successful applicants are required to provide an enhanced disclosure.

Title: Teacher Assistant
Working schedule: per diem, day shift, variable hours, up to 40 hours per week
Employer: Concord Hospital
Service Area: The Learning Centre
Minimum requirements: Must be at least 18 years of age and have a minimum of 9 credits in Early Childhood Education, or 3 ECE credits and 1,500 documented hours in a licensed childcare facility or completion of a 2 year vocational course in Early Childhood Education
Certifications: Current certification in Infant and Child CPR, and Basic First Aid preferred, or must be obtained within 6 months of employment.
Responsibilities: Works in close cooperation with classroom team members to encourage the social/emotional, cognitive and physical development of the children. Assists in planning and offering individual and group activities, participates in the orientation process for each new family. In the position you will be working with a teaching team caring for infants 8 weeks up to kindergarten aged children.

Title: Early Childhood Educator
Terms of employment: temporary, part time, day
Employer: Developmental Disabilities Association
Work setting: Child care centre
Salary: £10.70 hourly for 27.5 hours per week
Anticipated start date: As soon as possible
Education: completion of college/CEGEP/vocational or technical training
Credentials: Early Childhood Education Diploma or Degree
Experience: 1–2 years; with children who have special needs, children with an intellectual disability
Responsibilities: plan and develop child care and nursery school programs; provide supervision and guidance of daily activities; assess the developmental level of children; prepare progress reports and discuss with parents and other staff members; bathe, diaper and feed infants and toddlers; prepare and serve snacks

Title: Senior Youth Worker
Working pattern: full time, contract position
Employer: Islington Council
Service Area: Children's Services/Young People's Division
Salary: £33,110 – £35,738/35 per week
Job description: Toffee Park Youth Club is a dynamic and innovative youth project. We wish to recruit an energetic and committed individual to help us achieve our vision which is to create a listening and responsive service for young people. You will have successful experience of working with culturally diverse groups and young people at risk, with a passion for developing children and young people's skills, talents and achievement. You will have designed projects to encourage participation and involvement and have a strong track record in engaging with and inspiring young people. Candidates should be qualified to a minimum of level 4 in youth work and understand the value of youth work in young people's development.

Grammar

Comparison of adjectives

		Comparative form		Superlative form	
Rule 1: Adjectives with only one syllable	old shy cute	-er	older shyer cuter	the + -est	oldest shyest cutest
and adjectives with two syllables ending in *-er*, *-et*, *-le*, *-ow* and *-y*	tend*er* qui*et* feeb*le* sall*ow* angr*y*	-r	tenderer quieter feebler sallower angrier*	-st	tenderest quietest feeblest sallowest angriest*
Rule 2: Three letter adjectives (not ending on *-y* or *-w*) double the end consonant before adding the ending, e.g. fat → fatter → fattest, wet → wetter → wettest, fit → fitter → fittest					
***Rule 3:** Adjectives with more than three letters which end in *-y* and are not preceded by a vowel: the *-y* is replaced by an *-i* before the comparative or superlative ending, e.g. dirty → dirtier → dirtiest					
Rule 4: Adjectives with two syllables that do not end in *-er*, *-et*, *-le*, *-ow* and *-y*, and adjecti-ves with more than two syllables	helpful gifted nervous important adorable	more	more helpful more gifted more nervous more important more adorable	the most	the most helpful the most gifted the most nervous the most important the most adorable
Exceptions to the rules:	good / well → better bad → worse far → farther / further little / small → less much / many → more				
There are some adjectives that can use both comparative forms.					

Task 2

Using the table in task one, compare the applicants' qualities and qualifications. Use the adjectives in the box to help you. You may also use the adjectives found in Module 1, Task 2. An example has been done for you.

active	experienced	interesting	lively	mature	old
recent	reliable	tolerant	well-suited	young	

Sandra Hare is the oldest applicant.

Language

Writing a curriculum vitae

A typical CV (curriculum vitae) in the United Kingdom or resumé in the United States does provide information about one's skills, work experience, education and special interests, as well as one's contact information, but it does not usually include a photograph, family status, age, nationality or racial background, as this could lead to discriminatory or preferential treatment in the application process. Above all, the CV and covering letter should be brief.

Claire Peters
5 Priory Road • Warwick
Warwickshire CV34 4 • United Kingdom
52 83 37 71 • Email: cpeters@googlemail.com

Skills:	• nineteen years of experience working with children, all ages • First Aid and CPR certification • ability to communicate in British Sign Language • knowledge of dietary needs of children with food intolerance • computer literate • basic knowledge of Spanish
Work Experience:	
1996–2002	Ingfield Manor School worked with young children with physical disabilities and learning difficulties
1994–1995	Warwick Children's Centre assistant teaching, worked with children 2-4 yrs
1990–1992	Au pair in Sydney, Australia cared for infant and twin five-year olds
Education:	
1992–1996	North Warwickshire College BTEC Diploma in Children's Care, Learning and Development (equivalent to Level 3 Diploma Children and Young People's Workforce)
1987–1992	Warwick School, Surrey completion of Key Stage 4
Interests:	cooking, travelling and spending time with the family

Writing a covering letter

Claire Peters
5 Priory Road · Warwick
Warwickshire CV34 4 · United Kingdom
52 83 37 71 · Email: cpeters@googlemail.com

The **return address** (**letter head**) with or without the sender's name, can either be placed on the left or right margin, or in the middle.

20 January 2018

The **date** belongs either on the right margin or the left margin, but is usually placed between the return address and recipient's address.

Ms Andrea Randall
Developmental Disabilities Association
Clinic Drive
Cotton Road
Nuneaton
CV11 5TY

The **recipient's address** is always on the left margin

Dear Ms Randall,

The British-style **salutation** is always followed by a comma.

Re: Your advertisement in the Warwick Courier, 14 January 2017

The **regarding** is **line** not necessary, but it is a good idea in a covering letter to show which job advert you are responding to.

As you suggested in our recent telephone conversation, I am enclosing my resume for your consideration.

You should begin your introductory paragraph with the purpose of your letter.

You are looking for a temporary part-time child care professional with experience working with young children with special needs. I would like to draw your attention to my six-year working experience and the professional skills I have acquired over the years.

Why are you applying for the job? Why should the employer consider you?

As a mother of two school-aged children, I would describe myself as mature, experienced and responsible when it comes to working with children. I currently hold a level 3 Diploma in Childcare and Education qualification. I have six years of experience which include working in a day nursery with young children with physical disabilities and learning difficulties.

What kind of person are you? What credentials do you have?

I particularly enjoyed building close bonds with the children and working closely with parents to ensure they were supported in leaving their child with someone other than a family member for the first time. I work on a 1:1 basis with children who have additional needs, and plan activities which can easily be adapted depending on a child's individual needs.

You should also know that I regularly attend training courses including Makaton, how to overcome communication difficulties, and safeguarding.

You may call me anytime at 52 83 37 71 should you have questions. I look forward to hearing from you.

In the final paragraph, you should welcome the potential employer to contact you. Show your eagerness.

Sincerely,
Claire Peters
Claire Peters

The **closure** is always followed by a comma.

Enc.: CV, professional licence, letter of recommendation

Enclosures, also Encl.

Here are some guidelines to writing covering letters:

The date is written either:
20 January 2018 (UK-style)

January 20, 2018 (US-style)

It's best to write out the name of the month to avoid confusions.

The British-style salutation is always followed by a comma. In American-style letters the titles Mr., Mrs., Ms. and Dr. are followed by a full stop (.) and the salutation takes a comma or a colon after the recipient's name.

Dear Mrs Smith/Dear Mrs. Smith,

If you don't know the name of the person you are addressing, use:
Dear Sir or Madam,
To whom it may concern,

The subject matter is introduced in the *Re:* (regarding) line with a few key phrases. This is placed immediately following the salutation.

Unlike German letters, the body of the letter begins with the first word of the first paragraph after the salutation, and this is capitalised. The closure of the letter may use

Yours truly
Yours very truly
Sincerely yours
Kind regards

If you do not know who the recipient of the letter is and your salutation is either, *Dear Sir or Madam* or *To whom it may concern,* then you must end your letter with *Yours faithfully.*

At the very end of your covering letter, you should remember to point out that you are enclosing documentation of your qualifications. Below the closure and signature, you should include the abbreviation for *enclosed*: *Enc. or Encl.* followed by the documents which are to be enclosed with the covering letter.

Here are some useful suggestions for your letter:

Introductory paragraph	*I am replying to your advertisement in the ....* *I read your advertisement in The Daily Paper and would like to apply for the position as ....*
Middle paragraph	*At present I am employed at ....* *I recently completed my three-year training course in ....*
Closing paragraph	*I would be very happy to discuss further questions in a personal interview.* *I am looking forward to hearing from you soon.*

Activity

Task 3

Use a newspaper or an employment database on the Internet to find a job that interests you. Then prepare your application as if you were applying for the job: write a CV and a covering letter. Trade job applications with a partner and compare.

Grammar

Asking questions

There are two types of questions: yes-no questions and specific questions. Yes-no questions seek a confirmation of information, whereas specific questions seek detailed information. Almost all questions require an auxiliary verb (e.g. be, have, do). Which auxiliary verb is needed depends on the type of main verb and its tense and aspect.

If the main verb is the stative verb *be* preceding a quality or attribute, another auxiliary verb is not needed. If the sentence already contains an auxiliary verb or a modal verb (e.g. can, will), the subject and auxiliary verb are simply inverted. Look at these examples:

***She is** disabled.*	***Is she** disabled?*
They are at home.	*Are they at home?*
I will help you.	*Will you help me?*
She will be home at six o'clock.	*When will she be home?*
She can speak three languages.	*How many languages can she speak?*

Sentences in the simple present and simple past tenses:

If the main verb is an action verb, the auxiliary verb *do* (*does, did*) is needed.

*They **live** in Cologne.*	***Do** they **live** in Cologne?*
*She **works** in Bonn.*	***Does** she **work** in Bonn?*
We don't live in England.	*Where do you live?*
*I **worked** in a kindergarten.*	*Where **did** you **work**?*

Sentences in the present and past progressive and present perfect:

The auxiliary verb is inverted with the subject.

*I **am getting** ready to go home.*	*Are you **getting** ready to go home?*
*He's **going** home at five o'clock.*	*When **is** he **going** home?*
*They **were playing** on the playground.*	*What **were** they **doing**?*
*I **have worked** at a nursery for two years.*	*How long **have** you **worked** at a nursery?*

Task 4

At a job interview you are asked many questions. Complete the questions below with an appropriate question word or auxiliary verb. Do the exercise on a separate piece of paper or in your notebook.

a. *When* did you finish your teacher training?
b. ...(1)... do you want to be a teacher?
c. ...(2)... are your strengths and weaknesses?
d. ...(3)... did you previously work?
e. ...(4)... did you quit your previous job?
f. ...(5)... would you define a good teacher?
g. ...(6)... would you define an ideal classroom?
h. ...(7)... you know CPR?
i. ...(8)... you qualified in sign language?

Activity

Task 5

In the last task activity, you prepared your job application. Congratulations! You have been invited to a job interview. This can be a daunting task, so you ought to be prepared. Make a list of questions you could expect to be asked at a job interview. How would you answer them? Conduct a mock job interview with a partner.

UNIT 2:
Protecting children

Module 1: What is child safeguarding?

What is the difference between child protection and child safeguarding?

Alison Watts works as a child safeguarding officer for schools and learning in the north of England. She explains what it means:

Until a few years ago, we talked about child protection, and it meant to protect children from abuse and neglect. Now we talk about child safeguarding. The two words have very similar meanings but the concept behind child safeguarding is broader. It includes the idea that as well as being protected from abuse, children also need to grow up healthy and well cared for, with nothing to impair their health or development.

Any organisation which offers services or activities to children has a duty – both legal and moral – to safeguard the children it works with. Safeguarding means "to keep safe from harm". In the workplace it means that you need to do everything possible to protect children's physical and emotional well-being while they are there. So you must do everything that you can to reduce the risk of children coming to harm while they are with you, but you should also know what to do if you believe a child to be suffering from harm from outside the workplace.

When we talk about safeguarding we also talk about keeping children safe from "significant harm". If we believe that a child is at risk of significant harm, it means that we think that the child might be suffering from abuse. It's very important that everybody who works with a child at risk (doctors, other health workers, care workers, social workers, educators and teachers) all communicate with each other and share important information. A lack of communication has led to problems in the past, although of course it is also important to remember confidentiality.

Even if children attend your workplace with one or both of their parents, you still have a responsibility to make sure that the children are safe. Accidents can happen even with parents there. That is why you should always carry out an assessment of all possible risks, and put a plan in place to reduce any risks to a minimum.

Comprehension

Task 1

Find four key words or phrases from the text which match the definitions below.

a. physical or sexual or emotional mistreatment
b. to fail to care for or pay attention to
c. in danger
d. to hinder
e. keeping personal information private

Task 2

Are the following statements true or false?

a. The verb *to safeguard* has a meaning that is almost the same as the verb *to protect.*
b. The term *child protection* includes more than *child safeguarding.*
c. *To come to harm* means to have something happen that hurts you in some way.
d. When you work with children, you only need to think about any harm which might come to them in your workplace.

Task 3

Work in pairs. Each of you chooses two of the words in italics in the questions below and explains them to the partner. Use a dictionary to help you if necessary.

Here is an extract from a risk assessment. It shows the type of questions which professionals (social workers, teachers, early learning workers, health visitors) might have to answer about a child they are working with.

a. Are there any *concerns?*
b. Is there any known history of abuse?
c. Does the child have a lot of *injuries?*
d. Has the child been in hospital for any of these injuries?
e. Does the child appear *well-fed* and clean?
f. Are there any other signs of neglect?
g. Does the child have any problems with his or her *behaviour*?
h. If yes, what kind of problems (e.g. aggression, *inappropriate* sexualised behaviour)?
i. Do you believe the child to be at risk?

Task 4

Have you ever heard about a case where child safeguarding went wrong? A case in Germany when people were working with a child at risk, but the child was still hurt? Discuss this with your neighbour.

On the telephone

Part A

- Hello, Children and Families, can I help you?
- Hello, could I speak to Aneesha please?
- Speaking.
- Oh hi, Aneesha. This is Sarah Redmond, I'm calling from Lorimer Children's Centre, I run the Family Learning Sessions there. I got a message to call you.
- Hi Sarah, thanks very much for getting back to me. Yes, I wanted to speak to you about a child who I believe attends your sessions. His name is Jaydon Blake. Do you know this little boy?
- Yes I do. He comes in with his mum, they probably attend around half the time.
- That's great. Do you think I could ask you some questions? His mother has given me consent for me to talk to you. The reason is that there are some concerns about Jaydon's well-being, and I'd really welcome your input. I've just started working with the family, and you've spent much more time with him and his mum.
- Yes that's fine, do you want to ask me now?
- I'm a bit busy right now, but perhaps we could chat later this afternoon, or tomorrow?
- Later today would be great, shall I give you a call around 4 pm?
- Yes, that's fine.
- Ok, speak to you then, bye.
- Bye!

Part B

- Well, thanks very much for your input Sarah.
- Is there anything that I should do?
- Just keep an eye on Jaydon, and see how he is in the sessions. If you see anything which gives you concerns, you should contact me as soon as possible. I have to write up a report, then we'll have to have a Team Around the Child meeting. Have you been to one before?
- Yes, once, about a year ago.
- Good, so you'll know what to expect. Everyone who works with the family must keep in touch with each other, although we should avoid giving any confidential details unless it's absolutely necessary. It's purely on a need to know basis, where we believe there is a risk of harm to Jaydon.
- Should I tell the other staff in the children's centre?
- No, you don't have to tell people who have no contact with the family. The only person you should tell is your line manager, who ought to be aware of what's happening. What we mustn't do is to alarm or frighten Jaydon. We are here to give help and support when it's needed, we mustn't be seen as punishing either Jaydon or his mother.

Comprehension

Task 5

Listen to the first part of the conversation and answer these questions.

a. Where does Sarah work and where does Aneesha work?
b. Who made the first contact, Aneesha or Sarah?
c. Which of the two professionals has the most contact with the little boy?

Task 6

Listen to the first part of the conversation again and complete the following phrases, useful for making telephone calls.

a. How does Aneesha identify herself on the phone? ...(1)...
b. How does Sarah identify herself on the phone? ...(2)...
c. How does Sarah say where she works? "...(3)... Lorimer Children's Centre."
d. How does Aneesha thank Sarah for calling? "Thanks very much ...(4)..."
e. How does Aneesha say that she doesn't have time to talk? ...(5)...

Task 7

Listen to the second part, an excerpt from their later conversation. Decide if the following statements are true or false.

a. Sarah has to write a report about Jaydon.
b. Those who work with the family shouldn't give each other any information at all, because of confidentiality.
c. Sarah ought to tell everyone else in the children's centre where she works about her conversation with Aneesha.
d. Sarah's line manager should know about the conversation.

Task 8

Listen again. What do you think the following phrases mean? Discuss this with a partner.

to keep an eye on – to keep in touch – a need to know basis

Task 9

Role-play the following telephone conversation with a partner.

Student A: You are a social worker who wants to ask Student B to a meeting about a three-year-old girl named Alice Jacobs.

Student B: You are a preschool worker, and there is a three-year-old girl named Alice Jacobs who attends your nursery every week.

Task 10

In pairs, decide what is the difference in meaning between the modal verbs *should*, *ought to* and *must*.

Grammar

Modal auxiliary verbs

Some modal auxiliary verbs are used to talk about things which are advisable (a good idea), or which are necessary/obligatory. These modal verbs are *should, ought to* and *must*. We also use *have to*, although it is not a true modal auxiliary.

Task 11

Find the modal verbs in Task 7 and decide which has which meaning.

a. it's necessary/obligatory
b. it's not necessary/not obligatory
c. it's necessary not to do it
d. it's advisable/a good idea
e. it's not advisable/not a good idea

Things to remember about modal verbs:

- Modal verbs are used with the infinitive of the main verb (e.g. we should *be* careful).
- Modal verbs have no *-s* on the he/she/it part of the verb (e.g. he *must* listen).
- Negatives are made by adding *not* or in contracted form *-n't* (e.g. you should*n't* ask too many questions).
- Questions are made by inverting the verb and subject (e.g. *must I* really write the report now?).
- There is no past tense of *must*, *should* and *ought to*.
- If you want to express obligation in the past, use the past of *have to* (e.g. I knew I *had to* meet him quickly).
- *Mustn't* and *don't have to* have different meanings (see Task 10 and Task 11).

***Have to* is not a true modal verb.**

- It changes in the he/she/it part (e.g. he *has to* do it).
- It forms negatives with *don't/doesn't* (e.g. she *doesn't have to* worry).
- It forms questions with *do/does* (e.g. *do* we really *have to*?).
- It has a past tense (e.g. I *had to* meet my manager yesterday).

Task 12

Complete the sentences with either *mustn't* or *don't/doesn't have to*.

a. The details of the case are confidential, so you ...(1)... tell anyone who is not directly involved.
b. As a preschool worker, she ...(2)... wear a suit to work.
c. There's a play group at the children's centre, so local parents ...(3)...travel far.
d. We ...(4)... overreact to this, there may be nothing to it.
e. Whatever you do, you ...(5)... lose the file.
f. It's a holiday tomorrow, so he ...(6).... go to work.

Activity

Case study

Imagine you are working with a child at risk. He is a six months old baby boy, whose mother is only 15 years old. His father is also young, and doesn't want to be involved with his son. The baby and his mother live with her parents – his grandparents, and his two uncles who are 12 and ten. The family has a three-bedroom flat, but the rooms are small and it feels very overcrowded.

Task 13

Work in groups of three or four. Think of five or six risks that this baby and this family might face. Design a risk assessment form in your notebook based on the format below.

Risk Identified		High/Medium/Low
1.	*Write the first risk you think of here.*	*Decide using the risk matrix below.*
2.	*Write the second risk you think of here.*	*Decide using the risk matrix below.*
3.		

RISK MATRIX					
	If something happens, how servere could it be?				
How likely is it that something will happen?	very slight	marginal	moderate	servere	very severe
very unlkely	low	low	low	low	medium
unlikely	low	low	low	medium	high
possible	low	low	medium	high	high
probable	low	medium	high	high	high
very likely	low	medium	high	high	high

Module 2: Making plans together

Working in a Sure Start children's centre

Natalie Bremner is 29 and works as an Early Years Educator at a children's centre in Birmingham. She has worked here for four years.

What is a Sure Start children's centre?

They were introduced by the government in 1998. The core aim is to get the best help to children right from the beginning of their lives, and to improve outcomes for young children and their families, with a particular focus on those who are most disadvantaged. Most centres offer childcare and early learning, but they do much more than this too. They bring together child and family health services, from health visitors to breastfeeding support clinics. Most centres give advice on parenting or run parenting courses. They also signpost families to other local childcare options, and help to access specialist services such as speech therapy, healthy eating advice or help with managing money. Some centres run sessions to help children with behaviour issues. Many also offer direct help to parents, helping them to find work or training opportunities, or give classes such as English for Speakers of Other Languages (ESOL).

Why do you think children's centres are important?

Evidence shows that development during a child's early years lays an essential foundation for progress throughout life. There are so many things children need at this age. Good childcare is important, but so are good parenting and a good home learning environment. Health and economic well-being also have an impact on child development.

What other services does your children's centre offer?

Our centre is one of the bigger ones, so you can see a dentist, dietician or physiotherapist, or you can visit the 'stop smoking' clinic. We also offer expert advice, support and short-term breaks if your child has learning difficulties or disabilities.

What qualifications do you have?

I have an NVQ Level 3 (National Vocational Qualifications = Ausbildungsgrad im englischen nationalen Berufsbildungssystem) in Early Years Care and Education.

Who else works at the children's centre?

We have family support workers, nursery assistants, nursery nurses and room leaders, a nurse-ry manager, a children's centre coordinator and a children's centre manager.

How old are the children that you work with?

Between three and five.

Tell us about your typical day.

I work with the children as part of a team of six. In the mornings we put out various activities for the children to choose from during the day. When they arrive we get them settled, and then they're free to play with whatever they like. We sometimes do focus activities, when we adults lead the activity and the children can come and take part in something, for example reading a story. We also sometimes move freely around, looking for chances to sit down and play with one or more children in ways which will help with their development.

Do you enjoy your work?

Oh yes, I love it!

Comprehension

Task 1

Replace the words in italics with words from the text that have the same meaning.

a. This first qualification will give him a good *basis* for working in childcare.
b. She hopes that her work will produce positive *results.*
c. In our work we *direct* families towards the services they need.
d. So far, there has not been much *movement* towards achieving our aims.
e. You need to show that you have *proof* for your claims.

Task 2

In groups of three to four, discuss the following questions.

a. Would you like to work in a children's centre?
b. Do you think it would be a good idea to introduce children's centres in your city or town? If yes, why?

Task 3

Look at the text of this email, and decide which word on this list would fit into each numbered gap.

grateful – attend – co-operation – sessions – concerns

???	***Felicia Okimbola, Social Services Children and Families***
???	***Yasmina Rahab, Pembury Children's Centre***
???	***12 October 2011***
???	***Child at risk***

Dear Yasmina
I'm writing to you concerning David Prentice, date of birth 03/06/2010. I'm aware that he comes to your play group ...(1)... on Wednesdays at 9 a.m.
I can disclose that some ...(2).... have been raised about David's well-being. Would it be possible for you to ...(3)... a Team Around the Child meeting at 10.30 on 15 October 2011? The meeting will be held at Pembury Children's Centre.
I would be very ...(4)... for your ...(5)... in this matter.
Best regards
Felicia Okimbola

Task 4

What else is missing from the email? Can you think what words should be written in the top left-hand corner?

Task 5

Is the tone of this email formal or informal? How can you tell?

Activity

Task 6

Write a reply to the email, saying that you will be happy to attend.

Task 7

Imagine that Felicia and Yasmina know each other very well and have worked together many times before. Rewrite the email so that it is in a much more informal tone.

Hint: Informal emails are usually much shorter than formal ones.

Confidentiality vs. sharing information

Information sharing is vital to safeguarding and promoting the welfare of children and young people. A key factor in many serious case reviews has been a failure to record information, to share it, to understand its significance and then take appropriate action. [...]

Where there are concerns about the safety of a child, the sharing of information in a timely and effective manner between organisations can reduce the risk of harm. Whilst the Data Protection Act 1998 places duties on organisations and individuals to process personal information fairly and lawfully, it is not a barrier to sharing information where the failure to do so would result in a child or vulnerable adult being placed at risk of harm. Similarly, human rights concerns, such as respecting the right to a private and family life would not prevent sharing where there are real safeguarding concerns. [...]

Practitioners should use their judgement when making decisions on what information to share and when and should follow organisation procedures or consult with their manager if in doubt. The most important consideration is whether sharing information is likely to safeguard and protect a child.

Adapted from: Department for Education: Information sharing: advice for practitioners providing safeguarding services to children, young people, parents and carers, 26 March 2015, www.gov.uk/government/publications/safeguarding-practitioners-information-sharing-advice.

Comprehension

Task 8

Answer the following questions from the text.

a. What do you think a serious case review might be?
b. In many serious case reviews, what has the staff failed to do?
c. What do you think the word *vulnerable* means?
d. In the UK, when can information be shared without getting consent?

Task 9

Discuss these questions in groups of three or four.

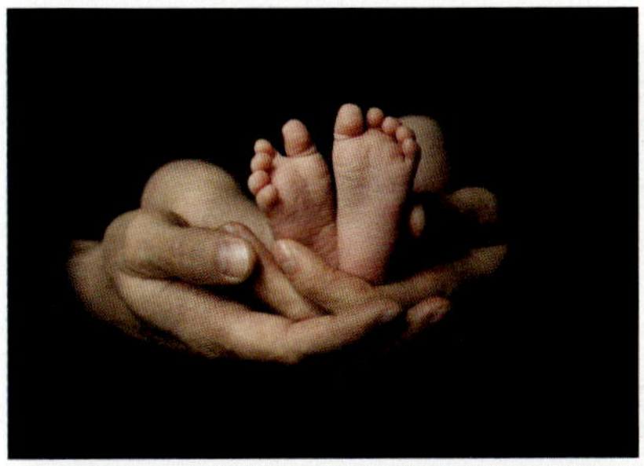

a. Do social workers and children's workers get unfair blame in cases when child safeguarding goes wrong?
b. Is the way that the media reports such cases helpful or unhelpful?
c. Refer to specific cases which you discussed in Module 1, Task 4.

Task 10

Here is an excerpt from the minutes of the Team Around the Child Meeting held about the little boy David Prentice. Find all the verb forms which express the future.

Felicia Okimbola (Social Worker) stated that David's mother Shaneka has already decided that she's going to attend a parenting course for teenage parents.

Jo Mink (Family Support Worker) agreed that she'll make sure that Shaneka gets appropriate budgeting and debt advice to help her to manage her money.

Jane Sillitoe (Children's Centre Coordinator) asked who will accompany David's mother to the housing office to apply for her own housing.

Jo Mink said that she'll do it.

Paul Giles (General Practitioner = family doctor) reported that he is going to refer David for an assessment on his hearing, in response to Shaneka's previous statement that she thinks he can't hear her when she talks to him.

Jacinta Shah (Health Visitor) said that she'll visit David and his mother once a week for the next month, to give advice and help on issues relating to healthcare.

Yasmina Rahab (Room Leader) agreed that she'll monitor David at the Wednesday play group.

Grammar

Future forms – *going to* and *will*

	going to	will
Form – positive	be (am/is/are) + going to + infinitiv	will ('ll) + infinitive
Form – negative	am not (I'm not) are not (aren't) + going to + infinitive is not (isn't)	will not (won't) + infinitive
Use 1	• Planned intentions • Decisions already made	• Spontaneous intentions • Decisions made at the time of speaking • Offering, deciding, promising, requesting
Use 2	Predictions based on visible evidence	All other predictions

Task 11

Put the verbs in brackets into the will ('ll) or the going to future.

A: I don't know how to input data into this system.
B: Oh it's quite easy, I (show) you.
A: Has Paul decided what to do when he finishes the NVQ?
B: Yes, he (work) in a nursery school.
A: Why are they looking at those catalogues?
B: They (order) some new books.
A: Should I bring a coat, do you think it (be) dry later?
B: No, I'm sure it (rain), there are lots of dark clouds.

Module 3: Solving problems

Two case studies, two problems

Tanya lives in a foster home. She's four years old, and has been in foster care for three months. She is in care because her mother has a problem with drugs and alcohol misuse and is now in a rehabilitation programme. Tanya attends a nursery three times a week, she comes with her foster mother but stays on her own. The nursery worker has a problem, because Tanya's behaviour can be challenging. As well as a social worker, there is a psychologist working with Tanya. She has reported that Tanya may have some form of Post Traumatic Stress Disorder as a result of the neglect she has suffered. The nursery worker needs to make sure that Tanya's specific needs are met, while at the same time considering the other children in the nursery.

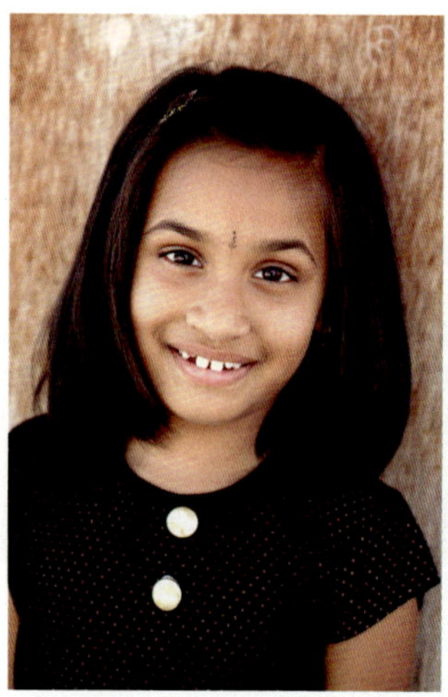

Sharmila is in hospital. She's four years old, and has been in and out of hospital since she was two because she suffers from a congenital heart defect. She doesn't always go into the same hospital, sometimes she's in her local children's hospital in Leicester and sometimes she's in a specialist hospital in London. Her parents are concerned that she's falling behind in her early development because of all this disruption. This is especially true now that she's due to start at her local primary school. She has a preschool keyworker in Leicester Children's Hospital School, who is working with her and her parents to address this problem.

Comprehension

Task 1

Answer the following questions, working in pairs.

a. Which of the two children is legally a looked-after child?
b. Which of the two children is disruptive?
c. Which of the two children would be termed to be a vulnerable child at risk? Or would they both?

Task 2

Find words on this list which match the definitions below.

challenging – disorder – disruption – to suffer – especially – in care – to address

a. in particular
b. undergo or feel pain or distress, illness or injury
c. when a child can't stay with his / her family so goes to a foster family or a children's home
d. try to solve
e. interruption in the progress of something
f. difficult
g. an illness or disability

Task 3

In groups of three, think of possible actions that a) the nursery worker and b) the keyworker could take to improve the situation for these two children.

Language

Asking for suggestions:

What shall I / we ...?
e.g. What shall we do tonight?
Do you have any ideas about ...?
What do you think we should ...?

Making suggestions:

How about + -ing / noun
e.g. How about going out?

What about + -ing / noun
e.g. What about the cinema?
We could ...?
e.g. We could go out for dinner?
Why don't we ...?
e.g. Why don't we go dancing?

Let's (let us) ...!
e.g. Let's have a party!

Accepting suggestions:
Yes, I agree.
Yes, great / fine / ok / that's a good idea.

Rejecting suggestions:
I think I would prefer to ...
I don't think that's a good idea.

Task 4

Complete the gaps with the words given below. The texts are excerpts from conversations that take place when the nursery worker and the keyworker meet their line managers.

First excerpt

we should – any ideas – how about – would be – could we – could try

Anne: Do you have ...(1)... as to how we can improve this situation?
Silvia: I think ...(2)... put an IEP (individual education plan) in place for this little girl. Anne: Yes, I agree. ...(3)... if we also get a specialist education support worker to work with her on a one on one basis?
Silvia: Yes, I think that ...(4)... a really good idea, some extra personal attention and input could really help her.
Anne: What else ...(5)... try to manage this situation?
Silvia: Well, I could put some strategies in place during my daily work with her.
Anne: Yes, that would be great. What sort of thing do you mean?
Silvia: I ...(6)... using positive modelling to encourage positive behaviour?
Anne: Yes, that's a very good idea.

Second excerpt

you could – would be – shall we do – don't you – else should

Pritpal: What ...(1)... about this little girl?
Jeannette: How about if we put an IEP in place?
Pritpal: I'm not sure we need to take that step just yet. She hasn't reached school age yet, and I think it would be better to do an IEP when she turns five.
Jeannette: What ...(2)... we do then, to make sure that she doesn't fall behind before she starts school?
Pritpal: Why ...(3)... do a smaller plan, not a full IEP? You could set some social targets, because she's missed out on some key social development by not attending nursery consistently.
Jeannette: Yes, that ...(4)... a good idea. Also, I can continue to spend time with her every morning.
Pritpal: Yes, and while you do that, ...(5)... make sure you read her plenty of stories, and play early learning games.
Jeannette: Yes, ok.

Task 5

Which conversation is between the nursery worker and his/her manager, and which is between the keyworker and his/her manager? Discuss and decide with a partner. How were you able to tell?

Task 6

Correct the mistakes in this dialogue. Each sentence has one mistake.

A: What about read a story to the children now?

B: I don't think are they ready to sit quietly.

A: Then why don't you setting up the painting activity?

B: Ok. What shall we ask them paint?

A: How about to ask them to paint their families?

B: Good idea, could you getting out the paints?

A: Ok, but let's to try keep the room clean!

Activity

Task 7

Role play

Student A: Imagine you work in a nursery. One of the children in your nursery lives in a children's home. He or she has some behaviour problems, and you don't know why.

Student B: You are a care worker in a children's home. One of the children you keywork has been upset due to recent contact with their family. Mum has mental health problems, which is why the child lives in the home.

What to do if a child discloses to you that he or she is a victim of abuse

Anne is a nursery manager. She wants to let her team know what to do if or when a child discloses abuse. She gives out the following guidelines:

1. **Listen.**
   Give the child your full attention, nod understandingly or make supportive sounds as the story comes out. Let them tell the story in their own words, don't press for details or 'interview' them. If you start questioning the child or ask for specific details, then this will cause problems with investigations later on.

2. **Take the child seriously, and say that you believe that the child is telling the truth.**
   The child is probably frightened about disclosing the abuse, because the abuser may have told them that if they tell this secret something bad will happen to them. Even if the abuser hasn't said this, children will often feel that the abuse is their own fault.

3. **Remain calm.**
   Control your own feelings of anger, horror or sadness. You'll make the child feel worse and more afraid if you react in a way that shows you are shocked or upset. Don't make any judgmental statements about the alleged perpetrator. The child may well love the person, and only want the abuse to stop.

4. **Reassure the child.**
   Tell them it is not their fault, and that they're doing the right thing in telling somebody. Let them know you will do something to help, and that they will be kept safe. However, only tell them things you are certain you can do. If you make promises that you can't keep, the child won't feel he or she can trust you (or anybody?) in the future.

5. **Explain what action you will take next.**
   Explain that you'll need to tell somebody else. If you promise that you'll keep the disclosure a secret, then you'll have to break that promise, because you do need to report this to someone else – you need to tell your line manager immediately.

Comprehension

Task 8

Answer the following questions.

Will the workers be helping the child if they:
a. look or act angry or become distressed?
b. criticise the alleged perpetrator?
c. listen openly to what the child freely wants to tell them?
d. conduct an investigation?
e. avoid asking too many direct questions?

Task 9

Copy this table into your notebooks. Decide which word matches which definition.

disclose	unhappy or distressed
supportive	give confidence to
upset	sympathetic and helpful
reassure	reveal

Grammar

Conditional I – what will happen if ...?

We use conditional I (if-clause type 1) to talk about things which may happen in the future. The things are not certain but they are possible. We often use this to give advice.

Form

if-clause	result clause
if + present tense	will/won't + infinitive of main verb

e.g.: If you eat healthily, you'll live longer. If you don't exercise, you won't get fit.

Task 10

Find six examples of conditional I in the guidelines "What to do if a child discloses to you that he or she is a victim of abuse".

Task 11

Complete these sentences with your own ideas.

a. If I don't go out too often ...
b. If I study hard ...
c. If my best friend has time this week ...
d. If I learn to speak English perfectly ...
e. If I live to be 90 ...

Activity

Task 12

Imagine that you have attended a Team Around the Child meeting about a child in a nursery where you work. The meeting took place because he has behaviour problems. You need to give feedback to your line manager at the nursery. Prepare this as a summary to give to the class. It should include the reason for the meeting, the desired outcomes and the action points which were agreed.

UNIT 3: Social background

Module 1: Children in poverty grow into adults with no prospects

More and more children are growing up in poor families. They experience exclusion very early on and have mostly poor educational opportunities and life chances.

The class trip has been organised. Five days in a youth hostel in Norderney, costing 180 Euros, says the letter to the parents. Already on the following day the teacher's assumption is confirmed: six out of the 29 children will not be going on the trip, just like last year and the year before that. In the parents' excuse notes it states that the children are in a difficult phase, which does not permit them to be taken out of their family environments. "We all know that the parents simply don't have the money to finance the trip", says the teacher in the Duisburg secondary school. He greatly regrets this, but can do nothing about it. "First of all we don't have the means, and secondly, the parents don't want to be seen as charity cases. We just have to accept this".

Bremen has the highest number of children living in poverty nationwide at 33 %. In Berlin the figure is almost 30 %, and in Leipzig 27 %. Even in wealthy Hamburg every fifth child lives in poverty.

Parental poverty always means child poverty, and because of this, exclusion from participation in the things that make life worth living or that give rise to educational opportunities and social mobility. According to statistics there are 2.7 million children living in poverty in Germany. "The problem has been recognised for years, but if you really want to help the children then you also have to engage with the parents and that doesn't happen", says Heinz Hilgers, president of the German Society for the Protection of Children.

Poverty has many sides: Every girl who has to wash herself with cold water a whole year long, who doesn't get hot meals and has to do without electric light because the supply has been cut off is poor. The boy who can't accept birthday invitations because there's no money to buy a present is poor. All those children who have no place to do their homework, who never go to the zoo, the cinema, or to the sports club whose sports gear the parents can't afford are poor. The obese boy whose coordination is underdeveloped and whose teeth are rotting because of inadequate nutrition and exercise is poor.

The consequences for children are devastating. Children who grow up in poverty are often badly integrated in many social spheres. “These children have no sense of self-worth”, says Martina Furlan, Chairperson of the Society for the Protection of Children, Dortmund. (Poverty level: 22 %). She has observed that an increasing number of families live in isolation. “For them nothing is easy. Living just to survive offers no prospect of a successful life.”

The fact that developmental programmes don’t take effect or reach people has many causes. Poverty is a complex phenomenon. Income poverty is often connected with insufficient school or professional qualifications, with individual health problems, and with ingrained behaviours that mean these people don’t meet the demands of the job market. The chairman of the Equality Council Bremen, Gerd Wenzel, explains: “Developmental programmes only deal with one problem and fail to take the complexity of the problem of poverty sufficiently into account. It would therefore be sensible, for example, to not only provide apprenticeship places for young people, but also at the same time to promote and support their social skills”. Many such programmes are, in addition, too short. Only a few run for several years and offer participants reliable long term prospects.

Adapted and translated from: Silke Hoock für ©ZEIT ONLINE (www.zeit.de): 22.07.2016 „Aus armen Kindern werden chancenlose Erwachsene“, https://www.zeit.de/karriere/2016-07/kinderarmut-eltern-einkommen-klassenfahrten-bildung/komplettansicht, accessed 5 September 2017.

Comprehension

Task 1

Find the words or expressions in the text which mean:

a. the state of being left out and unable to avail of opportunities
b. a belief that something will happen in a certain way
c. letters that parents write for their children when they can’t participate in a class activity
d. money, funds, financial resources
e. people who lack the money to meet their living expenses and have to rely on the financial generosity of others to help them out
f. rich, well off, affluent
g. the possibility of improving your standard of living, quality of life or social/professional status
h. school exercises that students are required to do outside of school and class time
i. catastrophic, disastrous, very destructive
j. areas of life that require certain social and interpersonal skills in order to allow you to relate to and interact successfully with other people
k. the feeling that you are a valuable person who is also valued and respected by others
l. the condition of being alone and cut off from other people and society
m. to produce a positive outcome or result
n. ways of doing things and habits that have negative effects but are difficult to change
o. requirements
p. logical, rational
q. opportunities to train as a tradesman, i.e. a carpenter, electrician, plumber etc.
r. your future range of career possibilities and professional opportunities

Task 2

Are the following statements true or false? Correct the false statements and indicate in the text the passages supporting the true statements.

a. Exclusion from society improves your chances of leading a successful and satisfying life.
b. Some parents don't allow their children to go on school trips because they can't afford the expense of sending them.
c. The school in Duisburg has a fund to finance the travel and accommodation of poor children who otherwise could not go on school trips.
d. In Hamburg, 20 % of children live in poverty.
e. According to Heinz Hilgers, the key to helping children in poverty is to involve their parents in finding solutions to the problem.
f. In Dortmund the number of families who find themselves cut off from their wider community is decreasing.
g. Most developmental programmes designed to deal with the problem of poverty run for years, allowing their participants the time they need to acquire the social and professional skills they need to improve their life chances and job opportunities.

Task 3

Answer the following questions.

a. Why would the poor parents of children in the Duisburg school not wish to have their children's school trip paid for by the school?
b. What are the child poverty rates in the cities of Berlin, Bremen, Hamburg and Leipzig respectively?
c. Name three of the negative effects that poverty and social exclusion has on the lives of poor people, citing an example from the text in each case to support your answer, e.g. *Poverty means that parents can't afford healthy food for their children, resulting in childhood obesity and decaying teeth.*
d. What is the connection between social isolation and low self-esteem?
e. What three problems are identified with the phenomenon of income poverty and why do the developmental programmes designed to address these problems so rarely produce successful results?

Grammar

Comparisons

When comparing things that are different, *than* is used.

Examples: *The standard of living in the outlying areas of London is* ***higher than*** *in the inner-city areas.*
Peter's report on child poverty ***is more cautious*** *in its findings* ***than*** *Robert's.*

We can also make comparisons using *as ... as*, or negative comparisons using *not as ... as*.

Example: *The population of Munich is* ***as great*** *as Manchester's, but* ***not as great as*** *that of London's.*

Task 4

Look at the table of statistics below, which show the levels of child poverty in different parts of Germany in 2015.

Kinderarmut in Deutschland, 2015

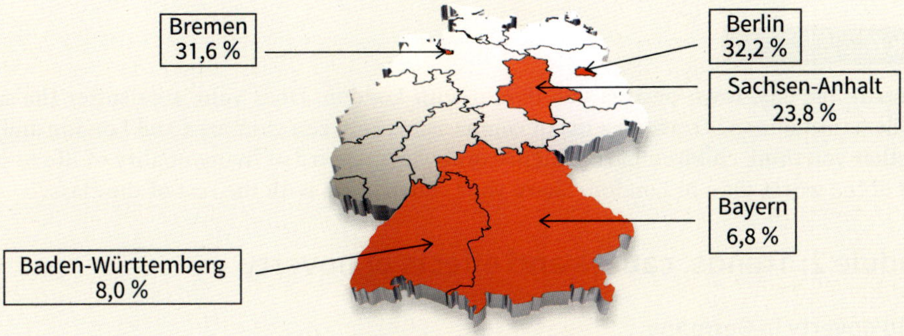

Source of statistics: Bertelsmann Stiftung.

Now, using some of the comparative phrases below, write sentences which compare the level of child poverty in one area with that in another area.

Example: The level of child poverty in Bayern (Bavaria) is the lowest in Germany.

as low as   the same as   lower than   the lowest   not as high as   not as low as   the highest   higher than   as high as

Task 5

Transform the adjectives in brackets in the text below into the comparative or superlative where appropriate.

Example: In Britain many families from immigrant backgrounds are (poor) than those who have lived in Britain for generations. The (poor) people of all are often those who are (educated).

In Britain many families from immigrant backgrounds *are poorer than* those who have lived in Britain for generations. The *poorest* people of all are often those who are *least educated.*

(Low) levels of education are often cited as one of the chief causes of poverty. People who lack skills and qualifications find it (hard) to find work than those who have received a good education or training. Poverty is also (prevalent) in urban than in rural areas. This is partly due to the fact that rents are (high) in towns and cities and the cost of living in general is (expensive) than in the countryside. Cities also have (big) immigrant populations than rural regions and immigrants are often amongst the (educated) social groups. It is not as (difficult) for native-speaking citizens to avail of educational and job opportunities. Immigrants who speak English as a second language experience (many) problems finding work than their native-speaking counterparts. When they do find work it is often of the (low) paid variety.

The Mayor of London has initiated the Childcare Availability Programme to help (poor) families achieve a (good) standard of living. He feels that this programme may offer the (good) solution to the problems experienced by the socially disadvantaged in the city.

Task 6

Compare the city, town or area you live in with London. Does your area suffer the same problems as London? Draw up a list of comparisons between your area and London and say whether you think children have a higher or lower standard of living/quality of life in your part of the world than in London. Share your conclusions with the rest of the class.

Module 2: Trends, causes and effects of poverty

Child poverty in Germany

The number of children living in poverty in Germany continues to rise, despite the country's thriving economy. The children of single-raising parents and immigrants are amongst those most at risk.

In three quarters of the world's most affluent countries child poverty levels have increased, sometimes considerably, partly as a result of the austerity policies pursued by governments since the global financial crisis in 2008. Another longer term cause of this rise is that governments' attempts to protect families and children from the circumstances that lead to poverty have declined since the end of the Cold War and the advent of globalisation. It may surprise many people that an increase in wealth has been accompanied by a rise in poverty. This development points to the fact that there has been a failure to distribute wealth evenly and fairly in society.

Western governments seem to have gradually abandoned the ideals they once held of wishing to create an egalitarian society where people are paid a fair wage for an honest day's work. Nowadays, the social and familial circumstances into which children are born often have a decisive influence on their future educational opportunities, employment prospects and earning power.

The lack of commitment at state level to creating opportunities for people from disadvantaged backgrounds has meant that many children are condemned to live in circumstances of persistent poverty throughout the period of their childhood.

Experts in this field have urged governments to make a greater commitment to combating child poverty. Germany, where about 15 per cent of children are classified as poor, has seen a steady rise in levels of child poverty over the past five years.

In Germany the problem of child poverty is particularly prevalent amongst single-raising mothers and immigrant families, especially those from the former Soviet Union. In total, approximately 1.9 million children are growing up in families in receipt of Hartz IV benefits.

Experts believe that the government must first take action to provide women with more opportunities to join or return to the workforce. Secondly the education system has to be reconsidered and improved at the lower levels and greater efforts made to integrate non-native speaking children into their school and social environments.

Statistics adapted from: Sagener, Nicole: Child poverty in Germany increasingly the norm, 13 September 2016, www.euractiv.com/section/social-europe-jobs/news/child-poverty-in-germany-increasingly-becomes-the-norm, accessed 17 September 2018.

Comprehension

Task 1

Answer the following questions.

a. According to the article, what has increased and what has declined in Germany over the past few decades? Try to explain the relationship between these two phenomena.
b. What do you think the German government should do to better address the problem of rising child poverty?

Task 2

Find words or expressions in the text which mean:

a. to be going up
b. fast/quickly
c. rich/wealthy
d. substantially/significantly
e. to have gone down/fallen
f. the start/beginning of something
g. a social system in which values such as fairness and equality are respected and nurtured (two words)
h. chances of finding suitable work (two words)
i. the ability to make sufficient amounts of money (two words)
j. ongoing/continuing/uninterrupted/constant
k. fighting against the effects of a problem
l. a considerable increase (two words)
m. especially common (two words)

Task 3

Listen to the following interview between a reporter and Sue Lynn, spokeswoman for a UK children's charity.

Have child poverty levels increased over the past few years?

Lynn: Yes, they certainly have. Since the effects of the latest economic crisis have begun to be felt, poverty rates have risen steadily. In 2008, just before the crisis struck, poverty levels stood at around seven per cent. Since then they have gone up dramatically by a further eight per cent to the current figure of 15 percent.

What factors, more specifically, have caused this rise?
Lynn: Well, the government has instituted a series of cutbacks that have hit the financial provisions for education, training and childcare facilities very hard. Reductions in educational and training subsidies have led to fewer people being able to take up places in universities and on training programmes. This has resulted in a more unskilled workforce who can't find jobs. The freeze in government funding combined with a fall in levels of income has given rise to a situation where parents either cannot afford or cannot find preschool places for their children.

How does the future look?

Lynn: With the crisis appearing to worsen and unemployment on the increase, it looks as if the continuing crisis will lead to rising rates of poverty.

Task 4

Answer the following questions.

By how much have poverty levels risen since 2008? What is the current percentage of the population living below the poverty line?
Explain the connection between government cutbacks, inadequate education, unemployment and poverty.

Grammar

Adjectives describe nouns and adverbs describe verbs.

Adjective:	There was a **dramatic increase** in poverty in London last year.
Adverb:	Poverty **increased dramatically** in London last year.

Formation of adverbs

Most adverbs can be formed by adding -ly, -y, -ally, or -ily depending on the spelling of the adjective or noun on which they are based:

Examples: **high/highly** **full/fully** **dramatic/dramatically** **day/daily**

Some adverbs and adjectives have the same form.

Examples: **daily** **fast** **monthly** **quarterly** **weekly** **hard** **late**

This publication on paediatrics is a monthly **journal. (adjective)**
This paediatrics journal is published monthly. **(adverb)**
He had an early **night. (adjective)**
He went to bed early. **(adverb)**

Adverbs can also be used to describe adjectives, past participles and other adverbs.

Adverb + adjective:	She is **really** careful when handling babies.
Adverb + past participle:	That child has been **well** raised by its parents.
Adverb + adverb:	She works **extremely well** with young children.

Verbs and adjectives

Some verbs are modified by adjectives rather than adverbs. These are often stative verbs rather than action verbs and typically relate to appearance or the senses.

Examples: **appear** **be** **look** **feel** **smell** **sound** **seem**

I'm glad John is no longer sick. He **looks healthy once** again. (i.e. not: healthily)
Jane sounded **happy** when I rang her today. (i.e. not: happily)

Good and well

Well is the adverbial form of good. **Well** is an irregular adverb.
Adjective: John is a **good** worker.
Adverb: John works **well**.

Mary is a good teacher.

Mary teaches well.

Task 5

Complete the following sentences by transforming the adjective in brackets into an adverb where appropriate. Not every adjective needs to be changed into an adverb.

Example:
Childcare services are (heavy) dependent on government funding.
Childcare services are **heavily** dependent on government funding.

a. He's really done his job very (good).
b. Poverty levels in some countries have declined (significant).
c. The post is delivered to our kindergarten twice (day).
d. I (full) agree with you that something must be done urgently to improve the quality of basic education in this country.
e. Many parents must work very (hard) to afford childcare.
f. She is (extraordinary) well paid for the work that she does.
g. When dealing with very young children she works (incredible) carefully.
h. Her job is (extreme) demanding as she has to put in long hours without a break.
i. We couldn't offer James a place at our kindergarten. His father looked very (disappointed) when we told him the bad news.
j. These parents always arrive (punctual) with their children at the kindergarten.

Describing trends and developments

Sue Lynn talks in the interview about poverty rates increasing and the number of job vacancies decreasing. We often use graphs to describe changes that have taken place in levels of income, living standards, employment rates etc. over a period of time. The graph depicts rises and falls, increases and decreases, and rates of growth and decline. To describe these upward and downward movements we use verbs and nouns to express the direction of the movement, and adverbs and adjectives to indicate the degree of change (e.g. great or small) represented by the movement:

- Child poverty levels have increased (verb) drastically (adverb) over the past few years.
- There has been a drastic (adjective) increase (noun) in child poverty levels over the past few years.
- Government support for families has slightly decreased since 2005.
- There has been a slight decrease in government support for families since 2005.

Language

Verbs indicating upward movement: increase, rise, go up, grow, reach a peak, boom, soar, climb
Nouns: an increase, a rise, a growth, a boom

Verbs indicating downward movement: decrease, decline, fall, shrink, drop
Nouns: a decrease, a decline, a fall, a drop

Adjectives indicating a big change: great, enormous, dramatic, substantial, considerable, significant
Adverbs: hugely, enormously, dramatically, substantially, considerably, significantly

Adjectives indicating a small change: moderate, modest, small, slight
Adverbs: moderately, modestly, small, slightly

Adjectives indicating a gradual/slow change: gradual, steady, constant, consistent
Adverbs: gradually, steadily, constantly, consistently

Adjectives indicating sudden/fast changes: sharp, sudden, quick, rapid
Adverbs: sharply, suddenly, quickly, rapidly

Prepositions used in graphs: **from, to, by, at**

Number of preschool places	
2016	2017
500,000	600,000

Examples:
The number of preschool places available increased from 500,000 in 2016 to 600,000 in 2017.
The number of preschool places increased by 100,000 between 2016 and 2017. (i.e. the difference between both figures)

In 2016 the number of preschool places stood at 500,000 and in 2017 at 600,000. (i.e. the number at a particular point in time)

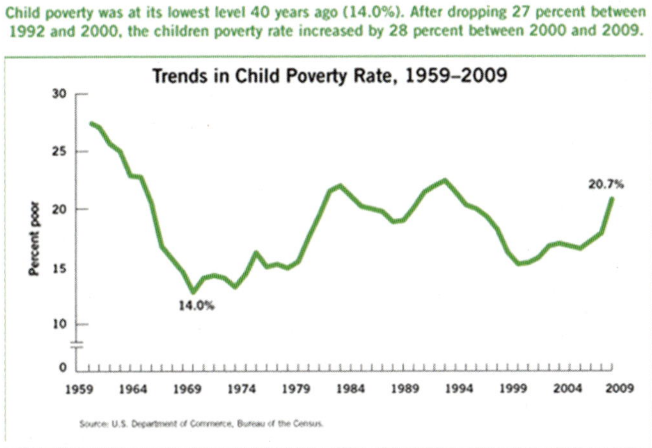

From: Children's Defense Fund: Child Poverty. State of America's Children® 2011. This material was created by the Children's Defense Fund (www.childrensdefense.org).

Source: U.S. Department of Commerce, Bureau of the Census.

Task 6

Look at the graph above and write six sentences describing its movements using the verbs, nouns, adjectives and adverbs on the previous page.

Examples:
Child poverty levels fell dramatically from over 25 % in 1959 to 14 % by 1968.
Between 2008 and 2009, poverty levels rose sharply by about 5 %, from 18 % to 23 %.

Task 7

Sue Lynn uses causative verbs in her interview to indicate the connection between causes and their effects.

"Reductions in educational and training subsidies *have led to* fewer people ..."
"This in turn *results in* a more unskilled workforce ..."
"The freeze in government funding combined with a fall in levels of income *has given rise to* a situation ..."

Causative verbs	
to lead to	to result in
to give rise to	to bring something about

What do you know of the prevalence of child poverty in Germany? Are some parts or regions of Germany more badly affected than others? With a partner, discuss what you think might be the causes of and effects of poverty on families and children in Germany. Then, using the verbs and phrases in the box above, write a text of approximately 80 words clearly illustrating the connections between the causes and effects of poverty (see example below). Finally share your thoughts, ideas and opinions with the rest of the class.

Example:
Low levels of education and training *have led to* vulnerable members of society being unable to find employment. This *results in* higher levels of poverty in these groups which in turn *gives rise to* their children suffering the effects of social disadvantage. Ultimately these developments *bring about a* self-perpetuating cycle of poverty across the generations which many find difficult or impossible to escape.

Module 3: The provision of day care places

Germany needs 300,000 more kindergarten places

450 parents and children caused traffic chaos in Leipzig last Saturday, as they stood patiently in line waiting to sign their children up for places at a new Kindergarten. The police had to intervene to get the cars past the queue. The facility for 45 infants and 120 young children had not yet even opened its doors – it will do so in August. The mass turnout of parents took the kindergarten's management completely by surprise.

The situation is indeed alarming – above all in western Germany: according to a study undertaken by the Cologne Institute for Economic Research, there is a lack of almost 300,000 places for very young children. *Bild Zeitung* was the first to report on this crisis. According to the Köln Institute the regional differences are particularly conspicuous. Whereas there is a shortfall of around 31,000 places in former East Germany, in the West the figure is over 260,000.

As a proportion of demand, parents in Nordrhein-Westfalen are those most likely to suffer disappointment in their search for a place for their children under three years of age. Despite their children's legal entitlement to a kindergarten place, demand here exceeds supply by nearly 77,500 places, a shortfall of 16.2 %. In Rheinland-Pfalz and Bavaria the shortfall is similarly high, at 16 % and 14.9 % respectively. The situation in Mecklenburg-Vorpommern is the least problematic. There the shortfall of places is lowest, at 3.1 %. Also in Saxony and Lower Saxony, the gap between supply and demand is under seven percent.

Ten years ago, only 35 % of parents took up kindergarten places for their children, but now demand is at 46 %. "This figure has continuously increased over the past ten years"; says Wido Geis from the German Institute for Economic Research. This can be attributed to the higher birthrate as well as to a change in values. "Women want and have to return to work earlier", says Geis. "At the same time, giving up very young children to the care of kindergartens is no longer perceived as negatively as it used to be".

In former East Germany, there was a well-developed childcare system and it was usual for women to work. In the West, on the other hand, the importance of parental care at home was emphasised. Following unification, these two approaches to raising children tended to merge, with the result that the shortfall of places in the East is not as great as in the West. However, the demand for places across Germany will continue to grow.

In the past few years, the government has tried to meet increasing demand for childcare places by building new kindergartens. But Geis observes that the rate at which new kindergarten places are being created has stagnated. "Despite the introduction of the law entitling children under the age of three to a kindergarten place, the creation of these places clearly does not enjoy the highest priority at local government level", says Geis. It was noticed by councilors that not as many parents as expected had sued to be granted a place, and for this reason councilors don't come under enough pressure to act.

Geis appeals to politicians not only to continue providing more childcare facilities, but to overhaul the entire system: "What is needed above all is a nationwide system of harmonised fees, opening hours and registration times". The differences between the various regions in these respects are still far too great.

Adapted and translated from: Lottritz, Kerstin: In Deutschland fehlen 300 000 Krippenplätze, in: SZ.de, 17 May 2017, www.sueddeutsche.de/leben/kinderbetreuung-in-deutschland-fehlen-krippenplaetze-1.3509237, accessed 8 September 2017.

Comprehension

Task 1

Find the highlighted words or expressions in the text which mean:

a. To get involved in a situation to control it or to prevent something from happening
b. the appearance of a large group of people for an event such as a protest march
c. very young children between the ages of zero and approximately eighteen months
d. to start business for the first time, especially a service provider that deals with the public
e. very worrying/concerning
f. conducted/carried out (e.g. a study)
g. an absence/an insufficient quantity of something
h. very noticeable/very obvious/very visible
i. the difference between supply and demand, when demand fails to meet supply
j. the feeling a person experiences when desires, hopes or expectations are not fulfilled
k. something the law gives you a right to have
l. a verb used to express the idea that one quantity is greater than another (e.g. when demand is greater than supply)
m. to identify the cause of a trend
n. to be seen or regarded in a certain way (often falsely)
o. to be stressed/highlighted/identified as important
p. the joining together of two things that have previously existed separately, such as East and West Germany
q. to blend two things together
r. to take legal action against a person or an organisation
s. to make something such as kindergarten places available
t. to completely revise or remake something from the start
u. to bring previously different things into agreement with one another, such as laws, guidelines and regulations/to standardise

Task 2

Answer the following questions on the above text.

a. Why did so many parents turn out in Leipzig in August?
b. In which states of the Federal Republic of Germany *(Bundesländer)* is the problem of the lack of kindergarten places (i) least serious, (ii) most serious?
c. What two reasons have caused demand for kindergarten places to rise from 35 % of parents ten years ago to 46 % today?
d. Why is the shortfall of places lower in former East Germany than in the rest of the country?
e. Why are local government authorities failing to provide a sufficient number of new kindergarten places for children?
f. What does Geis say is needed above all to help solve the crisis nationwide?

Parents speak out

Three-year-olds are supposed to be offered a year of preparation before going into primary school. But finding a suitable place in some areas has become very difficult.

Mary: I have tried to get my fifth child into a nursery school nearby, but she did not gain entry as she did not meet the criteria. The system is unfair. The unemployed seemed to get preference over everyone else.

Jennifer: I would like to know the reason why families who work only get part-time places in nurseries, whereas families who don't work get full time places. Surely families who don't work have more time to look after their children than families who work.

John: I can't get my child into our local school. Our family have been involved with the school for 40 years. Children who can't speak English seem to get in. Classroom assistants have to learn Polish over the summer. Parents who speak out are called racists.

Brenda: I am absolutely disgusted that my daughter has been turned down by our local nursery school where my entire family have attended. I feel I am being discriminated because both myself and my husband work, not like others who claim unemployment benefits while also working.

Adapted from: Lack of pre-school places leaving children unprepared, in: BBC News UK, 6 May 2010, http://news.bbc.co.uk/2/hi/uk_news/northern_ireland/8665777.stm, accessed 17 September 2018.

Comprehension

Task 3

Answer the following questions.

a. Why do Mary, John and Brenda feel unfairly treated by the admissions policies of the pre-school system in Northern Ireland? Do you agree with their point of view? Why or why not?
b. Do you think John's attitude about the issue of language is racist? Explain.

Task 4

Complete the following text using the terms below.

gain entry   criteria   part-time   classroom assistants   preference   discriminated
unemployment benefits   turned down

Many parents are finding it very difficult to secure kindergarten places for their young children. This is not only a problem in Germany, but in many European countries such as Britain. In order to ...(1)... to a kindergarten, families have to meet certain ...(2)... such as having a low income level and being socially disadvantaged. These families can get ...(3)... for scarce places over their wealthier rivals. Many children from better off families are only offered ...(4)... places, meaning that they have to be picked up from the kindergarten by their parents in the middle of the day. Alternatively they are offered nothing at all and are simply ...(5).... Many working parents feel ...(6)... against and are angry that the children of jobless parents claiming ...(7)... are favoured over their own offspring. Some parents complain that ...(8)... have to learn a foreign language in order to communicate with their young charges.

Grammar

Present perfect

The present perfect is formed using the present tense of the verb *to have* plus the past participle of the main verb.

I/you/we/they **have taken** the job.
He/she **has taken** the job.
It **has happened** twice this week.

When we refer to events that have taken place in the past and have no connection to the present, we use past tense. When, however, we refer to events that have taken place in the past that have a direct influence on or connection to the present, we use present perfect.

Examples:
John ***worked*** at this preschool for many years.
Mary ***has worked*** at this preschool for many years.

In the first sentence John is no longer working at the preschool. The sentence uses the simple past tense and therefore must refer to a situation which has finished.

Mary, however, is still working at the preschool, although she started working there many years ago. The sentence uses the present perfect and therefore refers to a situation which started in the past but is still ongoing.

since/for

Since is used together with the present perfect to indicate a point in time when an event or situation began.

Example: Mary has worked here **since** 2002.

For is used with the present perfect to indicate the period of time up to the present over which an event or situation has taken place.

Example: It is now 2012. Mary started working here in 2002. That means she has worked here **for** the past ten years.

Task 5

Complete the following sentences using *since* or *for*.

Example: ***She has worked with these children*** *since* ***they started here two years ago.***

a. Robert has been the director of this facility ...(1)... the last three years.
b. Franziska has worked in the field of early learning ...(2)... over ten years.
c. ...(3)... our voluntary worker Chris left last week the children have really missed him.
d. We have been able to completely reequip and refurbish our kindergarten ...(4)... we received extra state funding last year.
e. I don't know where Chris is working now. I haven't seen him ...(5)... ages.

Task 6

Rewrite the sentences using the negative form of the present perfect, with *for* or *since*.

Example:
The last time I saw Chris was two months ago.
I haven't seen Chris for two months

The last time we received a new intake if pupils was six months ago.
The last time we received a government subsidy was January 2009.
The last time we bought new equipment was a year ago.
The last time we raised our teachers' wages was in 2010.

Activity

Imagine that you run a kindergarten in a German city with a substantial immigrant population. You have just one place remaining in your kindergarten for the coming year. The following families present themselves to you, each wishing to have their three-year-old child accepted for admission at your kindergarten:

Family A: a working German couple. Both parents work during the day and need a place for their child. Between them the parents earn an average income and cannot easily afford to pay for private day care, although could manage to meet this expense if they save money in other areas of their lives. They need a full-time place for their three-year-old son. They have no other children.

Family B: an English-speaking couple. The father is well-educated, earns a good income, works for a German firm and is on a three-year contract. The mother hopes to take up full-time work next year, but has a two-year-old child to take care of at home and wishes to attend private German language classes this year to improve her proficiency in the language. They want their son to be immersed in a German-speaking school environment so that he can make friends and develop socially amongst other children during their time in Germany.

Family C: an immigrant family that arrived in Germany five years ago. Both parents are moderately well-educated and speak reasonably good English but only rudimentary German. Their child, a girl, mainly speaks the parents' language and only a few words of German. The father works long hours on low pay in a local factory. The mother is unemployed but is taking German lessons at the local vocational college and hopes to find full-time work in a low-skilled job in the near future. The parents are anxious for their child to attend your kindergarten, both to give them the time to work and, equally importantly, to provide their child with the opportunity to become socially integrated in a German-speaking social environment. The parents see the admission of their child to your school as essential to her future in the country. They have no other children.

Task 7

In pairs, draw up a set of admission criteria which will help you to decide between these three families. There are a number of factors you should consider when setting out your criteria, e.g.:

a. How well will each of these children fit into your existing group of children (mainly German children from middle to high income families in the local area)?
b. What is the level of need for each of the three families?
c. How easily can these families avail of alternative forms of care and schooling?
d. Which child will receive the greatest benefit in educational and developmental terms by being placed in your kindergarten?

Task 8

Now, with another pair playing the role of one of the families, conduct an interview to determine how well or how poorly the child in question fulfils the admissions criteria you have set out in the previous exercise. Be sure to phrase your questions tactfully. After you have considered the case, make a decision either to accept or turn down the child for admission. Explain to the parents the reasons behind your decision. Then switch roles with the other pair and, choosing a different family to role-play, repeat the exercise.

Task 9

Consider the following questions on your own, then discuss them with a partner and share your ideas and opinions with the group.

a. What do you think the real function and value of a preschool is?
b. Is a preschool really a day care facility whose main purpose is to provide a safe, controlled and supervised environment where children can play with each other while their parents are away working?
c. Are preschools essentially educational establishments whose chief purpose is to provide children with a crucial grounding

in the social, cognitive and academic skills that will later be further developed at primary and secondary school level?

d. Do preschools really provide pupils with a significant head start in school-life over children who have not had the opportunity to attend one?
e. Would most children be better off remaining at home with a parent or grandparent up to school-going age, or do they benefit emotionally and socially from being away at home in the company of other children and adults?

UNIT 4:
Living in a family

Module 1: What does a family mean to you?

Families are a basic component of societies. What we think of as family (especially in Western societies) has changed significantly over the last 50–60 years. We no longer think of a family only being made up of mother, father and children. The definition and scope of this institution and word has broadened and developed enormously with the changing times. Or is it just the appearance of the family that has changed? In this unit, we will explore living in a family in the twenty-first century.

Task 1

Reflect and write a short comment on the following questions. Discuss your answers with a partner or in a small group.

a. What does a family mean to you?
b. Who do you include in your family?
c. How do you think your future family will be like?
d. Who is the most important person in your family? Who was the most important person in your family during your childhood?

Try to use the following idioms.

I think that a family is ...
I consider a family to be ...
I believe that ...
My point of view is ...
In my opinion ...

There are some verbs that can be used to present your opinion, what you believe etc. that are never used in the continuous form. For example, *I believe, I think* (not pondering but expressing general opinion), *to believe, to consider, to find*, and so on. They are not action verbs and are used for mental or emotional states.

I *believe* ... (correct)	I am *believing* ... (incorrect)
I *like* ... (correct)	I am *liking* ... (incorrect)
They *think* ... (correct)	They are *thinking* ... (incorrect)

What is a family?

A family has a formal definition that can be found in a dictionary or other reliable sources but cannot possibly cover the full extent of this ever-evolving societal concept. This concept not only differs from culture to culture but also from individual to individual. According to Oxford Dictionaries, 'family' has several meanings. One is: "a group consisting of two parents and their children living together as a unit" or "a group of people related by blood or marriage".

Taken from: Definition of family, in: Oxford Dictionaries, https://en.oxforddictionaries.com/definition/family, accessed 07 September 2018.

This definition has been altered from the very traditional one that only mentioned a mother and father but still does not include and thus cannot cover the whole range of possibilities of what a family can be. It is a very basic definition of this unit of society, which may help to create an individual definition of family.

However, there is much more to this complex idea of a family than blood and legal rights. A family is two or more people who are committed to one another and often live in the same place and dwelling. Members of a family usually share values, beliefs and traditions as well as activities and experiences. They provide each other with unconditional support.

The family unit is a changing concept and the expectations people have of family relationships vary. Since the 1950s, the concept of family has changed a lot with the emancipation of women and the recognition of homosexual pairs, to mention just two areas. In Europe, the marriage rate has decreased by 50 % and the divorce rate has more than doubled since the middle of the twentieth century. More children are being born outside of marriage. People are living longer and deciding to stay single. Women study, have careers and have children a lot later than they used to, if they have children at all. Since women can support themselves through their professions, there is less pressure to get married. Couples often don't have children for many different reasons.

A family can be the good friends who are there when you are feeling down after your beloved pet cat got poisoned by an angry neighbour. Some find their families in religion, a type of spiritual family. Others find their family in an after-work hobby, for example, playing in an orchestra that meets and performs on a regular basis. This group can often offer not only a social platform but also a place where you can be yourself. Many childless people consider their pets as their family. There are even people who create online families that share hobbies, values and beliefs although they have never met. Whether or not these groups are families is only for the individuals directly involved to decide or judge, not anybody else.

Cf. Blessing, Michelle: Meaning of Family, in: lovetoknow.com
https://family.lovetoknow.com/about-family-values/meaning-family, and Mayntz, Melissa: Definition of Family, in: lovetoknow.com, https://family.lovetoknow.com/definition-family, accessed 19 September 2018.

Comprehension

Task 2

Answer the following questions about the above text.

a. What is the very basic definition of family, according to Oxford Dictionaries?
b. What families are not included in this basic definition?
c. What reasons does this text mention for the change in the structure of a family? Are there other reasons that may have played a role?
d. The author mentions several different groups that could be considered as families. Can you think of other groups that may be considered families?

Task 3

Match the following definitions to phrases that were used in the texts above.

a. What a person thinks is important in life.
b. The legal dissolution of a marriage.
c. The state of being dedicated to something, a relationship, a job, a person, etc.
d. To supply something useful or important.
e. To live permanently in a particular place or home.

Activity

Task 4

Do one or both of the following activities with a partner.

a. Create your own family tree.
b. Write questions to ask somebody else in the class about their family and do an interview. Write a short presentation about your classmate's family to present to the rest of the group.

A woman talks about her family

I am American and have been living in Germany since 1999. My *immediate family* stayed in the USA. They are spread out all over the entire country. My parents still live in the area where I grew up in Upstate New York. My father's parents came from Lebanon and my mother's from Italy. At the turn of the twentieth century they emigrated to America. Unfortunately, they have all *passed away*. Both of my parents were born and raised in Utica, New York. They even went to the same high school, but did not meet until afterwards. To avoid a big wedding in a church, they ended up *eloping*. For their *honeymoon* they went to Niagara Falls. My mother worked as a nurse until she started having children. My father is still working as an accountant.

I am the sixth child out of seven. I have five sisters and one brother, who is the oldest. Since I have been an adult, I can say it was quite nice growing up in a big family. Of course, I did not always think that way. At home I never had space for myself and had to share everything all the time. However, I always had somebody there for me, my sisters. They are still there for me even though I live so far away.

My brother and three of my sisters are married and have children. My brother has one child of his own and two *stepchildren.* He is also a grandfather of three grandchildren. Three of my sisters have two children each, ranging in age from seven to 13. I am an aunt to four nieces, three nephews, one step-niece and one step-nephew. Despite the distance, they know who I am, and I have been speaking with them on the telephone a lot more lately. They are my family and I love them.

I have a partner, but live alone and have no children of my own. Besides my *biological family* in the States, I have a family made up of my friends here in Berlin. To me, family includes the most important people in my life, not only *biologically related* ones. I consider myself very lucky to have a family which spans the whole world.

Task 5

Answer the following questions on the text.

a. Where did her grandparents come from?
b. How many nieces does she have?
c. How many siblings does she have?
d. What does family mean to her?

Task 6

There are italicised words in the text. Translate them into German and write a definition of these terms in English.

Family types

Families in the Western world nowadays come in different shapes and forms. No longer are families only extended from biological or marriage ties. What we used to call non-traditional or dysfunctional are now common and prosperous groups of people who live together. In the following box are some of the main types of families.

Nuclear families

This family consists of mother and father with one or more children. This form used to be one of the most common in Western societies. This is no longer the case. The average number of children in European households is 1.6 (as of 2008) and that of North American households is about 2.1.

Extended families

Extended families have changed a lot over the years. In the past, an extended family consisted usually of parents, children and grandparents and/or aunts and uncles and their children all living under one roof. Nowadays extended families usually do not live in one house but may live many miles away from each other. Because of the economic downturn, extended families under one roof are on the rise.

Single-parent families

Over the past 20 years, the number of single parent families has increased. Mainly headed by mothers, the number of single-parent families headed by the father has also been increasing. The reasons for single-parent families have changed. In the middle of the twentieth century, death was the cause of most single-parent families. In the 1970s and 1980s, divorce was the main reason. The 21st century has parents who do not get married and/or who want to raise their children alone.

Blended families

Blended families consist of two previously married parents and their children from their former marriages. Two families blend to form a new step or blended family. In a blended family you have both a step and biological mother and father and step and biological children.

Patchwork families

In a patchwork family, each person is an individual patch in a patchwork quilt. Each person can stand alone, and stands for each person's unique self. When someone becomes part of the family – by birth, adoption, due to divorce and remarriage – the individual person is not changed, but can enrich the family (quilt). In this kind of a family, the interaction between the individuals shapes and forms the family unit.

Comprehension

Task 7

Are the following statements true or false? Correct the false statements.

a. A blended family always has biological and step-parents.
b. In a patchwork family, the family group is the most important unit.
c. Extended families do not exist anymore.
d. Single-parent families are an important part of many societies today.
e. Nuclear families are the main form of families in European countries today.

Task 8

Answer the following questions based on the text describing the different types of families.

a. Why do you think that extended families were important? Why do you think the number of this type of family then decreased for awhile and is on the rise today?
b. Why do you think the reasons for single-parent families have changed several times? Why do you think there has been an increase in this type of family?
c. What is the difference between a patchwork family and a blended family?
d. How would you describe your family?
e. In what way is the experience of being a mother today different than it was in the past (i.e. 60 years ago)? Lone mothers are quite a new concept. What do you think a lone mother is?
f. What is the average number of children people have in Germany? What about other parts of the world? Why do you think the average is different in various parts of the world?

Task 9

Answer the following questions based on the knowledge that you already have.

a. Do you know any other types of families?
b. Can you think of another way to call or describe the other family members?

Number of adoptions decreases

More and more people are waiting longer to have their own children. Women want to first fulfil their wishes and dreams before settling down or instead of having children of their own. Couples often do not want to produce more consumers in a world full of hate and uncertainty. Other people are unable to bare their own children because of infertility or because it is biologically impossible. Foster and adoptive children are two alternatives that not only grant the wish for a child but also give the child the chance to live with people who want to have children and have the means to have them.

In Germany, the number of traditionally adopted (non-biological) children has decreased by 50 % over the past 25 years. At the same time, the number of adoptions involving one of the partner's child has increased. This could be because women use contraception more and also because single mothers are not stigmatised like they used to be. Another reason could be that there is more support from the state for families with reduced means. In addition, fewer couples want to adopt a child. The Federal Ministry of Family Affairs in Germany believes the reason is modern reproductive medicine. This claim has not been statistically proven yet, but the number of artificial inseminations has increased in the same period of time in which the number of adoptions decreased considerably.

Because of modern medicine and the resulting drive and urge for self-optimisation, the pressure and wish to raise a healthy child has risen. As a result, it is difficult to find adoptive families for children with special needs, such as older and disabled children.

Cf. Becker, Wibke: Weniger Paare adoptieren Kinder. In: FAZ.NET, 5 February 2017, www.faz.net/aktuell/gesellschaft/familien-weniger-paare-adoptieren-kinder-14846277.html, accessed 19 September 2017.

Comprehension

Task 10

Are the following sentences true or false?

a. The number of adoptions has increased in Germany in the last 25 years.
b. Single mothers are still stigmatised.
c. It is easy to find an adoptive family for a child with a disability.
d. It is believed that modern medicine is one of the reasons why the number of adoptions has decreased.

Task 11

Answer the following questions based on the text above.

a. What are some of the reasons why people do not have children?
b. Can you think of any other possible reasons?
c. What are possible reasons for the decrease in the number of adoptions in the last 25 years? Why are these reasons considered possible?
d. What kind of adoptions have increased during this time? Why do you think this has happened?

Task 12

Read through the list of adjectives. Which ones do you know? Do you know their opposites?

a. close
b. traditional
c. dysfunctional
d. active
e. harmonious
f. close
g. estranged
h. broken

Task 13

Answer the following questions and exchange ideas with a partner.

a. Which adjectives would you use to describe a perfect family?
b. Which adjectives are missing? How would you describe your family?

Module 2: Single-parent families

The number of single-parent families has increased throughout Europe. On the one hand, the stigma of such families is not how it used to be. On the other hand, these families are especially at risk for poverty and unemployment. As a consequence of these two factors, depression (for both parents and children) and a lower performance in school plague these families.

Task 1

Discuss the following questions with a partner or a small group.

Why do you think that poverty and unemployment are especially high for these types of families? Do you think the number of single families are higher in some European countries than in others? Which ones and why? How does the EU support these kinds of families?

Children of divorce

In the EU, the number of marriages has decreased since the 1960s and the number of divorces has increased. No longer seen as a taboo, divorce may be an easy way out for the parents but may be devastating for the child.

Parents need to remember that divorce is not only stressful and complicated for the parents involved, but also for the children. Change in any form can be stressful. How long this stressful transition period lasts, depends on how the adults deal with it and each other. Usually children want their families to stay intact. When parents decide to part ways, they could lose contact with one of their parents or conflict between the parents could be a result as well. Divorce also increases the risk that the children will suffer psychologically and behaviourally and thus develop problems with anger, depression, etc.

Believe it or not, most children of divorce do not develop these kinds of problems. Children are resilient and can cope with change. Later on, they may report painful memories and worries that continue into their adulthood. Children cannot be fully protected from divorce and its effects and they should not be. This kind of pain and grief is not a mental disorder that needs to be healed. They should be allowed to feel their emotions. Only then can they fully deal with the changes that divorce creates.

Cf. Laumann-Billings, L. &. Emery, R.E. (2000): Distress among young adults from divorced families. *Journal of Family Psychology, 14*, 671–687.

How to help kids survive divorce

I have always had a poor memory. A blank look sweeps across my face when my family reminisces over childhood experiences [...]. That said, I remember 29 March 2003 with great clarity. It was the night my parents told me they were getting divorced.

My brother and I were looking forward to our favourite meal. [...] A big fat hug in a bowl, resplendent with saturated fats and washed down with a pint of Coke. At 11 years old, that combination could not be defeated.

I had seen the breakup coming. Their relationship had deteriorated, punctuated by a row whose aftershocks still reverberated during the family holiday to Disney World. The most extreme rides [...] served as welcome respite from the omnipresent tension. It was with a sense of inevitability that I took my mum aside before we sat down that Saturday evening to find out how things were. She gave me a rueful look that has stayed with me, conveying everything I needed to know. My sister, then eight, was told separately.

I remember the date with such precision because [...] we were told of the divorce the evening before my mum's birthday. I entered the kitchen the following morning to find her on the phone to my grandmother. Midway through discussing plans for the day ahead, she burst into tears. [...] She covered her mouth as if to stop her heart from spilling out on to the floor. Her parents had separated when she was three, leading to a divorce, and she had vowed never to follow suit. I could see the pain of having, in her eyes, broken that promise.

For the first few months, my parents kept things "amicable", a word they would so often deploy [...]. As with all breakups, reality began to bite. A new relationship was embarked on and the residual feelings of resentment, sometimes anger – the unwelcome affiliates of a deep love for a person – began to surface. Old friends chose sides, and the distance between them widened as their shared experiences faded. Staying "amicable" proved (almost) impossible. [...]

Adapted from: Whale, Sebastian: How to help kids survive divorce, in: The Guardian, 16 September 2017, www.theguardian.com/lifeandstyle/2017/sep/16/how-to-help-kids-survive-divorce, accessed 07 September 2018.

Task 2

Answer the following questions about the text.

a. What happened on 29 March 2003?
b. Why do you think the author remembers this date so vividly?
c. Why did his mother have pain in her eyes and tears in her eyes when they were discussing?
d. What is meant here as amicable?

Case study

[...]

Grace Mainwarin, 17, London: Be kind to those who are also grieving around you

"I lost my father to terminal brain cancer when I was 15 in August 2014. It took two years between diagnosis and death for him to go. During this time, he became paralysed down his left side and had a series of seizures. He died half way through my GCSEs, so it affected my relationships, mental health and just the normal way a teenager is supposed to grow up. It was devastating. I was dealing with something so serious that many people don't have to cope with until they are much older. Something that stands out when you lose a parent as a child is how little your peers your own age can grasp what you're going through. I felt very isolated. I was 13 when he was diagnosed so I could almost feel when I told other people my age what had happened that they were thinking of films they'd watched. Death is often so abstract for those who've never experienced it.

My dad was a very good person who was a hard-working lawyer and loved me and my sister so much. He was funny and kind, and I have so many fond memories of him. His courage and resilience during those two years was amazing. He kept on trying to walk, he kept on trying to adjust and adapt to his situation as much as he could, because he loved us so much.

If I could give myself advice at the time it would only to be kinder to those who were also grieving around me. I would say: "Don't make their suffering worse. You need each other."

[...]

Clive, 27, Bristol: My mum told me of her cancer over crumpets

In 1997, my mother told me of her cancer over crumpets. Needless to say, I was devastated or as much as one can be at such a young age. It's not something I have ever really gotten over but it just becomes history. I became a shy kid as a result, although I try not to think too much about that time as it was so traumatic. I hated being the center of attention, with people asking me continuously if I was OK. They were all so kind but I just wanted to be alone. To this day I hate to be the center of attention.

My mum was lovely and softly spoken. She had red hair and wore flowery dresses and hats – I wish I could remember more but I don't and that upsets me. My biggest regret is not going to see her when she had passed away, I just couldn't do it, but I wish I had.

I try to stay positive, you either laugh or cry, I realise that life is too short and [try] not to hold on too tightly to superficial things."

Taken from: Marsh, Sarah & Guardian readers: 'When I heard he was dead I went numb': stories of losing a parent in childhood, in: The Guardian, 26 July 2016, www.theguardian.com/lifeandstyle/commentisfree/2016/jul/26/losing-parent-in-childhood-prince-harry, accessed 07 September 2018.

Task 3

Answer the following questions based on the two case studies above.

a. How did these two teens lose one of their parents?
b. What would Grace tell her younger self?
c. What does Clive regret the most?
d. How has this affected their lives now?

Grammar

Noun and verb agreement

Collective nouns, like *family, team, crowd* and *staff* may be either plural or singular, depending on how they are being used in the sentence.

Examples:

My **family is** great. (the unit)
My **family get** along very well. (the individuals)

The **staff** at the preschool **is** in a meeting. (staff as a unit)
The **staff are** in disagreement about how to deal with the bullying of a specific child. (the staff as individuals)

Task 4

Choose the right form of the verb in brackets.

a. The staff (work/works) together well.
b. The whole staff (is/are) not available today.
c. The family (live/lives) in Berlin.
d. The family (talk/talks) to each other at dinner every evening.
e. The club (is/are) meeting tonight.
f. The couple (is/are) coming tonight.
g. The couple (is/are) breaking up.

Module 3: LGBT Families

In more than 20 countries, L(esbian) G(ay) B(isexual) T(ransgender) couples can legally get married and adopt children. Having two fathers or two mothers in some cultures is not so unusual anymore. It has been a long fight for these couples and families and will continue to be so for at least the immediate future, unfortunately.

Task 1

Discuss with a partner or small group one of the following questions. Prepare your results to present to the rest of the group.

a. What is meant by the term LGBT families?
b. What does marriage mean to you?
c. Where is gay marriage legal?
d. What was the very first country to legalise LGBT marriage?
e. Why do you think it is not legal everywhere?
f. How do you think these families are different to non-LGBT families?
g. How do these types of families affect the children involved?
h. What are the advantages of marriage compared to a lifelong partner?
i. Is marriage important to you and to your family? Why or why not?

Activity

Task 2

Read through the list of reasons for marriage. Rank them with your partner or group from the most understandable to the least understandable. Can you add any other reasons?

pressure	pregnancy	love	physical attraction	financial security	biological clock
tax reasons	similar interests	for a visa	to have children	to live longer	

Germany finally legalises same-sex marriage

On 30 June 2017, a bill was passed in the German Parliament legalising marriage between two men and two women, finally adding Germany to a list of over 20 other countries which have already recognised gay marriage, including England, Wales, the USA and Ireland. Coming into effect on 1 October 2017, this law will also grant same sex married couples full rights to adopt children. Since 2001, same sex couples have been legally recognised as registered life partnerships, giving them rights and obligations in areas such as inheritance, health insurance, and immigration. (In 2004, this law was amended to also give registered gay couples stepchild adoption rights, allowing one of the partners only to adopt the other's biological child.) This right was extended to successive adoption in 2013, allowing one partner to also have the right to become the adoptive parent of the other's adopted (non-biological) child.

Starting in October 2017, homosexual couples will have full adoption rights, giving the adopted children more rights. Now these families will be finally recognised by law as a family unit and will enjoy the same rights.

Children's rights are attached to the family unit. Until now, same sex partnerships were not considered legal families in Germany and they did not have the same rights as married couples. It can be argued that marriage is in fact good for children's rights. The Convention on the Rights of Children reflects on the importance of the family for children noting in its preamble that a child should grow up in an atmosphere of love, understanding and happiness. The Convention refers to parents and legal guardians but in international law, the emphasis is on protecting the child's family relationships rather than entitling the child to be raised only by their biological parents. The right to know their identity is separate from the question of who provides for this child. Research increasingly shows that the quality of children's relationships is what affects children's lives and life chances. Legalising marriage equalises the position of all children.

Cf. Connolly, Kate: German parliament votes to legalise same-sex marriage, in: The Guardian, 30 June 2017, www.theguardian.com/world/2017/jun/30/germany-poised-legalise-same-sex-marriage-bill-law.

Cf. United Nations: Convention on the Rights of the Child, www.ohchr.org/en/professionalinterest/pages/crc.aspx, accessed 18 September 2018.

Comprehension

Task 3

Answer the following questions in full sentences with a partner and write down the answers.

a. What happened on 30 June 2017 in the German Parliament?
b. What other countries have already legalised same-sex marriages? Why do you think it took until 2017 for Germany to pass this bill?
c. What is stepchild adoption? Compare this to full adoption.

Task 4

Elton John, an English singer, pianist and composer, is openly gay and supports LGBT marriage. He and his partner have adopted two children. Can you think of an example (either from your life or from the media) of a LGBT family, who have a child or children? Describe this family on paper.

Language

Prepositions of time: *while, during* and *for*

During is used with a noun to express when something happened:
During my childhood and teens my mother rarely, if ever, spoke badly of my father.

While is used to express the same thing but with a verb:
While I was growing up, my mother never spoke badly of my father.
For is used to talk about the duration of periods of time an event has taken place:
My mother never spoke badly of my father *for* 15 years.

Task 5

Complete the sentences using *during, while* or *for*. Do the exercise on a separate piece of paper or in your notebook.

a. Gay marriage in Ireland has been legal ...(1)... 2 years.
b. ...(2)... my childhood, my parents got married.
c. ...(3)... their marriage they never fought.
d. ...(4)... they were living together, they travelled a lot.
e. I fell asleep ...(5)... the film.
f. We were on welfare ...(7)... 30 years.

UNIT 5:
Stages of development

Module 1: Concepts of development in early childhood

Theories of development and learning

In order to develop good pedagogical practice in the preschool, it is first necessary to acquire an understanding of the stages through which young children grow and develop. Child psychologists and educational specialists have developed theories concerning the physical, cognitive, emotional and social development of children at the preschool age. Many of them have identified specific stages that all children go through as they grow and mature, developing new skills and a deeper understanding of the world they live in. The development of these skills and understanding enables children to increasingly control and interact with their immediate environment, and to assert and express themselves as individuals within it.

Amongst the best known developmental and educational psychologists are John Dewey (1859–1952), Maria Montessori (1870–1952), Jean Piaget (1896–1980), Erik Erikson (1902–1994).

In his works, John Dewey emphasised the importance of basing learning programmes on the immediate experience of the children, as well as on the teacher's observations of what interested the children. He believed that the learning experience should be closely related to the life experience of the children. He was also a strong advocate of the guiding role of the teacher and was opposed to the tendency he saw in progressive teaching methods of allowing children too much freedom to have fun and do as they please. He felt it was important that teachers have the confidence to use their own understanding of their pupils, as well as their own experience of the world to provide a meaningful context for learning. He felt that without clear guidance, direction and structure, learning programmes could have little real educational value.

Maria Montessori's ideas have become so widespread in the field of early childhood education that they are now often perceived as self-evident. When she first published her ideas at the turn of the twentieth century, her pedagogical concepts were revolutionary and controversial. Montessori believed that children had a natural desire and impulse to learn and would do so independently if the conditions were created for them by their teachers.

Jean Piaget is well known for his work on explaining the cognitive development of children. He believed that children passed through certain clearly defined stages of intellectual development. The development phase that children go through between the ages of three and seven he termed the "preoperational stage". This stage of development is characterised by the child's egocentric perspective on the world and his place in it. Piaget conducted a number of experiments in which he demonstrated that children in this age were incapable of seeing something from another person's perspective. He also showed that children in the preoperational stage can only focus on one aspect of a thing at a time. For example, a child in the preoperational stage finds it difficult to understand that his own mother also has a mother, i.e. that his grandmother is also his mother's mother.

Erik Erikson concentrated on the psychological development of human beings and observed that children go through a process of establishing their independence between the ages of two and three. The child may develop feelings of shame and doubt at this stage, if it is thwarted by adults in its attempts to establish autonomy. At the next stage of development, between the ages of four and five, children are at a stage of developmental maturity where they are ready to acquire a sense of purpose. At this stage the danger is that instead of developing a healthy sense of initiative, the child may be reprimanded by adults for mistakes it makes and, as a result, be burdened with a sense of guilt.

All of these developmental psychologists believed in the importance of providing children with concrete situations in which to test and develop their experience and understanding of the world.

Comprehension

Task 1

Match the words and expressions in italics in the following sentences with the appropriate words or expressions from the box below.

widespread – advocate – self-evident – reprimanded – autonomy

guidance/direction – immediate – thwarted – a sense of initiative – enables

a. The ideas of pioneers, such as Maria Montessori, in the area of child psychology and development were considered revolutionary in their day, but are now so *common* that they are seen as very *obvious.*
b. John Dewey was a *supporter* of the idea that teachers had an important role to play in the development of children. He felt that teachers had a responsibility to use their own experience and knowledge of the world as a means of providing structure and *orientation* to their pupils' development.
c. Dewey also believed that pedagogical concepts and teaching practices should be based fundamentally on the children's *direct* experience of the world they live in.
d. The learning and application of new skills *facilitates* children in exercising more control over their environment, and to interact more productively with it.
e. Children are often *frustrated* by adults in their efforts to achieve *independence.*
f. When children are *criticised* for making mistakes, it often discourages them from developing *the power to make and act on their own decisions.*

Task 2

Some preschool teachers feel that the theories of child development they learn while studying aren't very relevant to the practical, everyday business of managing a class and dealing with the desires and demands of their young pupils.
With a partner discuss the question of whether or not the principles of theory can be usefully applied to the processes and procedures of classroom practice.
Report your ideas and opinions to the rest of the class.

Erik Erikson's eight ages of man

Erikson's stages of psychosocial development		
Age	**Stage**	**Strength**
0–1 year	Trust vs. Mistrust	Hope
2–3 years	Autonomy vs. Shame and Doubt	Willpower
4–5 years	Initiative vs. Guilt	Purpose
6–12 years	Industry vs. Inferiority	Competence
Adolescence 13–19	Identity vs. Role Confusion	Fidelity
Young adulthood 20–39 years	Intimacy vs. Isolation	Love
Middle age 40–64 years	Generativity vs. Isolation	Care
Old age 65 +	Ego Integration vs. Despair	Wisdom

Erik Erikson divided human development into eight distinct but interconnected stages, from birth to old age. His work was based on that of Sigmund Freud, but also considered the vital role social and cultural influences play in developing our sense of self, and in determining how we interact with the people who make up our social environment. Erikson believed that at each stage of life (listed in the table above), a person has to successfully resolve what he called an identity crisis in order to develop healthily and move on to the next stage of their psychosocial development. For example, in the first stage of life, babies need to develop a sense of trust in the people around them by feeling that they are being properly cared for and loved. Once this sense of trust has been instilled, the infant is then ready to deal with the crisis awaiting it in the next phase of its development. Thus Erikson saw human development as a cumulative process in which the successful resolution of one stage provides the inner strength necessary to meet the challenge of the next.

In their first year of life children learn to develop a sense of hope and optimism within themselves, if given the proper level of care and love by parents and other caregivers. According to Erikson it is particularly important for the child at this stage to enjoy a close relationship with its primary caregiver who should always be available and willing to comfort the child when it feels insecure and needs lots of loving attention. The presence and availability of the caregiver will reassure the child that it is safe and can always rely on the caregiver to protect it from danger or harm. Children who are raised in an environment where their need for security is neglected grow up with feelings of anxiety, fear and insecurity towards the world. They tend to distrust instead of trust, and develop a sense of doubt rather than hope in a world they fear will harm them or let them down.

Between the ages of one and three Erikson emphasised the need for parents and caregivers to allow the growing child the freedom to explore their environment and to do things on their own. Children at this age will feel a natural desire to develop a sense of independence, and they experience a great sense of pride and joy in any task they manage to accomplish by themselves. A sense of self-worth develops in children in this phase, if they are allowed the scope to develop their ability to do certain things by themselves. Of course, it is also important for caregivers to get the balance right and not allow the child so much freedom that it places itself in danger. Erikson felt that the main risk to the child's development at this stage was presented by authoritarian or overprotective caregivers, who – out of a misplaced anxiety for the safety of the child – may criticise him for acting on his own impulses and for exercising his will. Such treatment will lead the child to develop feelings of shame towards itself which will undermine its will to do and achieve things for itself.

Erikson believed that between the ages of three and six, children should be allowed to plan simple activities such as play dates with their friends and encouraged to contribute to the organisation of events like their birthday parties. This sort of freedom and scope for action instils a sense of initiative in the child. The child will thus feel encouraged to make its own suggestions and know that they will be positively received and taken seriously by the people from whom the child seeks affirmation and approval. In this phase the child who is allowed to plan and make proposals about how events and activities should be organised will develop a sense of self-belief and purpose. "I did it all by myself" is a proud claim made by children at this age. Problems at this stage arise when parents are critical or contemptuous of the child's ideas or lack confidence in its ability to achieve the goals it sets itself. This will result in the child thinking, its ideas and opinions are valueless and not worth acting on. Thus failure to resolve the identity crisis at this stage of psychosocial development can produce an adult who constantly apologises for himself and is afraid to offer an opinion for fear of being ridiculed or criticised.

Comprehension

Task 3

Answer the following questions on the texts above.

a. What did Erikson believe is the main thing a person has to achieve in each stage of the psychological and personal development outlined in his theory?
b. In Erikson's first stage of development, explain how the effects of proper care and upbringing can instil feelings of trust in the child.
c. Why is the development of feelings of trust crucial to the establishment of personal autonomy in the next phase of development (from one to three years)?
d. How can the behaviour and actions of parents and caregivers produce feelings of shame and doubt in a child at this age?
e. What can parents and caregivers do to help to instil a sense of initiative and purpose in the developing child?

Task 4

Match the words below with words or expressions from the text.

a. very important/essential/indispensable/crucial
b. the developmental issue that needs to be resolved at each stage of psychosocial growth
c. the belief or feeling that things will turn out well
d. the person in a child's life that is most responsible for its care
e. to fail to do something that should have been done
f. to get to know an environment by moving around and examining it
g. an adjective that describes people, often parents, who believe in the importance of obeying rules
h. the impulse and willingness to realise an idea or wish
i. to be thought well of by someone
j. to be laughed at or mocked

Task 5

First reflect on your own experience of childhood between the ages of three and six or on the experience of a child of that age that you know well or with whom you work closely. Think of common, everyday situations at home or activities at school where children have the opportunity to assert their initiative in making decisions to perform a task in their own way. This could be, for example, allowing the child to decide what she wants to eat for breakfast and permitting her to prepare the meal the way she wishes.

Note down your answers to the following questions, then discuss them with a partner and finally with the class.

a. In what ways can children at this age be supported and encouraged to develop a capacity for independent decision-making and action?
b. What concerns and anxieties of parents and caregivers might obstruct this process and produce guilt feelings in the child, rather than a healthy sense of self-esteem?

Module 2: Applying theory to classroom practice

Applying Erik Erikson's theory in the preschool classroom

Two of the psychosocial developmental crises identified by Erik Erikson occur in early childhood, at the ages in which children attend preschool. The second of these crises involves the child developing a sense of initiative, which is itself essential to the generation of a feeling of purpose. Preschool caregivers should be aware of these crises and how to manage them to help ensure that the child will develop in the right way. This is a crucial stage in the development of children. If handled badly the child may grow up with a feeling of guilt and a lack of self-belief. If dealt with correctly the child will develop a sense of competence and confidence in its own abilities to perform and complete tasks independently.

It's important at this stage to strike the right balance between allowing children the freedom to make their own decisions, while not presenting them with tasks and activities that are excessively challenging. For this reason, it is vital to provide children with structured, planned activities that are broken down into small, manageable steps. Each step involves the child making a small decision in the carrying out of a concrete, practical activity.

In order to support children's development at this stage, teachers should: encourage children to act independently; focus on the progress the child makes and not on its mistakes; set expectations that are commensurate with each child's abilities; focus on setting activities that involve the performance of real tasks.

Classrooms should be set up to allow the children to act with as much independence as possible. Children should be able to fetch and reach drawing materials and tools themselves. This allows them the power to decide for themselves, for example, what pencils and crayons to choose for an art activity.

According to Erikson it is important to send a signal to children that their efforts are taken seriously and valued. For example, in a writing activity, where the children were encouraged to draw a sequence of pictures to tell a story, the children were told that their first efforts were merely a draft. They were told by the teacher that in drafts you can experiment with ideas, especially crazy ones, and it didn't matter if you made mistakes and had to cross out a picture and begin again. This approach encouraged the children to focus on the progress they were making with the activity and that making mistakes and changing your ideas were all part of the creative process.

Erikson also emphasised the importance of designing activities that cater to the individual capacities of each child, and being sensitive to the needs of the individual at any given time. For instance, if Heike has a new brother and has to share her parents with this newcomer, it might be unreasonable to expect her to share a toy or book with another child. If Heike is forced to share this may give rise to guilt feelings concerning her unwillingness to share Mum and Dad with her little sibling.

Erikson, together with Montessori, emphasised the importance of providing children with real activities to perform. This could be preparing a meal in the kitchen. By performing tasks such as these the children feel a sense of pride and achievement in doing something "grown-up", and therefore real and useful. Learning to use real utensils properly, such as sharp knives, gives the children a feeling that they are trusted and boosts their sense of competence and responsibility. Learning a real skill helps them to feel that they are moving forward in their development into grown-ups. A real skill can also be practised at home and elsewhere, increasing their feeling of control and competence.

Comprehension

Task 1

Answer the following questions.

a. According to Erikson, what kind of process influences and shapes the development of human identity at each psychosocial stage?

b. Why is it so important that teachers focus on the child's conflict with itself at each stage of its development?
c. What kind of conflict characterises the third psychosocial stage?
d. Explain how inadequate, insensitive or inappropriate upbringing can lead to the production of guilt feelings in the child.
e. Why is it important at this stage in their development that young children are presented with activities that are broken down into small steps?
f. Explain the logic behind giving children real tasks to do and concrete goals to achieve.

Language

When breaking a process down into its component steps, we often use signal words such as *first ..., second ..., then ..., next..., after that ...* and *finally,* to clearly distinguish each step of the process from the next and indicate what point of the process has been reached.

Example: Planning a painting activity

- First, ask the children to select an object to paint. This could be a ball, a simple toy, a colourful box, a kitchen utensil or a flower.
- Secondly, clearly inform the children about the activity and what you would like them to do.
- Then, ask the children to put on their aprons.
- Next, ask the children if they know where the painting materials are stored and get them to fetch them themselves.
- After that, ensure that each child has provided itself with a paintbrush and has access to the full range of paint laid out on the activity table.
- Then, ask each child to look closely at the object in front of them and to note its shape, size and colour.
- Next, ask them to try and reproduce the object on the sheets of paper in front of them using their brushes and paint. Tell them they are free to use their imagination in their representation of the object. They can change or add details to the object in their painting as their imagination dictates.
- Then, ask the children to remove and clean their aprons, and to hang them up.
- Finally, gather the children together in a circle and ask them to talk to the group about their experience of creating their painting. The children should be listened to attentively and praised for their efforts, in order to promote their sense of self-confidence.

In the example above, the process is presented as a sequence of instructions. To give instructions, the imperative is often used. There is only one imperative form for both singular and plural cases, and this is simply the infinitive form of the verb.

Examples:
Take the first left, go straight on and the kindergarten is on the left.
Children, go to the cupboard and **fetch** the paints and brushes.
Fill some beakers with water, Jenny, so we can clean the brushes.

Task 2

Complete the following sentences using the imperative form of an appropriate verb selected from the "painting activity" text above.

a. ...(1)... an object for the children to paint.
b. ...(2)... the children to put on their aprons.
c. ...(3)... each child has a paintbrush of their own.
d. ...(4)... the children are free to use their own imagination.
e. ...(5)... the children together in a circle.

Task 3

Erikson, like Dewey and Maria Montessori, emphasised the importance of creating environments where children can play and learn using real objects and achieve concrete results by performing meaningful tasks.
With a partner, think of an activity requiring peer interaction and teamwork, like the painting activity above, such as the making of papier mâché Halloween masks.

a. Think the activity through carefully and list all the steps involved in the performance of the activity.
b. Work together on writing out the process, as in the example given above, using verbs in the imperative and signal words to help indicate the beginning of a new step in the process. The activity should be organised in such a way that the individual tasks are manageable for the children, while allowing them the freedom to complete the tasks independently.
c. Read out your activity plan and discuss the logic of how you chose to structure and organise it.

Grammar

Ability, possibility and permission – the verb *can*

Can is used to talk about ability, possibility and permission. The negative form is ***cannot.*** It refers to both the present and the future and is followed by the infinitive form (active or passive).

Examples:
I ***can*** *plan* (active infinitive form) a classroom curriculum (i.e. I have the ability to perform this task).
The classroom ***can*** *be converted* (passive infinitive form) into a play area by moving the furniture aside (i.e. it is possible to change the function of the room).
You ***can*** use this knife to cut the cake, if you wish (permission).
This room ***cannot*** be used as a play area because it is too small (impossibility).

Can has no infinitive or present perfect form. Instead the expression ***be able to*** is used.

Examples:
I'd like to ***be able to*** plan a classroom curriculum properly, but haven't yet received the training to allow me to do so.

The children ***haven't been able to*** go outside and play for the past week because the weather has been so bad.

Task 4

Complete the following sentences using *can*, *cannot* (or *can't*), *be able to* or *been able to*, and say whether the sentence refers to the ability to do something or the possibility of doing something.

a. We ...(1)... send the children out to play today as the weather is fine.
b. I have ...(2)... plan my classroom activities far better since I attended a weekend seminar on this subject.
c. She ...(3)... work with us, I'm afraid, because she doesn't have sufficient training.
d. The children ...(4)... be trusted to use the sharp cutting tools responsibly, because we've already taught them how to do so.
e. The children would like to ...(5)... go to the technical museum today, but ...(6)... because it's closed.

Activity

Task 5

Think of a concrete learning activity, such as learning to prepare a simple breakfast. You have a group of 4 six-year-olds. Explain how you would organise the activity to enable the children to act on their own initiative without overchallenging them.

a. What individual steps would you break the activity into?
b. How would you take account of the children's individual abilities t to get each child to do what he's interested in?
c. How would you correct mistakes without making them feel they've done something wrong?
d. Write out the activity as a series of steps. How you would deal with the issues listed above?

Module 3: The development of a pedagogical concept for preschoolers

The ideas of Maria Montessori

The theories of Maria Montessori have probably had more influence on the methodology and practice of early childhood pedagogy than those of any other educationalist. Trained in paediatrics Montessori's work brought her into contact with children who were regarded as uneducable, i.e. with children who did not seem willing or able to respond positively to any teaching methods. Knowing that problems arising through poor education and upbringing in childhood lead to the development of psychological and behavioural difficulties later in adulthood, she set about devising teaching methods that would prove to be very effective with children who did not respond to conventional teaching techniques.

Montessori laid great stress on the importance of observing how children behaved by themselves and interacted with one another. She believed that it is crucial to create an environment that is conducive to learning. The educationalist considered it as essential to make the kindergarten a child-oriented environment. This means setting up the rooms in the kindergarten in a way which appeals to children and allows them the freedom to function independently, without the assistance or interference of adults. This can be done by using child-sized furniture, equipment and tools, and ensuring that shelves in the rooms are set low enough so that their contents are accessible to every child.

The human aspect of the learning environment however is as important as the physical. This means that the kindergarten teachers need to be properly trained, sympathetic to the children's needs and committed to meeting those needs through using the right kind of approach. Montessori emphasised these environmental factors because of her conviction that children learn naturally from their own experience of their immediate surroundings, if left to their own devices.

Montessori thought that the experiences and activities made available in the learning environment should be as real as possible if they were to have any true developmental value. Performing real tasks with real tools is much more preferable, in her opinion, to carrying out pretend tasks using toy tools, which can't be used outside the context of imaginary play. This is why she insisted that the utensils and implements that the children were given actually functioned as intended. Knives should be sharp to allow the children to prepare their own snacks and meals. Hammers should be heavy enough to drive real nails into blocks of wood. Montessori felt confident that children could be trusted sufficiently to use such tools safely and responsibly. She also felt that children should be allowed the space and time within the kindergarten curriculum to work and play independently, in order to allow them the freedom to explore, experiment, learn and develop on their own and through their interaction with each other.

Comprehension

Task 1

Answer the following questions on the text in your own words.

a. What early professional experiences led Maria Montessori to the area of child education?
b. Why is it so important to create the right kind of environment for children to learn in?
c. Describe some of the ways in which such an environment can be created.
d. Why is it important to give the children real tasks to perform?

Task 2

Match the words and expressions in italics in the following sentences with the appropriate words or expressions from the box below.

methodology – laid emphasis on – is conducive to – conventional teaching techniques
immediate surroundings – uneducable – devised – curriculum – left to their own devices – carrying out – observing – conviction

a. Maria Montessori developed a *set of techniques* to help children who were thought to be *unteachable* to learn effectively.
b. She *developed/put together* a pedagogical system that was designed to replace *normal teaching methods.*
c. Carefully *watching* the behaviour and interactions of children *is helpful to* the creation of an appropriate *programme of educational tasks and activities.*
d. When *left alone* children can independently learn a great deal from their *direct environment.*
e. Montessori *emphasised* allowing children the freedom to explore, play and experiment on their own.
f. Most educationalists entertain a firm *belief* in the pedagogical value of independent learning.
g. By *performing* meaningful activities and enjoying the achievement of meaningful goals, children develop their ability to accomplish tasks and meet new challenges.

Language

In the comprehension text above, verbs such as *believe, feel, think* and *insist* convey the beliefs, opinions, ideas and convictions of a certain person:

Montessori *believed* that it was first of all crucial to create an environment that is conducive to learning.
Montessori *thought* that the experiences and activities made available in the learning environment should be as real as possible.
Montessori also *felt* that children should be allowed the space and time within the kindergarten curriculum to work and play independently.
She *insisted* that the utensils and implements that the children were given actually functioned as intended.

Task 3

Using the verbs above and some of the vocabulary in Task 2, write a short essay of approximately 250 words expressing your own ideas on the most important factors concerning the education of young children. In your essay consider the issues of peer interaction, independent play, the significance of the physical environment and, most importantly, the role of the teacher in the education of young children.

The Spreesprotten Kinderladen – a pedagogical concept

The concept of the kindergarten in Kreuzberg, Berlin, is based on many of the ideas and teachings of Maria Montessori.

Childhood is characterised by physical growth and change, the development of a sense of self and increasing independence, the building of relationships with adults and other children, playing alone and together, learning to accommodate others, experiencing the world and learning.

Every child is born with a multiplicity of needs and abilities: the need for contact and to explore, the will to survive and live, taking joy out of life, the capacity to understand and react, and the capacity to recognise the connections between things.

The expression "the child is an actor in his own development" means for us that the child has a need to develop and grow, and is provided with an environment that respects this need and can be relied upon to meet the individual child's requirements. In this way, the child can play a part in her own development, but is also subject to outside influences and factors.

We accompany and support the developmental process of the child, offering a feeling of security and protectiveness. We have developed the environment of our kindergarten in such a way that the child can learn holistically, become independent, develop a sense of self-confidence and acquire social skills. We respect the personality of the child, but exercise an influence on its behaviour and development, in accordance with the tenets of our concept, as well as through active engagement with the child. We nurture the child's freedom of movement; its freedom to experiment; its freedom to express feelings; its freedom to choose; and its freedom to be independent of adults.

Comprehension

Task 4

Answer the following questions in your own words.

a. Identify the elements of Montessori's teaching that the Spreesprotten Kinderladen have used to create their concept.
b. Using your own ideas, suggest ways in which you think the needs of the child as an individual can be reconciled with the necessity of developing and integrating the child as a social being within its peer group.
c. In what ways do you think this concept and its implementation can provide children with the support they need to positively resolve the identity crises that Erikson believed occurred at stages two and three of a child's psychosocial development? (see Module 1, Task 2)

Listening

Interview with Gabi, Antonia and Kathrin, caregivers at the Spreesprotten Kinderladen

Please tell me something about the pedagogical concept you have developed for your kindergarten.

Gabi: Well, we are basically "minimalists". We focus on developing relationships, individuality and independence. One of the best aspects of our philosophy is that the staff members are also keen to develop themselves and find out more about who they are, so that each one of us, by understanding who we are, can relate to the children in an authentic way. It's more important for us, as caregivers, to develop meaningful relationships with the children than to follow a precisely formulated programme, point for point and goal for goal.

Kathrin: Yes, I think it's very important that the children learn how to get on with other children and to learn that others, apart from themselves, also have needs. This doesn't always work of course. Sometimes the children understand and accept others, and sometimes not.

Gabi: It's also important to emphasise that we don't take a "moral" approach to resolving disputes. There's no "you're bad" or "I'm bad", but rather we try to encourage the children to accept each other as they are.

Do you think the concept you've created is appropriate for the developmental needs of every child in your care?

Gabi: Yes, we do! It's appropriate for everybody, because if you treat the other person with respect, tolerance and openness, that person feels valued. This is the basis of a healthy relationship through which each person can help develop themselves and each other.

How do you see the role of the caregiver in the development of the children?

Gabi: We have to try out a lot of different things. It isn't the case that we can simply say right from the beginning that it works in such and such a way. Maria Montessori developed materials that are complete in themselves. This means that there doesn't have to be someone standing by who constantly provides correction. The child itself can use the materials in its own way and when it doesn't work, it can try it out again and again.

Maria Montessori wrote that teachers should "teach less and observe more". Do you sometimes find it difficult to stand aside and allow the children to do their own learning?

Antonia: It really depends very much on the specific situation. When the children are involved in a learning process and trying something out it's easy for me to sit on the margins and observe their play and interaction. But in conflict situations my instinct is to leap in and immediately intervene. It can be difficult in these situations to stand aside, but this gives you an opportunity to reflect on where your limits lie and to ask yourself why you feel the need to intervene at a certain point.

Gabi: Yes, the concept has a great deal to do with us, the caregivers, and who we are as people. You have to ask yourself questions like "why is it difficult for me to be patient with a certain child", and so you have to examine what your own reaction is and see what it has to do with your own personality.

Do your pupils in the three-to-six age group learn a lot from each other?

Kathrin: Well, we recently had a situation where there was a conflict. One child was lying on the floor crying, while another sat on top of him and refused to move. The whole group were involved in dealing with this conflict. They all tried in different ways to resolve the conflict by saying things like "get off him please". One of them tried to push the offending child off the other, but was beaten away by him. Then one of the children came to us and said "we need help". We said that there were already more than enough people involved, and stood aside to observe the situation. In the end one of the boys came over and pulled the boy off the other from behind. The child who was crying was then comforted by three others and after two or three minutes they were all playing happily together again. Of course we could have quickly settled the conflict ourselves, but not in the way the children dealt with it. And we thought, yes, that's exactly how it should work, with the children being free to come to terms with each other without our interference.

Thank you so much for your time.

Task 5

Answer the following questions in your own words.

a. Why, according to Gabi, is it important for caregivers to understand and develop themselves?
b. What does Kathrin think is important for children to learn about each other?
c. In what kinds of situations does Antonia find it difficult not to involve herself?
d. How can these situations help Antonia better understand what kind of person she is?
e. How, according to Kathrin, did the children themselves resolve a conflict between two boys? Do you agree that this was a better way of resolving the crisis than the direct intervention of the Spreesprotten staff? Explain.

Activity

Task 6

You and a partner wish to set up a kindergarten together. In order to do so, you first need to develop a clear concept on which to base your pedagogical practice. Using the Spreesprotten concept above as a model, think up and write out your own.

The concept should contain information such as:

- the principles your concept is based upon,
- your understanding of the most important factors of a child's development,
- how the teaching practices you employ, based on the theoretical principles you've outlined, can support and promote the emotional, cognitive and social development of the children in your care,
- the overall developmental goal of your pedagogical practice, e.g. you seek to help the children develop into happy, confident and motivated individuals.

UNIT 6:
Working with children under three

Module 1: Emotional relationships – a matter of trust

Choosing the right childcare

Fewer families today can afford to live on one salary alone, so they rely on affordable childcare to reconcile work and family life. In an effort to allow mothers and fathers to return to the workforce quickly, the federal government of Germany devised a scheme to provide access to day care for 35 % of all children under the age of three by the year 2013, while guaranteeing day care places to all one-year-olds. The government's efforts of the most recent years are proving effective. According to statistics provided by the German Federal Ministry for Family, Seniors, Women and Youth, the proportion of the children under the age of three enrolled in a day care rose from 13.6 % in 2006 to 32.7 % in 2016.

And although the number of children under three in day care increased by 5.7 % between 2015 and 2016, the demand for childcare continues to increase as the birthrate and the number of immigrant children in this age group grow. The federal government has earmarked considerably more money for childcare for the upcoming years.

The qualitative differences within Germany are considerable, notably the discrepancy in staffing ratio between the eastern and western states. 52 % of all under three-year-olds attend day care in the East, while only 28 % do in the West. However, the child-carer ratio is overall significantly lower in the West.

Due to the shortage of day care facilities in some areas of Germany, parents often do not have many options as to whom to entrust with the care of their children. Those who do have the choice find it difficult to decide whether a nursery or a childminder would be best. The needs of children and their parents are different and the choice in day care is based on the suitability of the carer or facility to meet these individual needs. Regardless whether childminder or nursery, when parents look for an appropriate setting, the most important criteria include safety and cleanliness, the number of staff, the variety of equipment and stimulating materials, but above all, the positive interaction of the carer with the child. A child's ability to develop a trusting and secure relationship with its carer is fundamental for its sound emotional and behavioural development. Also the parents' trust in the carer to validate and support their child's emotions is reflected in the stability of the child-carer relationship and is key to a positive working relationship.

Comprehension

Task 1

Which statements are not true? Correct the false statements with information from the text above.

a. Fewer children are being born today.
b. The federal government was able to fulfil their pledge to provide day care for 35 % of all children under the age of three by the year 2013.
c. The federal government plans to spend more money on childcare in the upcoming years.
d. More children under the age of 3 attend day care in the West than in the East.
e. The relationship between carer and child plays a significant role the child's development.

Task 2

Discuss the following questions with a partner, then share your answers with the group.

a. Why is the demand for childcare increasing?
b. Why is providing affordable day care so important?
c. Why is the positive interaction between carer and child so important?

Case study

Evelyn tells her story about finding day care for her one-year-old, Freddy.

We thought that Freddy would be better off at a nursery school, but it was very difficult finding a place for him at twelve months at a nursery school we felt comfortable with. Many of the nursery schools in our area weren't accepting one-year-olds because of the shortage of staff members.

We finally did happen to find a childminder in our area who, in her early sixties, was looking to take on two young toddlers. Although she had no formal education as a childcare professional, she was experienced, having raised two girls by herself as a single mom. She liked Freddy immediately, and Freddy warmed up to her quickly, too. She was willing to mind Freddy from nine o'clock in the morning till three in the afternoon. This wasn't always that convenient for us, but between the two of us, we managed to pick him up punctually every day.

The childminder's apartment was clean, but small and on the third floor. She had a cat, too, which was not very fond of children. Freddy was the first child in her care, so she didn't have any problem carrying Freddy up and down three flights of stairs until she took on a second toddler, Luisa, who couldn't walk yet. Though Freddy could walk, he wasn't ready to climb up and down three flights of stairs by himself yet. The childminder had to rely on the help from a neighbour to mind one child while she fetched the other. And when a neighbour wasn't available, Freddy was made to crawl up and down the stairs by himself. We were concerned about Freddy's safety and didn't like the idea of him being left alone in a crib while the childminder carried Luisa down the stairs, but there wasn't much we could do about it.

As the year progressed, we noticed that the childminder was reluctant to answer all of our questions and didn't seem to appreciate our concerns and suggestions. Although Freddy seemed to be enjoying himself, we began to doubt her competency as a childminder. When the childminder announced that she would be taking a two-week summer holiday, we were faced with a problem. Neither of us could afford to take two weeks off from work to stay at home with him. Furthermore, we didn't think that it would be good for him to be in someone else's care he wasn't familiar with. After an emotionally difficult nine months, we made the decision to remove Freddy from the childminder's care. Freddy, now two, absolutely loves nursery school and we are very satisfied with the nursery and its professional staff.

Task 3

Discuss the following questions with a partner, then with the group.

a. Evelyn was dissatisfied with her choice of day care for Freddy. Why was she unhappy with the situation? What could have been better?
b. The parents' choice in day care for their child is based on the suitability of the carer or facility to meet their individual needs. Make a list of the advantages and disadvantages of childminders and nurseries for children under the age of three.
c. If you had a young child, what kind of day care would you choose?

Task 4

Complete the sentences with a preposition. If you need help, look for clues in the first two texts of this module.

a. A majority of families cannot live ...(1)... one income anymore.
b. Traditionally, mothers were expected to stay at home for the sake ...(2)... their children.
c. Problems in a child's emotional development can sometimes be attributed ...(3)... a disturbed relationship between carer and child.
d. Many nursery schools do not take ...(4)... children under the age of two.
e. Ten per cent more children under the age of three will have access to day care ...(5)... 2013.
f. Many people believe young children are better ...(6)... at home with their mothers than in day care.
g. We are not fond ...(7)... the idea of leaving our child with a childminder.
h. Working parents have to rely ...(8)... competent professionals to care for their children.
i. Without day care for their children couples are often faced ...(9)... financial problems.

Grammar

Past progressive

When we want to say that something (an action or situation) was in progress at a particular time in the past, we use the progressive aspect of the past tense – the past progressive form of a verb. It looks like this:

was/were + (verb)-ing

Only actions or events that are not instantaneous can be used in the past progressive tense. For example, the verb *stop* expresses an action that occurs immediately; it does not require time to progress. The verb *stop* is therefore almost never used in the past progressive form.

The verb phrase *to have a snack,* on the other hand, does not occur instantaneously. It requires time to have a snack. We can say that at one particular moment of the day this action or event was in progress. Look at this example:

What **were** the children **doing** at ten o'clock?
At 10 o'clock the children **were having** a snack.

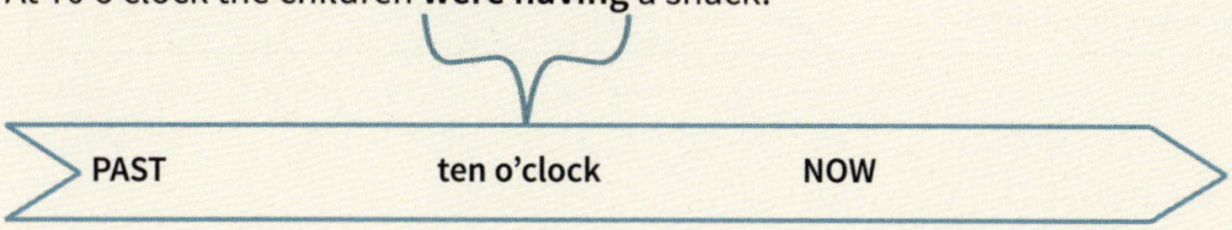

Snack time might have begun at ten o'clock, but it continued beyond ten o'clock, perhaps until quarter past ten.

At ten o'clock the children **were not napping** yet. (weren't napping)

Task 5

Freddy just turned three. He has learned a lot in the past three years. Look at the timeline on the next page and write sentences in the past progressive to describe the milestones in his development during his first 36 months. An example has been done for you.

birth	responds to voices	*After birth Freddy was responding to voices.*
6	passes objects from hand to hand	
9	learns to crawl	
12	takes first steps	
15	says his first words	
18	learns to say his own name	
21	uses more than 200 words	
24	speaks in three-word sentences	
27	rides a tricycle	
30	counts to ten	
33	understands concepts of time	
36	gets dressed without help	

The childcare dilemma

Academics, childcare experts, politicians and parents have been in disagreement for decades about the question whether full-time day care for children under the age of two is harmful or beneficial. Over the years studies and news articles have presented contradicting conclusions about the linkage between day care and the emergence of aggressive and risk-taking behaviour later in life. A study published in 1986 by Professor Jay Belsky sparked a heated debate about the long-term effects parental separation had on infants and young toddlers. Belsky found evidence that young children who spent many hours in day care facilities every day displayed higher levels of aggression, had poorer relations to teachers, and were more likely to use drugs and alcohol later in life. Although Belsky admits that the negative effects are marginal on an individual basis, he warns that the multiplicity of aggressive behaviour in older children and teenagers can have a large-scale impact. Other research, however, has shown that nursery day care can have positive effects in cognitive and language skill development among the under two-year-olds.

Most parents grapple with the decision to return to work and are already laden with guilt for leaving their child with a childminder or in a nursery at an early age. This period of transition into day care is stressful for both child and parent. The results of a Dutch study in 2006 did not pacify parents' anxiety. The researchers (Vermeer and van IJzendoorn) found that cortisol levels in children younger than 36 months who attended a day care facility were considerably higher than in those who were cared for at home. Cortisol is a hormone that is released in stressful situations. Although no longitudinal studies have been done to reveal the long-term effects of high cortisol levels, the researchers speculate that the interactions in a group setting is stressful for a young toddler. Some experts suggest that abnormal cortisol levels can not only cause aggression and disobedience, but also emotional insecurity, fearfulness and hyperactivity.

British psychologist Dr Penelope Leach is concerned about the non-maternal childcare in the first year of life. She states that the advantages of day care in nursery settings only become evident between the age of 18 and 30 months. Leach makes reference to psychoanalyst John Bowlby's attachment theory, which establishes that children between 8 and 36 months often suffer from separation anxiety from their primary caregiver. The research of Bowlby and Belsky has led to a greater emphasis in training childcare professionals on the importance of establishing continuity in the care-giving relationships and the provision of attachment-friendly care. This involves assigning the child to a key person in the day care setting to whom it is able to develop a stable emotional relationship.

Comprehension

Task 6

Complete the table with the missing word forms. Write a sentence using one of the other word forms.

Noun	Verb	Adjective	Adverb
		beneficial	
aggression	–		
anxiety	–		
	suggest		
provision		–	–

Task 7

Answer the following questions in your own words. Then discuss your answers in a group.

a. Why is it believed that day care for the under two-year-olds can lead to more aggressive behaviour?
b. Why is a nursery setting stressful for toddlers?
c. How can day care in a nursery setting benefit toddlers?
d. What can practitioners do to make the nursery experience less stressful for a toddler?

Module 2: Language and motor skills development

Language development through movement

In the first three years of its life, a child is constantly multi-tasking as it grows and learns. It is learning to use self-control and coordination over its own muscles, experimenting with physical movement, and discovering the meanings of words through interactions with others. Everything it experiences and does is connected to language. Each new movement and each new sound or word is the assertion of the infant's own self. Without the use of its body as a medium, a child could not define itself through language as an autonomous person in a social environment.

First language acquisition is closely connected to the process of sensory perception. A child must use its sense of vision, hearing, touch, taste and smell to perceive its environment before it can learn to express its observations or feelings. The sensorimotor area of the brain requires exposure to feeling and movement to stimulate the development of neural connections. The left and right hemispheres of the brain communicate across the corpus callosum when language is conveyed through movement, facilitating the development of all cognitive skills.

Although many childcare practitioners are aware of the importance of movement and play for language development, nursery and preschool teachers are feeling pressured to create structured curricula which are often inappropriate for young children. Preschools are placing a stronger emphasis on traditional methods of early literacy and language arts rather than physical education and free play in order to satisfy the expectations that children achieve benchmarks.

Childcare practitioners can promote language development in toddlers by focusing on activities which combine language and movement. Children do this naturally without the guidance of adults when they play. When they invent games and rules for those games, they implicitly practise their negotiation skills while they expand their vocabularies. By adding elements of rhythm and music, learning through movement becomes a kinaesthetic experience; children grasp and retain the concept of nouns, verbs, adjectives and prepositions more quickly and develop a keener sense of their meanings.

Comprehension

Task 1

Collocations are two words that are commonly used together as a fixed expression. Find the words in the right column that collocate with the words in the left column. Look for clues in the text to help you.

a. free	1. callosum
b. language	2. education
c. corpus	3. acquisition
d. cognitive	4. play
e. language	5. skills
f. physical	6. arts

Task 2

Which word makes sense? Choose the correct word in the brackets to complete the sentence. Look for clues in the text, or use your dictionary to help you.

a. Most experts agree that (exposure/disclosure) to television is harmful for under two-year-olds.
b. The (exposure/disclosure) of confidential information without permission is unethical unless a person is in danger.
c. Babies are born with the innate ability to (grasp/understand) objects.
d. Very young children do not (grip/grasp) the difference between reality and fiction.
e. Email has replaced the letter as the most common (medium / facility) of correspondence.
f. Although it is quite unusual, some adults (retain/keep) their baby teeth their whole lives.
g. Many parents (retain/keep) their children's baby teeth as a keepsake.

Task 3

Answer the following questions in your own words. Then discuss your answers with a partner.

a. Why is physical movement advantageous for language learning?
b. Why are more nurseries and kindergartens designating more time to language arts than free play?
c. Why is free play important for the development of language skills?

Grammar

The past progressive vs. the simple past

We often use the past progressive in sentences which also use the simple past tense for a different action. The verb in the past progressive form refers to a longer action, i.e. something that was *going on already* when the shorter action or event occurred. The shorter action or event uses the simple past. Look at this example:

The children **were playing** on the playground **when it started to rain.**

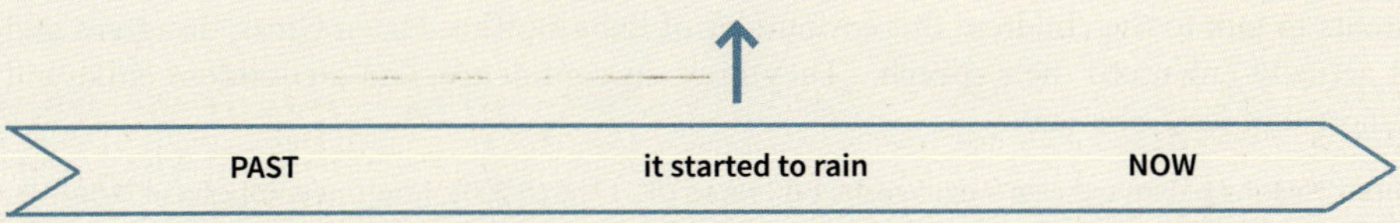

The children went out to play before it started to rain. Their playing was in progress when the rain started at once.

We can express the sentence differently. If we put the shorter action before the longer action in the sentence, we use the word *while* rather than *when* to connect the sentences.

It **started to rain while** the children were **playing on the playground.**

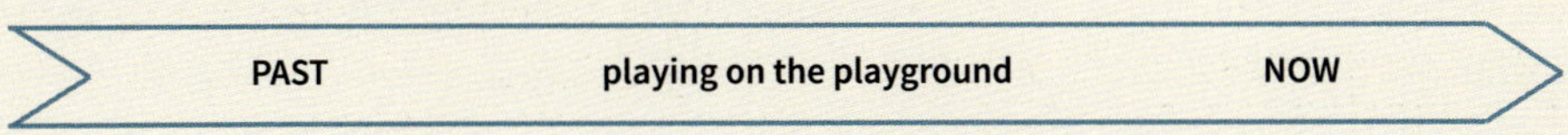

Task 4

Complete the sentences with the simple past or past progressive form of the verbs in the brackets.

a. Leonard (get) himself wet. He (drink) water from a cup and (spill) some on his jumper.
b. Victoria (hurt) herself. She (play) on the playground and (fall) from the swing.
c. Sarah (sleep) still when her mother (come) to pick her up.
d. Max (say) he (hit) Kyle because Kyle (tease) him.
e. We (plan) to take a walk to the park when it (start) to rain heavily.
f. "(See) you Jonathan's toy car?" "Yes, I think Henry (play) with it."
g. The practitioner (not + see) the accident happen because she (not + pay) attention.

Hearing babies use sign language

A group of mothers have started their own sign language group for hearing babies to try to communicate with them before they learn to speak. Simple actions accompany pictures at the Baby Boffins sessions in Hastings, East Sussex, using an idea originally pioneered in the US. It has been set up with the help of the government's Sure Start programme, which means it is free. Co-founder Sarah Stone said signing relieved the frustration in babies. She said her children were signing sentences to her from the age of 13 months, and communicating their basic needs very clearly.

The method of signing with hearing babies by hearing parents was developed by Dr Joseph Garcia, an American child development expert. After working as an interpreter, he noticed how hearing babies of deaf parents could communicate their needs at a much earlier age than children of hearing parents who did not use signs. He also noticed how it reduced levels of frustration in a child and helped build up the bond between parent and infant.

Language experts have expressed concern the use of signing could take priority over the need for parents to talk to the children. But co-founder of Baby Boffins, Helen Cross, disagrees and says it actually enhanced their speech. "They grow in confidence, and a confident child will speak more, not less," she said.

Taken from: Hearing babies use sign language, in: BBC News UK, 1 March 2005, http://news.bbc.co.uk/2/hi/uk_news/england/southern_counties/4307333.stm, accessed 21 September 2017.

Comprehension

Task 5

What are the arguments for and against teaching sign language to babies and young children? Discuss with a partner and make a list.

Activity

Task 6

In a group of four or more people, have a debate about whether baby sign language can help improve language skills. The class divides into two teams. One team will support the motion that baby sign language can improve language skills, and the other team will oppose the motion. Refer to Unit 3, Module 3 about the rules of debate.

Grammar

The modal verb *should*

The modal verb *should* has several different uses.

We use *should* to make a recommendation, or to express an opinion. Here are some examples:
You **shouldn't** go to work if you are ill.
You **should** stay home and rest.

We also use *should* to talk about an obligation, or things that are good or important to do.
We **should** call the child's parents.

Should is also used to express something that is probable.
We **should** be back by four o'clock.

We use *should* to make a prediction, or to say what we expect will happen.
The weather **should** be nice tomorrow.

To talk about what a child, for example, is expected to do by a certain age, we use *should* followed by *be able to*.

should + be able to + infinitive verb

At three months a baby **should be able to smile** when it sees its mother.

Task 7

Look at the table of milestones in language development below and write a sentence using *should be able to* to express what a child can be expected to do at each phase of its development.

a. at 9 months	communicate with gestures, like waving its arms
b. at 12 months	use a few words like "dada" and "dog"
c. at 18 months	name some body parts
d. at 24 months	say two and three word phrases
e. at 30 months	ask questions with "what?", "where?"
f. at 36 months	speak in three- and four-word sentences

Module 3: Hygiene and toilet training

Good hygiene practise in childcare settings

Toddlers are more susceptible to illness than older children and adults because their immune systems are still too weak to ward off all bacteria and viruses. Therefore, childcare practitioners must observe public health guidelines and regulations, and maintain good hygiene practise in their settings at all times. Although day care staff may be aware of the importance of proper hygiene, in reality, some may be too busy to practise it consistently. Here's what some of them say:

"I carry and comfort the little ones all day long. When they cry, I wipe away their tears and when they have a cold, I clean their runny noses. Of course small children don't cover their mouths and noses when they cough or sneeze, so I am in constant contact with germs and body fluids. I have to remember to wash my hands frequently to try to prevent the spread of colds."
Cynthia, Leeds

"The children at our nursery not only have their own cubbies for their belongings, each of them also has a hook and shelf space in the washroom for their flannels, towels and toothbrushes, which is marked with a picture of the child. That way there is no confusion about whose is whose. The flannels and towels are washed every other day."
Miles, Plymouth

"Because the babies are always putting the toys in their mouths, we sterilise the toys regularly to reduce the risk of cross-contamination. Each child also has its own set of bed linens for its cot."
Judith, Cornwall

"Our nursery has a nappy changing policy. Nappies are checked and changed if needed every two hours, or sooner if the child is soiled. All staff wear disposable gloves and aprons for each change. The changing areas are cleaned with disinfectant after each use. The soiled nappies are double wrapped in nappy sacks before they are put in the covered waste disposal bin. The childcare practitioners are expected to wash their hands with warm water and liquid soap after they have finished."
Bret, Carlisle

Comprehension

Task 1

Find a word in the text to replace the word in italic print. Use the dictionary to help you.

a. The childcare practitioner must *comply with* state regulations.
b. The children's personal belongings are hung separately to try *to curb* the spread of germs.
c. Each child naps in its own *bed*.
d. The towels and linens are washed every day *to minimise* the chances of transmitting illness.
e. *Dirty* nappies must be wrapped in two plastic bags before they are disposed of.
f. The practitioners teach the children about the importance of *cleanliness*.

Grammar

Reflexive pronouns

Reflexive pronouns are pronouns used following transitive verbs, or verbs that take objects, to show that the object and subject are the same person or thing.

*The girl looked at **herself** in the mirror.*

In this sentence the subject is the same person as the object.
It should be noted that English has far fewer verbs that take reflexive pronouns than other European languages. There are some verbs in German, for example, that are followed by reflexive pronouns, but not in English.

The boys washed themselves their hands. (incorrect)
The boys washed their hands. (correct)

I interest myself for music. (incorrect)
I am interested in music. (correct)

A reflexive pronoun is not used after prepositions of place or position.
*The girl took her teddy **with her** to bed.*

If the subject is plural and the verb is a reciprocating action, then a reciprocal pronoun, *each other*, or *one another,* is used.
*Lucy helps Louis, and Louis helps Lucy. Lucy and Louis **help each other.***

Compare these sentences:
*The children **helped themselves** to fruit.* (reflexive pronoun)
*The children **helped each other** pick up the toys.* (reciprocal pronoun)

In the second sentence, the verb is a reciprocating action.

We also use reflexive pronouns to show that the action is done without help from someone else, or alone.
*A child should never be left **by itself.***
*The boy was proud that he could climb the ladder **by himself.***

Reflexive pronouns are also used to emphasise something, usually the subject.
*I'm caring for an ill child, though I feel ill **myself.*** (also)
*I was going to call the child's mother, but the mother called me **herself.*** (personally)

Task 2

Look at the sentences below and decide whether the reflexive pronoun or reciprocal pronoun is necessary. Rewrite the sentence correctly only if the sentence is incorrect.

a. After breakfast the children brushed themselves their teeth.
b. The baby recognised itself in the mirror and giggled.
c. Maggie isn't able to dress herself yet.

d. The children sat themselves down in a circle.
e. The children were playing hide and seek, and James hid himself behind the curtain.
f. Simon hurt himself on the playground.

Task 3

Translate the following sentences from German into English.

a. Die Kinder freuten sich über ihre Weihnachtsgeschenke.
b. Zoë musste sich selbst umziehen.
c. Er hat sich wahrscheinlich gestern im Regen erkältet.
d. Sie versteht sich gut mit den anderen Kindern.
e. Wir haben uns alle beim Zirkus amüsiert.
f. Leo hat sich mit der Schere geschnitten.

Task 4

Together with a partner, write a list of guidelines for maintaining good hygiene for the staff members at your preschool. Present the guidelines on a poster to the class.

Case study

Three-year-old Zoë Rosso, like many children her age, was having difficulties making it to the toilet in time. She had been potty training for a few months, and was dry by the time she started preschool. But when Zoë started preschool, the stress of the new situation caused her to have accidents from time to time. Zoë's mother saw no reason for concern until the Montessori preschool Zoë was attending in Arlington, Virginia, suspended her for one month. The principal of the preschool claimed that Zoë was having too many accidents at her age; the county had a policy for the admission to preschool programs requiring three-year-olds to be fully toilet-trained. If a child had more than eight accidents in a month, it would be suspended. After the suspension Zoë returned to the preschool and shortly thereafter started having accidents again – too many. For fear that Zoë would be suspended again, her parents found a spot at a new preschool that worked with children who were potty-training. Zoë's mother assured her that she would be going to a preschool where the teachers wouldn't be angry with her for having accidents. Zoë never had an accident after that.

This text is based on the story "Three-year-old suspended from Arlington preschool for too many potty accidents" by Brigid Schulte that appeared in the Washington Post on 30 January 2011.

Comprehension

Task 5

Discuss the following questions with a partner.

a. Why do you think Zoë began having accidents?
b. Should being toilet trained be a criterion for the admission to a preschool? Why, or why not?
c. How should potty training be managed at a nursery or preschool?

Task 6

Discuss the following questions as a group.

a. How would you react if a child had an "accident" and didn't make it to the toilet in time?
b. How should the accident be dealt with?

UNIT 7:
Growing up

Module 1: Growing pains

Growing up involves a lot of changes, new responsibilities and learning on many different levels. These changes are usually accompanied by conflicts, discussions and debates. In this unit, some problems of growing up will be discussed.

Task 1

Reflect and write a short comment on the following questions. After you finish answering them, discuss your answers with a partner.

a. What did you enjoy about growing up? What did you dislike about growing up?
b. What is better now at your current age compared to when you were younger? What is not as good as when you were younger?
c. What would you change if you knew then, what you know now?
d. Did you have a happy childhood? Why or why not?

Quotes on growing up

"A grownup is a child with layers." – Woody Harrelson, actor

"It is only because of problems that we grow up mentally and spiritually." – Morgan Scott Peck, psychiatrist

"We grow neither better nor worse as we get old, but more like ourselves."– May Lamberton Becker, journalist and literary critic

"All children are artists. The problem is how to remain artists once they grow up." – Pablo Picasso, artist

"To exist is to change, to change is to mature, to mature is to go on creating oneself endlessly."
– Henri Bergson, philosopher and writer

"When I grow up I want to be a little boy."
– Joseph Heller, writer

"If you haven't grown up by age forty, you don't have to."
– unattributed

Task 2

Discuss with a partner the meaning of the quotes. Which one can you relate to most? Share your ideas with the whole group. Can you come up with your own quote about childhood or growing up?

Caught between childhood and adulthood: the life of a teenager – it's all in the mind

Growing up isn't easy, and adolescents are stuck in the middle of it. They aren't quite adults yet, but they aren't children anymore either. Teens are in a period of metamorphosis called puberty that erupts in their brains when they are about ten, and not only causes rapid physical growth, but also erratic mood swings and unpredictable behaviour. They go through a process of maturation that takes them through many ups and downs – conflicts with themselves and with others.

Teenagers often feel misunderstood by their parents and resent their parents' involvement in their lives. They seek their independence and demand the freedom to discover their identity and role in society. But the rules their parents lay down for them always seem to prevent them from doing just this; conflict is inevitable. At the same time, teens secretly yearn for their parents' guidance and support at one of their most vulnerable stages of their lives. Although many parents feel their efforts are futile, their constant lecturing about responsible decision-making and proper social conduct is crucial for their offsprings' development and for their safety.

Scientists say that teenagers are not to blame for their less than desirable patterns of behaviour. Research on the development of the adolescent's brain has unfolded that it undergoes a wave of overproduction of brain cells and synopses during puberty that is similar to that in infants in the first year of life. The executive centre of the brain, the pre-frontal cortex, does not fully mature until the mid-twenties. During adolescence, this part of the brain, whose job it is to plan and think about consequences and to control impulses from other parts of the brain, is deluged by hormones, making it practically impossible for teens to think clearly, understand consequences of their behaviour, and understand and follow rules of social conduct. Unlike an adult, an adolescent is unable to control impulses; instead, he seeks thrills and adventure and engages in activity that involves risk, without being able to recognise the risk. These activities are usually prompted by group dynamics and a teen's eagerness to win the respect of his peers.

The miscommunication between adolescents and their parents also seems to be caused by a teenager's inability to interpret emotions through facial expression. While adults use the pre-frontal cortex – the rational part of the brain – to read emotion, adolescents use the amygdala, the part of the brain that stores memories of emotional events and controls instinctive responses such as fear or the fight-flight response to threat. A teen has difficulty interpreting social cues, such as body language, facial expression and even the tone of voice. So, when a parent asks their child to clean up their room, this is probably not interpreted as a request, but rather as a threat or insult.

The tendency to overreact to harmless remarks makes teenagers particularly vulnerable to bullying and humiliation by their peers. They go to all lengths to "fit in" with their clique and to avoid negative attention. This usually expresses itself through their preoccupation with their appearances. Particularly girls become very self-conscious about their bodies and often have a distorted perception of themselves. Because they still lack self-esteem, teens are easily embarrassed and hurt by their peers' criticism – even if it's a spiteful gaze.

Teenagers are fragile. Their brains take them on a roller-coaster of emotions that are more intense than at any other time of their lives. Although all people go through this stage of confusion and frustration, the adult, whose mature brain has made their behaviour more placid, often regrets later in life not being able to experience life with the same intensity as when they were teens.

Comprehension

Task 3

What are the meanings of the words in italics in the following sentences? Choose the correct synonym from the box.

calm – changeable – embarrassment – flooded – signals – unavoidable – useless – weak

a. During puberty, teenagers experience not only rapid physical growth, but also *erratic* mood swings and unpredictable behaviour.
b. The rules parents lay down for their children always seem to prevent them from venturing their independence; conflict is *inevitable*.
c. Teens need their parents' guidance and support at one of their most *vulnerable* stages of their lives.
d. Many parents feel their efforts in being a good parent have been *futile* when their children act irresponsibly.
e. During adolescence, a teenager's brain is *deluged* by hormones, making it practically impossible for them to think clearly and to understand the consequences of their behaviour.
f. A teen has difficulty interpreting social *cues*, such as body language, facial expression and even the tone of voice.
g. The tendency to overreact to harmless remarks makes teenagers particularly vulnerable to bullying and *humiliation* by their peers.
h. Once an adult's brain matures by his mid-twenties, his behaviour becomes more *placid*.

Task 4

Answer the following questions based on your understanding of the text.

a. What happens to a teenager during puberty?
b. Why do conflicts often evolve between teenagers and their parents?
c. In what ways are a teenager's brain different from an adult's brain?
d. Why do teenagers often overreact to their parents' comments and requests?

Growing up

What does it mean to grow up? Growing up can be divided into three major categories:

- **Growth** is associated with an increase in physical size, and can be measured by height, weight and circumference of the head.
- **Physical development** refers to the increasing ability and function of the body, including motor skills, skills of coordination and balance.
- **Emotional and social development** relates to how children understand themselves as individuals and as part of a social group (i.e. friends, family). It also involves how they become more independent and self-confident and are able to express and control their emotions. This aspect of development affects relationships with others most.

Comprehension

Task 5

Match the following skills or abilities to one of the three major categories of growing up. Can you name any other skills or competences?

a. hand-eye coordination
b. self-esteem
c. weight
d. body proportions
e. self-concept
f. autonomy
g. balance
h. motor skills
i. sensory development
j. friendship
k. relating to others

Grammar

Comment adverbs for viewpoint and opinion

Comment adverbs are words or phrases that express the speaker's or writer's opinion or attitude about the stated information.

Some comment adverbs evaluate the statement so as to reflect the speaker's or writer's preferences or viewpoints (i.e. *fortunately, honestly, importantly, luckily, personally, regrettably, surprisingly, thankfully, understandably, unfortunately).* These adverbs are placed at the beginning of the sentence and separated from the rest of the sentence by a comma to show they modify the whole sentence, rather than just the verb.

Some comment adverbs show how likely we think something is (i.e. *apparently, certainly, clearly, definitely, surely, probably*). If it is placed after the subject to add emphasis, commas are used to separate it from the rest of the sentence: *Our son,* clearly, *had no idea what he was doing.*

Other comment adverbs show our judgement of someone's actions (i.e. *carelessly, kindly, politely, stupidly, wisely*):
He **stupidly** got himself in trouble with the law.
She **wisely** chose not to leave school.

Comment adverbs should not be confused with **adverbs of manner**, which sometimes look the same, but are meant to modify the verb or verb phrase and are placed either before the verb or after the verb and its object.

Comment adverb: **Happily**, she was able to find an apprenticeship that suits her.
(I am happy that she found an apprenticeship.)

Adverb of manner: She **happily** found an apprenticeship that suits her.
(She is happy to have found an apprenticeship.)

Viewpoint adverbs are quite similar to comment adverbs, but are used to make it clear from what point of view we are speaking (i.e. *politically, financially, physically, biologically, from a medical point of view*):
From a scientific point of view, teenagers are not to blame for their rebellious behaviour – their brains are.

Task 6

Rewrite these sentences so that the word or phrase in italics is replaced with an appropriate comment or viewpoint adverb. Make any necessary changes to complete the sentence.

a. *It was understandable that* her parents were upset about her behaviour.
b. She *regretted* not having finished school.
c. I am not *biologically* related to my uncle.
d. You have few *legal* rights as a minor.
e. It's *probable* that she ran away from home.
f. It was *kind of her* to ask me about my mother's health.

Teenage confessions

Listen to Emma (17), Stephen (18) and Jane (16) talk about how they struggle with their problems. As you listen, take down notes on a separate piece of paper to answer the questions in the grid. The transcription of the audio can be found on page 200.

	Emma, 17	Stephen, 18	Jane, 16
What problem do they have?			
What are the causes for their problems?			
How are their problems similar?			
How do their problems affect them?			

Task 7

After you've listened to Emma, Stephen and Jane speak about their problems, compare your notes with a partner's. Discuss the answers to the questions.

Task 8

Do the three teenagers understand how serious their problems are? Do they understand the consequences of their behaviour? Write a comment using comment adverbs to state your opinion about each teenager.

Task 9

Can you relate to the portraits of these three teenagers? Have you ever had a similar problem? Write a composition of no more than 300 words explaining the problems you've had to face as a teenager.

Module 2: Experimenting and risk-taking

Children and teenagers need opportunities to test new things for themselves. They also need to be encouraged to take risks, despite the chance of failing. Through experimenting with lots of different things, they will get to know what they enjoy and what they are good at and also what is difficult for them. They will also be able to encounter their own limitations which is important in development to become more confident about who they are. It also teaches them to make safe, informed decisions and to avoid people and situations that are potentially harmful or not good for them. Along with trying out new hobbies, activities and social encounters, alcohol, drugs and cigarettes are among the substances teens tend to experiment with.

Task 1

Discuss the following questions with a partner.

a. Why do you think they want to consume these substances?
b. Do you think this consumption by teens has changed over the last fifty years? If yes, how?
c. When did you experiment with these substances? How did it come about? How do you think about this experiment now?

Binge drinking

A health study in Germany has actually shown that alcohol, drug and cigarette *consumption* among teens are at their lowest since they began these studies in the 1970s. However, what is a problem now amongst adolescents is *binge* drinking, which is a heavy consumption of alcohol over a short period of time with an intention of becoming *intoxicated*.

A “study from the government's drugs commissioner, which surveyed the alcohol consumption habits of 5,000 young people in 2012, showed 44 percent of 18 to 25 year olds drinking heavily at least once a month.

It also found 17 percent of 12-17-year-olds drank to excess every month.

Drugs commissioner Marlene Mortler said the widespread overuse of alcohol among young people represented a 'substantial health risk,' highlighting that in the past year over 26,000 young people had had to be treated in German hospitals for alcohol poisoning."

From: The Local: Half of young Germans binge drink regularly, 7 April 2014, www.thelocal.de/20140407/half-of-young-germans-binge-drink-regularly.

According to other studies, German teens binge drink more than British and American. Because of this, a school programme called „Klar bleiben" (keep a clear head) was designed and *carried out* among 10th graders, where the participants did not binge drink for nine weeks. Signing *a contract* not *to binge* drink, they recorded their drinking behaviour every two weeks as a class. The adolescents who had already consumed alcohol took part in binge drinking at a significantly lower amount. They concluded that such a programme could have a significant effect on the frequency and intensity of binge drinking, especially amongst the adolescents who have already consumed alcohol.

Adapted from: Hanewinkel, Reiner; Tomczyk, Samuel; Goecke, Michaela; Isensee, Barbara: Preventing Binge Drinking in Adolescents: Results From a School-based, Cluster-randomized Study, 21 April 2017, www.aerzteblatt.de/int/archive/article/187987, accessed 07 September 2018.

Comprehension

Task 2

Match the following definitions to one of the words in italics in the text above. The tenses of several of the italicised words need to be changed. One word from the text is used two times.

a. A period of time of excessive indulgence.
b. The act of using something.
c. To be placed in a medical facility for care or observation.
d. To execute.
e. Something deemed harmful, usually legally restricted.
f. Another word for being drunk or high.
g. An agreement between two or more parties, usually written and signed by those involved.
h. To cause to lose control of one's facilities and behaviour.
i. To indulge excessively over a certain period of time.

Task 3

Answer the following questions based on the text above. Discuss the answers with a partner.

a. What is binge drinking?
b. How has the consumption of alcohol, cigarettes and drugs among adolescents changed since the 1970s in Germany? What could be the cause of this?
c. Why do you think binge drinking has become a problem? Brainstorm this question without using help from the Internet, etc.

Language

Linking words to express a contrast: while, whereas, although, though

In order to express a contrast, linking words can be used. Here are some examples:

Binge drinking is drinking excessively in a certain period of time, **while** binge eating is eating excessively.

Teenagers tended to drink more in the 1970, **whereas** teens today tend to drink less.

Teens try drugs, **although** they are illegal.

Children and teens experiment with illegal substances, **even though** their parents do not want them to.

Task 4

Complete the following sentences using while, whereas, though or although.

a. Teens experiment with drugs, ...(1)... they can be harmful.
b. My mother lets me drink wine at special occasions, ...(2)... it is not really allowed.
c. ...(3)... Tom is not old enough to drink, his mother allows him to sip her beer once in awhile.
d. Adolescents who had already drunk tended to binge drink less ...(4)... those who had only occasionally something to drink started to binge drink.
e. You have to be 21 to drink in the US ...(5)... you can drink at 18 in Germany.

Task 5

Write down the negative and positive aspects of risk-taking.

Children of alcoholics

Growing up with an alcoholic parent is not so easy. It is not just the alcoholics themselves who are affected by the addiction, but also the people around them, especially family and friends. Because the children alongside the addict are often left to fend for themselves, the impact of alcoholism on children was highlighted by the National Association for Children of Alcoholics.

This organisation's helpline received 32,000 calls and emails in 2016, with children asking for bedtime stories because their parents were too drunk to do so. One child, a seven-year-old girl who called on Christmas Day while hiding from her drunk parents under her bed, asked to be told a story about her imaginary dog, Bruce.

The charity also helped a five-year-old whose addict mum locked herself in the bathroom and was found dead by paramedics. An all-party parliamentary group has been working to ensure government policy is in place to support these children's needs. They have called for a national strategy to deal with the issue that affects 2.5 million children in the UK.

According to Sky News, children of alcoholics have been shown to be four times more likely to become heavy drinkers themselves, five times more likely to develop an eating disorder and three times more likely to consider suicide.

Task 6

Discuss the following questions in a group.

a. Why do you think the children of alcoholics are often forgotten? How are they forgotten?
b. Why do you suppose that children of alcoholics are more likely to be heavy drinkers or have other problems?
c. What are possible signs of a child of an alcoholic?

Module 3: Media consumption

The impacts of media on children

Hand-held devices are everywhere nowadays. Smartphones, tablets and other hand-held devices are in almost every German household. Between January 2009 and April 2016 the number of these devices increased more than eight times. Even the smallest of children have access. Due to the sinking price of these devices and the sheer necessity of having access to the Internet in the 21st century, the number of devices in families with small children has risen.

What is practical and necessary for adults may have adverse effects on our smallest children. Recent studies have been showing the possible negative impact on our young children. Research from the University of Toronto and the Hospital for Sick Children in Toronto found that for every 30 minutes of screen time, the risk of delayed speech increases by 49 %. A recent study by University College London found that the sleep of infants is affected due the blue light from the screen affecting the natural body rhythm and thus possibly harms the brain development. Every hour an infant spends on hand-held devices was linked to 16 minutes less sleep. Since sleep is important for the development of the brain, this lack of sleep could have drastic negative impacts.

It is easy to give in to a child's wishes to watch one more YouTube video or play one more game. Physical playtime and face-to-face contact is not only very critical for both brain and body development but also helps to form a relationship between the child and parent. This relationship will be altered if hand-held devices are used as a digital babysitter. Infants can experience their first addiction. Not only does the blue light present or disturb the sleep of the child, it may also spark tantrums.

Adapted from: Knapton, Sarah: Tablets and smartphones damage toddlers' speech development, in: The Telegraph, 4 May 2017, www.telegraph.co.uk/science/2017/05/04/tablets-smartphones-damage-toddlers-speech-development, accessed 21 September 2017.

Comprehension

Task 1

Are the following statements true or false? Correct the false statements with information from the text.

a. The number of hand-held devices has gotten smaller over the years.
b. The blue light from screens encourages sleep.
c. Results of recent studies have shown negative effects of such devices on small children.
d. Such devices have no proven effect on the child's speech.
e. Brain development is affected by over usage of smartphones and tablets.
f. Playing offline and having real-time contacts are not so important for the brain and body.
g. Tablets and smartphones can be damaging for small children.

Task 2

How do you think communication has changed since many people have smartphones? Do you think it has changed since you were younger? If yes, for the better?

Communicating online

Modern teens are communicating the most while looking at a screen, not another person. Even when a group of teens are physically together, their eyes will all be attached to a smartphone. Social media is involved in every aspect of a young person's life, not just in their free-time. 90 % of 14–29 year olds are registered on at least one social media platform, with Facebook, Google+ among the top networks. Here they can chat, text, meet others, share pictures and videos – all in the comfort of their rooms at home.

Adolescents communicate on social media with photos, videos and memes. Naturally some of this can be positive. Teens need the chance to explore their own identity without having their parents or teachers present. They need to feel like they belong to a group of their own outside of the immediate family.

On the other hand, this way of communicating can cause poor decision making. This culture of instantaneous likes or dislikes on every post can lead to life-changing decisions that are rarely fully thought through. Moreover, because they are afraid of getting caught, many teens now have secret ways of communicating. They establish groups which cannot be found by non-members and in order to become a member, one must receive an invitation. These secretive groups can lead to other problems, causing teens to overshare and maybe get caught up in a world "all about the likes" rather than real life.

Comprehension

Task 3

Answer the following questions based on the text above.

a. How do most teens communicate nowadays?
b. What are the positive aspects of social media listed in the text? Can you think of any others?
c. What are the negative apects talked about in the text? Are there any others that you know of?
d. What are your experiences with social media?
e. What is meant by a world "all about the likes"?
f. How do you think that this form of communication will affect other areas of teens' lives?

Task 4

Imagine you were babysitting a child who would not stop watching videos on a tablet. How would you react? What other alternatives could there be instead of using a tablet?

Cyberbullying

One teenage issue that has been concerning not only parents is cyberbullying. According to Wikipedia, cyberbullying (known in Germany by the term "cybermobbing") is a form of bullying using electronic forms of communication and has become increasingly common, especially among teens. Since smartphones and the internet are now found almost everywhere, communication with peers has become possible anytime and anywhere. Along with the obvious advantages, there are also disadvantages. Quarrels, power struggles and teasing can now be shifted and intensified at any time to the internet and take on dramatic dimensions.

Since 1980, youth and children in Germany in distress can receive anonymous assistance by calling the free hotline "Nummer gegen Kummer" (literally: "Number against Distress"). On an average of one to two times a day, the calls specifically concern cyberbullying: in 2013 alone, this telephone counselling service recorded almost 500 cases. Not only are adolescents and children affected by this phenomenon, but also parents' fear that this could happen to their own child has been a growing concern, especially because they do not feel like they are being adequately informed and supported.

Cyberbullying, which can come in even more forms than traditional bullying, e.g. harassment, spreading rumours, hacking user profiles, to name just a few, is believed by just over 50 % of German teens to be worse than face-to-face bullying, which was a result of a survey completed by YouGov. In addition, about 18 % of German teens say they have experienced bullying through social media. What sounds at first harmless is a widespread problem that has the potential to get out of control. Or has it already?

Unfortunately, there is still no definition of cyberbullying at a European level, meaning it is difficult to come up with measures that can protect young people. Spain is the only country in the EU that can claim that cyberbullying is in their legislation.

Moreover in Germany there are no central structures for the prevention of cyberbullying, nor any binding standards, such as a scientific evaluation, for the quality assurance of relevant approaches. At a local level, schools try to deal with this problem in their own individual way but no one knows exactly if this local intervention is actually effective. Along with the Federal Ministry for Family Affairs, Senior Citizens, Women and Youth, researchers and other organisations have created a Germany-wide contact point for internet risks, for example, the so called "Bündnis gegen Cybermobbing" (www.buendnis-gegen-cybermobbing.de/).

Over the past few years, dozens of pilot projects have been launched and workshops and project days have taken place at schools. In Berlin, researchers at the Freie Universität have developed the training programme "Media Heroes". Nevertheless, the demand everywhere is greater than the supply and often they can be funded only on a short-term basis.

Another successful way to deal with this phenomenon is to train young people to be experts in this field. Often the victims have too much anxiety to turn to adults for help. Or they fear that their parents will immediately seek to get contact with the parents of the perpetrators, which could often be seen as a further loss of control. Students in upper forms are therefore sometimes a better contact point. Several programmes in Germany train young people to be "digital heroes" and then become active as mentors and help to sensitise younger ones to the dangers of cyberbullying.

These programmes and projects have helped to put this problem into the media and it made people talk about it in public. However, much more has to be done at a national and European level to conquer this new area of bullying.

Adapted and translated from: Herbold, Astrid: Cybermobbing - Wenn soziale Medien zum Pranger werden, in: goethe.de, December 2014, www.goethe.de/de/spr/unt/kum/jug/som/20456247.html, accessed 21 September 2017.

Cf. Vodafone & YouGov: Cyberbullying - Germany. Online survey carried out in September 2015. http://docs.dpaq.de/9635-ppt_for_vodafone__cyberbullying_-_germany__060_9_9_15.pdf.

Task 5

Answer the following questions based on the text above.

a. Can you think of any other forms of cyberbullying which the text does not mention?
b. Why do you think that quarrels, power struggles, etc. can take on dramatic dimensions on the internet?
c. Do you think the projects mentioned in the text are enough to deal with such an ever-growing problem?
d. What exactly is "Media Heroes"? Try to find out more information on this project on the Internet.
e. Why is this form of bullying potentially more dangerous than the traditional face-to-face form?
f. Write an email to Dr. Schultze-Krumbholz, a researcher in Berlin who worked with the Federal Ministry for Family Affairs, Senior Citizens, Women and Youth , asking about her success (or lack of) with the German government.
g. Can you find a specific programme that trains students to become experts/mentors in this area? Use the internet or any other source of reliable information.

Task 6

Translate the following first aid tips.

Du wurdest im Internet oder per Handy angegriffen? Jetzt nicht den Kopf verlieren:

- Auf keinen Fall auf SMS, E-Mails, Kommentare antworten.
- Informiere den Betreiber der Online-Plattform über den Vorfall.
- Lasse den Täter sperren oder blockiere ihn.
- Sammle Beweismaterial – mache zum Beispiel Screenshots.

When would these tips come in handy?

Activity

Task 7

Have a classroom debate on the appropriateness of talking about cyberbullying in preschool. Split into two teams. One team will support education in this area, while the other team is opposed to it. Before you open the debate, each team should collect and prepare their arguments. Once both teams have presented their arguments, decide as a whole which team is more persuasive.

Task 8

You and your partner are preschool teachers and you would like to implement a cyberbullying curriculum for children aged 4 to 6. What do you feel is appropriate to tell children about and how? Plan a few activities in which you introduce young children to cyberbullying and bullying in general.

UNIT 8:
Food and health

Module 1: You are what you eat

Task 1

Do you know which countries these different dishes come from?

1.

2.

3.

4.

5.

Task 2

Here are the names of the dishes. Can you match them to the pictures?

a. Curried goat
b. Pirozhki (fried buns stuffed with meat or vegetables)
c. Gnocchi (potato dumplings) with butter and sage
d. Sushi
e. Vegetarian side dishes

Task 3

Discuss the following questions:

- Which of the above dishes do you – or would you – most like to eat?
- Do you have any favourite foods?
- Which do you think has the most calories?
- Which is the most balanced meal? Why?

Hummus shortages after shops remove dip from sale over 'taste issues'

Lovers of Middle Eastern cuisine are bracing themselves for a new kind of double dip recession as both Sainsbury's and Marks & Spencer face a shortage of hummus. Customers at branches of both supermarkets from York to Essex to Chiswick have complained of a lunchtime crisis after finding shelves empty of hummus and have published a barrage of pictures online. Some tweeted heartbreak emojis, while others used the hashtag #firstworldproblems.

The shortage came after a series of complaints that the dip had an unpleasant flavour, which one Twitter user described as metallic. "Please fix your hummus production issue. I've never been more heartbroken in my life than when I found the hummus aisle so empty," another customer tweeted Sainsbury's.

M&S and Sainsbury's both withdrew some lines from sale after what Sainsburys described as taste issues, and Tesco customers also noticed the problem. One branch of Sainsbury's decided to help ravenous hummus fans by sticking a recipe to one of the empty shelves, helpfully including where to find the necessary chickpeas, tahini and herbs.

In a statement, Sainsbury's said that the problem was down to "a production issue at our supplier." Own-brand hummus at all three supermarkets is supplied by the food-manufacturing company Bakkavor. [...]

A survey in 2013 marked Britain as the hummus capital of Europe, with 41 % of people having pots in the fridge, almost twice as many as any other country. Waitrose was the first British supermarket to stock hummus in the 1980s, with others following in the next decade. Chefs such as Yotam Ottolenghi, Claudia Roden and Anissa Helou have done much to popularise Middle Eastern foods in recent years, and shoppers now view hummus as a grocery staple.

"It's filling and sustaining but still has a healthy image, which is justified in many ways because chickpeas have lots of protein and tahini is a much better source of oil than many others. But in all honesty, I think it's mainly the flavour," Ottolenghi said at the time of the survey.

Last year, however, a health group said many healthy-sounding savoury products including hummus were "salt and fat traps" laden with excess calories. [...]

to brace yourself for = sich vorbereiten auf

Extract from: Khomani, Nadia: Hummus shortages after shops remove dip from sale over 'taste issues', in: The Guardian, 25 April 2017, www.theguardian.com/business/2017/apr/25/humour-bypass-as-houmous-runs-dry, accessed 17 September 2018.

Comprehension

Task 4

What are you doing if you are tweeting?

a. eating sweets
b. imitating a bird
c. posting on social media

Are the following statements true or false? Correct the false statements.

a. Hummus fans reacted with humour to the situation.
b. The problem was that the hummus tasted too sweet.
c. UK consumers see hummus as a basic food, similar to bread or milk.

Task 5

Look at the picture on the right. How many foods can you name in English? What other things do people eat for breakfast? Compare lists with your neighbour/s and see if you can extend your food vocabulary.

Task 6

Now copy the food pyramid into your notebook, and put the food words on your list into the main food groups in the pyramid.

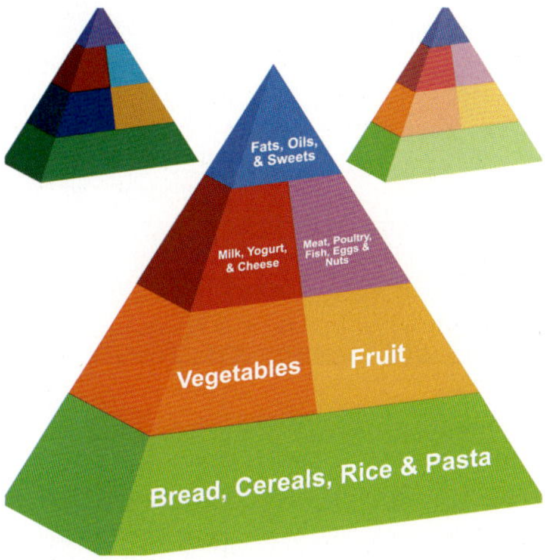

Task 7

Look at the following list of food nouns from the module. Divide them into nouns which are countable, uncountable or can be both.

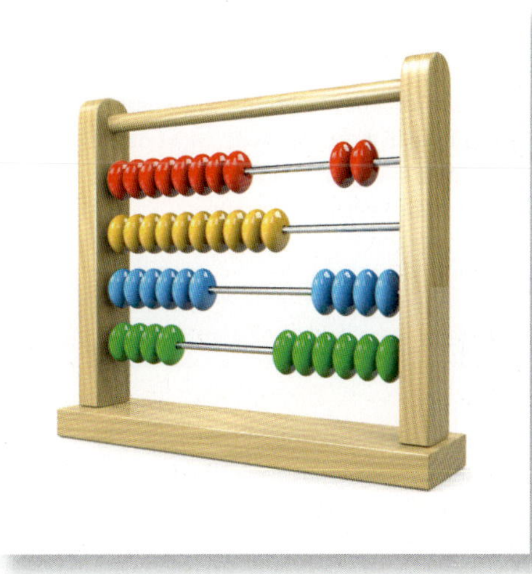

1. butter	8. herb
2. calorie	9. hummus
3. goat	10. oil
4. chickpea	11. protein
5. curry	12. sage
6. fat	13. salt
7. gnocchi	14. sushi

Examples:

Countable – vegetable/vegetables
Uncountable – sugar
Can be both – food/foods

Grammar

Countable and uncountable nouns with *some/any*, *much/many*, *a lot of*

USE	EXAMPLES
Countable nouns These nouns can be counted We use a/an with the singular There is a plural form	*Last year I read 200 books.* *It makes a big difference!* *Ian has 19 grandchildren.*
Uncountable nouns These nouns can't be counted. We don't use a/an, and there is no plural.	*Some milk with your tea?* *Children need fresh air.*
Nouns which can be both Some nouns can be both, depending on the meaning: Usual use (uncountable) To refer to different types (countable)	*We drink wine every evening.* *The wines of Italy are famous.*
Some (and somebody, something, somewhere) *Some* is used in positive sentences, with both countable and uncountable nouns *Some* is also used in requests and offers.	*Mac did some general research.* *We saw some interesting sights.* *Could I have some more coffee?*
Any (and anybody, anything, anywhere) *Any* is used in most questions, with both countable and uncountable nouns. *Any* is used in negative sentences.	*Do you have any questions?* *Has anybody seen Petra?* *I didn't bring any money.*
Much *Much* is used with uncountable nouns especially in negatives and questions.	*She doesn't eat much pizza.* *How much help do you need?*
Many *Many* is used with countable nouns, in positive sentences but especially in negatives and questions.	*Jack does many part-time jobs.* *Does she eat many takeaways?* *There aren't many people there.*
A lot of *A lot of* is used in positive and negative sentences, and questions, with both countable and uncountable nouns.	*Phil has a lot of health issues.* *She doesn't have a lot of time.* *Are there a lot of new students?*

Task 8

Complete the sentences with *some* or *any*.

a. There are ...(1)... types of fat which are healthier than others.
b. There isn't ...(2)... evidence that what you eat causes ADHD.
c. Do you have ...(3)... pets?
d. There is ...(4)... research which suggests that fish are very intelligent.
e. Could I have ...(5)... more time to finish the essay?

Task 9

Complete the sentences with *much, many* or *a lot of.* Sometimes more than one answer is possible.

a. It's true that there are ...(1)... ways to make a good impression.
b. She can't be unhealthy when she gets so ...(2)... exercise.
c. Do you have to make so ...(3)... telephone calls?
d. There are as ...(4)... experts as there are opinions.
e. Hurry up, we haven't got ...(5)... time left.

Task 10

Find and correct the mistake in each of these sentences.

a. The school counsellor gave me a lot of useful advices.
b. There isn't some way that he is going to agree to that!
c. Q: What does surplus mean? A: That there are too much of something.
d. I didn't see somebody I knew at the party.
e. Big football stars earn too many money.

Module 2: Keeping a healthy weight

Celebrity chefs promote healthy eating for school kids

Two well-known faces from the world of television have joined forces to lead a drive towards healthier lifestyles among US schoolchildren. Peter Waylie and Julia Cope are familiar faces from their hit TV programmes '*Bake against the Clock*' and '*123...Cook*.' Now they're working together to improve awareness of the importance of balanced nutrition in childhood, combined with convincing North American children to get more exercise.

"We were inspired by Michelle Obama and her 'Let's Move' campaign," said Julia at a press conference on Wednesday. "We'd love to build and consolidate on her great work in tackling the epidemic of obesity among our kids," she added. Mrs. Obama's campaign had the aim of reducing obesity to 5 % by 2030, via a program which provided nutritious food in schools, helped to give families access to healthy affordable foods and encouraged physical activity. In terms of food, Peter said at the press conference "This means not only improving the sort of school dinners which we serve, but also trying to reduce the on-site sales of sugary snacks and drinks. It's ok to have these as a treat, but they should only make up a limited part of children's regular daily food intake."

According to the World Health Organization, childhood obesity is "one of the biggest public health challenges of the 21st century." "One in five US children is now obese" said Ian McEnroe, chief executive of the NGO 'Active kids: Happy kids.' "Unfortunately, children who become overweight are more prone to illnesses such as diabetes and heart disease, and they will probably also remain obese as they become adults," he explained. "Children today are simply not active in the way that children were in the past," said Julia, "and that's a big problem. A key aim of Mrs. Obama's campaign and of ours is to inspire kids to get out there and take up sports and do other physical activities."

Comprehension

Task 1

Fill the gaps in the following sentences with 4 words from the text.

a. Some types of food are not ... (1) ... for low-income families.
b. Now that many parents are avoiding vaccinations, children everywhere are more ...(2)... to diseases such as mumps and measles.
c. Three key ways to boost your immune system: get enough sleep, pay attention to ...(3)... and do lots of exercise.
d. The government has pledged itself to ...(5)... childhood illness.

Task 2

Discuss the following questions:

- How can we make sure that children stay physically active nowadays?
- Would it help to limit the time children spend looking at screens?
- How could we do this?

Case studies – Two cases of unhealthy eating

Case study A

Maggie Olwen is a nutritional adviser, and she has just started to work with the Parsons family. The family's eleven-year-old daughter Chantel is obese and has been diagnosed with childhood diabetes. They have two younger children aged six and four who are also heavy for their age. The family eats a lot of takeaways and not too much fresh produce. The news of the diabetes has been a great shock and the parents really want to make lifestyle changes.

Case study B

Peter Clarke is also a nutritional adviser and he has been asked to meet with the Edwards family, whose two children Jack, twelve, and Josie, ten, are underweight. The parents are very interested in what their children eat and are currently following the 'paleo' diet. They tell Peter that they believe that people should only eat foods which were available to hunter-gatherer societies before the start of agriculture. They are also worried about the risks of obesity and teach their children that sugar is like a dangerous drug.

Grammar

Conditional II: What would happen if ...?

We use conditional II (if-clause type 2) to talk about a different possible world. It is used to describe things which are unlikely or impossible.

if-clause	**result clause**
if + simple past tense	would/might/could + infinitive of main verb

e.g. If you ran marathons, you could eat what you wanted and you would stay slim.
e.g. If you didn't eat so many sweets, you wouldn't need so many fillings.

Task 3

This is advice for the Parsons or the Edwards. Put the verbs in brackets into either conditional I or conditional II.

a. The children's bodies (not develop) properly if you (not eat) balanced meals which include things from all of the different food groups.
b. It (help) if you (find) some fruits and vegetables which you all like and (include) them regularly.
c. If you (stigmatise) a food it may be that your children (want) to eat more of it. It's better to eat all types of food, but in appropriate quantities.
d. If you (not buy) so much fast food, you (save) money as well as improve the whole family's health.

Task 4

Think of endings for these sentences.

a. If children ate fewer snacks between meals, ...
b. There wouldn't be so much obesity if ...
c. If children get too worried about their body image, ...

Task 5

a. Imagine that Jamie Oliver is going to do a school dinners' TV programme in Germany and he is looking for kindergartens to participate in the show. You work in a nursery; write him a letter saying why you think he should choose your workplace to film his programme.

b. Your kindergarten has been chosen, and Jamie and his team are going to visit to film. Plan a menu for five lunches for the children at the nursery so that they eat five healthy balanced meals. Write out this menu. Remember to include a mixture of different things to eat so that all of the main food groups are represented.

Module 3: Food allergies

Task 1

Quiz – food allergies

1. People are commonly allergic to:

a. potatoes
b. rice
c. wheat

2. How many food allergens are there which must be labelled in the EU?

a. 12
b. 14
c. 16

3. Which of these foodstuffs contain gluten, the trigger for coeliac disease?

a. wheat and flour
b. barley and rye
c. all of the above

4. In the EU, there are six more officially listed allergens than in the US. These include:

a. celery and celeriac
b. crustacean shellfish
c. peanuts and tree nuts

5. People who are allergic to fruit often experience symptoms

a. around their mouth
b. in their ears
c. on their hands

Task 2

Discuss the following questions

- Do you know anybody with a food allergy?
- Have you read anything in newspapers about food intolerances, for example to gluten?

Task 3

Match the headings (a-j) below the text with the correct section of text.

Food allergy and intolerance myth buster

There is much in the media about food allergies and intolerances, but what is the difference? And more importantly, how accurate is the information we read? Here we sort fact from fiction.

1) ______________________________

FALSE: Food allergy and food intolerance are quite different things. A food allergy is a reaction produced by the body's immune system when it encounters a normally harmless substance. This tends to happen relatively quickly, sometimes within minutes, but more likely within 1–2 hours. An intolerance does not usually involve the immune system and is when a foodstuff (such as lactose) causes an unpleasant reaction (such as diarrhoea) and effects are rarely immediate. [...]

2) ______________________________

TRUE: It is thought that allergies to food are rising. For instance, the number of children admitted to hospital for food-related anaphylaxis has risen by 700 % since 1990. Food allergy is thought to affect 5–8 % of young children and 3–4 % of adults. It is not known why allergies are rising, but theories include changes in diet and improved levels of hygiene, which leave children's immune systems underexposed to germs.

3) ______________________________

TRUE: It is true that most children will grow out of their allergy to eggs, milk, wheat and soya – generally by about the age of five. [...]

4) ______________________________

FALSE: An allergy to peanuts, seafood, fish and tree nuts is very rarely lost. [...]

5) ______________________________

TRUE: This is true in theory, but in fact just a handful of foods are to blame for 90 % of allergic reactions to food in the UK. They are: celery, cereals containing gluten (including wheat, rye, barley and oats), crustaceans (including crabs and prawns), eggs, fish, lupin, milk, molluscs (such as mussels and oysters), mustard, nuts (including brazil nuts, hazelnuts, almonds and walnuts), peanuts (groundnuts or monkey nuts), sesame seeds, soya, sulphur dioxide or sulphites.

6) ____

FALSE: It may be that symptoms of an allergic reaction appear immediately, but it can be several hours before they present themselves. It is also the case that symptoms can be more or less severe on different occasions.

7) ____

TRUE: People with allergies can have a reaction called anaphylaxis (pronounced anna-fill-axis), sometimes called anaphylactic shock. Anaphylaxis can be fatal if it isn't treated immediately, usually with an injection of adrenaline (epinephrine). This is why it's extremely important for someone with an allergy to take their medication with them wherever they go.

8) ____

FALSE: It is thought that a much higher number of people will believe that their symptoms are being caused by a food allergy or intolerance than is actually the case. [...]

a. Food allergies can be fatal
b. Levels of food allergy are rising
c. Most people will grow out of allergies to peanuts, seafood, fish and tree nuts
d. A food intolerance is just a less severe type of allergy
e. Most children grow out of their allergy to eggs, milk, wheat and soya
f. A food allergy or intolerance can be easily self-diagnosed
g. Symptoms of an allergic reaction will always appear immediately after eating the food that caused it
h. You can be allergic to any foodstuff

Extract from: Food allergy and intolerance myth buster, in: NHS Choices 2014, www.nhs.uk/Tools/Documents/Food%20allergy%20and%20intolerance%20myth%20buster.htm, accessed 23 July 2018.

Interview: What to do when a child has an allergic reaction

Maria-Jesus Martinez works at the health board of North Norfolk, and advises preschools about handling food allergies.

How do you know if a child is having an allergic reaction?

You should know all of the symptoms to watch out for. Children may develop an irritating skin rash; their face, tongue, lips or throat might swell up; they may start coughing and wheezing and/or vomiting or having diarrhoea. Children may also experience difficulties breathing and could experience a drop in blood pressure, causing them to feel dizzy or to faint.

What should you do?

If the allergy is known to the parents, they will have provided a note from their family doctor and medication in case the child has a reaction. In that situation, follow the doctor's instructions and give the medication. If the reaction is serious you should immediately use the adrenaline in the auto–injector pen. Of course a child could also have an allergy which may not have appeared before. If you think this is happening, phone an ambulance at once.

What are the best preventative measures?
If you have children with food allergies at your kindergarten you can't be too careful. It's extremely important to make sure that everybody knows about it, and that all staff are trained in allergy awareness. It's also a good idea to let other children know – this could be done in a sensitive way. You must read all labels very carefully so as to avoid the potential food triggers. Some preschools ask that all the children avoid bringing snacks containing allergens. If this isn't considered appropriate, you will need to watch children to make sure they don't swap food or take other children's snacks. And of course the basic rules of food hygiene are of vital importance; all staff must wash their hands before handling anything any child might eat.

Comprehension

Task 4

Which answer is correct?

According to Maria-Jesus:

- A child might feel *a) cold b) tired c) itchy* with an allergic reaction.
- Staff should give a child adrenaline when they suspect a reaction is *a) mild b) acute c) faint.*
- It's important to prevent children from *a) exchanging b) making c) buying* food.

Task 5

Listen again and tick the words you hear:

may		*might*		*mustn't*		*can*		*could*		*may not have*	

Grammar

Modal verbs to express *possibility* and *probability*

	Form	Example	Meaning
Present	must + infinitive	*The children* ***must be*** *tired.*	I really think this.
	might/might not + infinitive	*They* ***might need*** *some quiet time after lunch.*	Possibly true.
	may/may not + infinitive	*They* ***may not understand*** *what we expect of them.*	Possibly true.
	could + infinitive	*They* ***could*** *be confused because it's different today.*	Possibly true.
	can't + infinitive	*You* ***can't be*** *hungry, you just ate.*	I think this isn't true.
Past	must have + past participle (PP)	*He* ***must have had*** *a good reason to miss the meeting.*	I really think this.
	might/might not have + PP	*He* ***might not have seen*** *the email.*	Possibly true.
	could have + PP	*He* ***could have been*** *held up.*	Possibly true.
	may/may not have + PP	*He* ***may have sent*** *a message we didn't get.*	Possibly true.
	can't have + PP	*He* ***can't have*** *just* ***forgotten***	I think this isn't true.

Task 6

Put the verbs in brackets into a correct form, using a modal verb.

a. The little girl (have) an allergy; she seems to have a slight rash on her legs.
b. The medication (be) out of date – we just got it!
c. The other parents (not like) the idea of having to avoid all snacks containing nuts.
d. He (be) delighted that he got the job he applied for.

Task 7

Match these sentence beginnings with the correct endings on the right.

1. He may not have really …	…a good team. Shame that you're leaving.
2. I might have known that…	…a joke about the new office having a gym.
3. She can't have been …	…she would be late. She always is.
4. That must have been …	…wanted the job after all.
5. We could have been …	…out of the office for long, her tea is still hot.

Case study

Lizzie Cribbin has a nut allergy. She had her first reaction when she was two years old, after eating some pesto sauce her mum bought from a deli, although up to then she had been fine eating supermarket pesto. Her lips and cheeks swelled up, and her parents took her to A&E where the doctor gave her medication. It happened one more time when she ate a biscuit containing nuts. Nowadays Lizzie is very careful what she eats, and carries her medication with her.

Summarizing a text using a framework

When summarizing a text, you need to choose only the most important information, and you also need to keep your summary brief. To help you in this, it is useful to use a framework.

Task 8

Look back at the articles in Modules 1 and 2: *"Hummus shortages after shops remove dip from sale over 'taste issues,'"* and *"Celebrity chefs promote healthy eating for school kids."* Choose one of the texts and summarise it, using the framework below:

Name of article, source and date.	
What was the main theme or point of the article?	*This should be described in one or two sentences. The sentences must not be too long.*
What main events were described in the article?	*You should limit this to a maximum of three events, so choose only the most important. Summarise each event in one short sentence.*
Give a little background information.	*This should be no more than two short sentences.*
ADDITIONAL INFORMATION	
What were your feelings when you read this article?	*For example, did you find it interesting, shocking, depressing?*
Think of a question to ask your classmates on this topic.	

Task 9

Find a newspaper article relating to any of the three modules in the Food and Health chapter. Use the framework to summarise it, then bring it to present to your class.

UNIT 9:
Disability and illness

Module 1: What is disability?

Comprehension

Task 1

Look at this word cloud. In pairs, put the words into three different groups.

hearing impairment	blind	sign language
muscle weakness	visual impairment	
guide dog	limb disability	paralysis
lip reading	lack of manual dexterity	
hearing aid	Braille	mobility impairment
partially sighted	speech therapist	

Task 2

In groups of four, write a survey to find out about attitudes to disability.

Your survey should have five questions. Think about the information you want to get. An example question might be: How would you feel if one of your siblings had a disability: very comfortable, quite comfortable, quite uncomfortable, very uncomfortable? Why?

Activity

Task 3

Move around the class and conduct your survey on your classmates.

Ask at least one person from each group of four, so that there is a good exchange of information between groups. When you have finished, compile your findings. For example: "Four of the six people we asked said that they would be very comfortable ..."
One or two of your group should then present this information to the class.

The social and medical models of disability

The diagram on the right shows the medical model of disability. This is the traditional way of viewing disability. It centres on the lack of physical, sensory or mental function, and it sees a disabled child as a passive receiver of services aimed at treating or managing their impairment. Emphasis is on the diagnosis and on the label, so that the disability becomes the focus of attention, not anything else about the child.

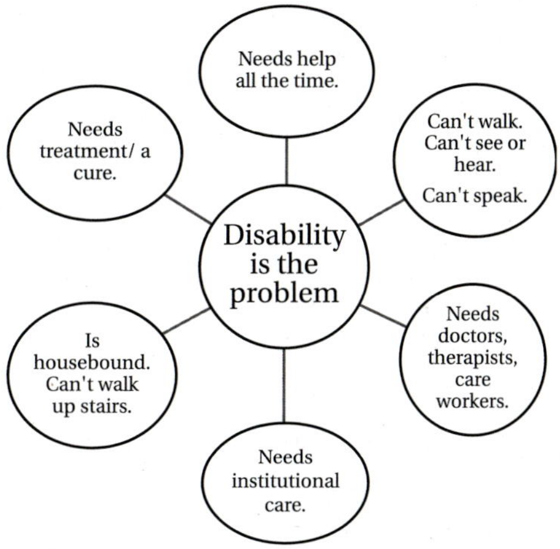

An alternative way of viewing disability has developed since the 1970s, led by disability rights' groups. This different way of looking at disability is known as the *social model.*

The social model says that the problem is not the disability, but society's barriers. These barriers stop people with impairments from taking part in society in the same way as other people. The disabled child is valued, and resources are made available to services.

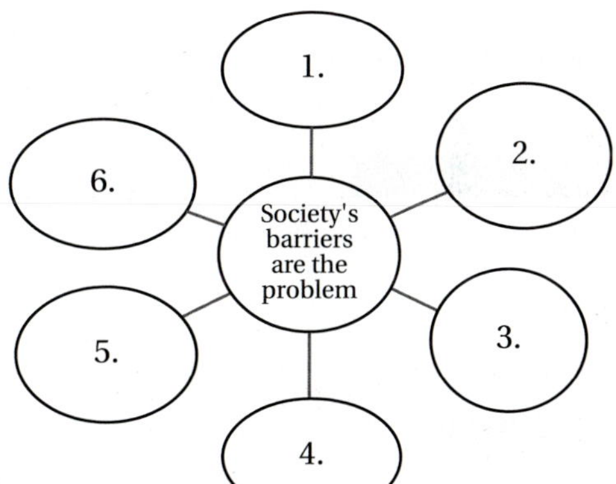

Comprehension

Task 4

Looking at the social model diagram, what do you think might be in circles 1–6?

Task 5

In groups of three to four, write down your answers to the following questions.

a. What do you think are the advantages of using the social model of disability?
b. Can you think of five barriers that are faced by disabled children and their families?

Three case studies from the UK

A. Jonathan is a four-year-old boy with cerebral palsy. He goes to a nursery for children with special needs called Winnie the Pooh Nursery. Here the children are seen by therapists (speech therapists, occupational therapists and physiotherapists) at least once a week. Activities and play are tailored to the needs of each child and their development. Opportunities are given to the children to explore and value the differences and similarities between themselves and others, and children are encouraged to express their needs by talking, pointing, eye pointing, use of pictures and signing.

B. Maylin is a five-year-old girl who has a severe hearing impairment. She is in the reception class at Kingston Primary School. Children are left to play a lot of the time, and learning activities are designed to be fun, for example maths sessions may be number rhymes. Maylin has a teaching assistant who works with her through signing, so that she can take part in the activities and play with her classmates.

C. Sinead is a three-year-old girl with Down syndrome. She attends Little Acorn Nursery in her home town of Hull. Little Acorn is an inclusive nursery. The children spend their time playing, but they are also taught pre-reading and pre-number skills as they play. The children are read to and encouraged to paint and draw. With Sinead, tasks are broken down to basics to help her learn the same skills as her peers.

Comprehension

Task 6

Answer the following questions.

a. Which of the children are educated alongside children without disabilities?
b. Which of the children has their own specific worker to help them?
c. Which of the children is taught basic numeracy?

Task 7

With a partner, answer the following question.

What do you understand by the phrase: "Opportunities are given to the children to explore and value the differences and similarities between themselves and others"?

Grammar

The passive voice

Use

We use verbs in the active voice to say what the subject of the sentence does.
e.g. The children **go** to the local kindergarten.

We use verbs in the passive voice to say what happens to the subject of the sentence.
e.g. The children **are looked after** at the kindergarten.

In the passive, the person or thing who/which performs the action is often not known, or not of primary importance. If we want to say who or what performs an action, we use *by*.
e.g. The children are looked after **by** the staff at the kindergarten.

Form

The passive is formed by the verb *be* and the past participle (the third part of the verb). *Be* changes its tense, the past participle stays the same no matter which tense is used.

e.g. The nursery **is cleaned** every day.	present simple of **be** + past participle
e.g. The nursery **is** currently **being cleaned**.	present progressive of **be** + past participle
e.g. The children **were taught** yesterday.	past simple of **be** + past participle
e.g. The boy **has been seen** by a doctor.	present perfect of **be** + past participle

Task 8

Look back at the three case studies of Task 5. Make a list of all the verbs which are in the passive voice, and all the verbs which are in the active voice.

Working in an inclusive Berlin kindergarten

Ritvan Celik works in an inclusive nursery in Berlin. He talks about the daily routine and the work he does there.

Our day begins at 8.30, when the first children arrive. A little after 9 we give the children breakfast. There are three groups of children and I work with the oldest group, the Little Einsteins.

After breakfast the children clean their teeth and then we take them through to the play room for the Morning Circle, when they sing songs and play speaking and counting games, for example practising the days of the week. We encourage each child to take part but we don't force any of them, and if they make mistakes we use positive modelling rather than correction.

Between 10 and 12 we lead the children through activities which are different every day, for example one day they might do sport and another day music. Alternatively, we help them to work on a special individual or group project. Our work fits in to a city-wide curriculum, and each activity has clear aims and objectives which we explain to the children.

At 12 we have lunch, and then after lunch the group has a quiet time while the younger children take a nap. We also have Book Hour, when the children look at books, or one of us reads a story to them. Later in the afternoon they have free play.

We're constantly observing each child's progress and evaluating that progress against previously agreed objectives. Every child has their individual Sprachlerntagebuch which is full of things such as interviews and photos. They get different projects to work on and put in the book, always guided by their own interests, curiosity and skills. The children who come to the kindergarten are from various different ethnic backgrounds, and there are also disabled children. Of course, we treat the disabled children in exactly the same way as the other children. Each child is an individual with skills and strengths, and in planning the children's objectives we've taken these strengths into account, rather than focusing on something which perhaps they can't do.

Task 9

Re-write the sentences from the text in the passive voice.

a. We give the children breakfast.
b. We encourage each child to take part, but we don't force any of them.
c. We use positive modelling rather than correction.
d. One of us reads a story to the children.
e. We're constantly observing each child's progress, and evaluating that progress against previously agreed objectives.
f. In planning the children's objectives we've taken these strengths into account.

Task 10

Why have inclusive kindergartens? In groups of three or four, discuss the advantages and disadvantages, and then write four sentences giving your group's opinion either for or against inclusive kindergartens.

Module 2: Children in hospital

If your child has to go to hospital

Hospitals can be strange, frightening places for children. Being ill or in pain can also make them upset. You might feel helpless, but there are things you can do to comfort your child.

Prepare them

Prepare your child as much as you can. Play doctors and nurses or operations using teddies and dolls, and read stories about being in hospital. It's good to do this even if your child isn't due to go to hospital. Many children have to go into hospital at some stage, and many are an emergency case. Explain as much as possible to your child. Even young children need to know what's happening to them. It's important to be truthful. What children imagine is often worse than reality. Don't say that something won't hurt when it will.

Some hospitals arrange visits for children and their families before a child is admitted for a planned treatment or operation. It's also important to let your child know when they'll be able to see you and whether you'll be staying with them. Explain to your child what being in hospital will be like. Tell them they'll be sharing a ward with other children of their own age and that it'll be different from their own bedroom at home.

Stay with them

It will help your child if you visit them in hospital as much as possible and, with young children especially, sleep there. Do all you can to arrange this. All hospital children's departments now have some room for parents to stay overnight with their children. Talk to hospital staff beforehand. Be clear about the arrangements and what will happen.

Talk to the hospital staff

Talk to one of the nurses or doctors who will be treating your child about anything you think is important. Inform staff of any special words your child uses (such as for needing to go to the toilet) and any particular ways you have of comforting them.

Take their comforter

Let your child take a favourite teddy or comforter with them into hospital. Be prepared for your child to be upset by the experience. They may continue to be upset for some time afterwards. Give them as much reassurance as you can.

Adapted from: If your child has to go to hospital, in: NHS Choices, 29 July 2011, www.nhs.uk/conditions/pregnancy-and-baby/going-to-hospital/, accessed 21 September 2017.

Comprehension

Task 1

Answer the following questions.

a. Name two ways how parents can use objects to help to make hospital less frightening and upsetting for their children.
b. Name two ways how parents can use language to help make hospital less frightening and upsetting for their children.

Task 2

Write an English sentence using the phrase *in pain,* and another using the verb *to hurt*. Compare your sentence with the person next to you.

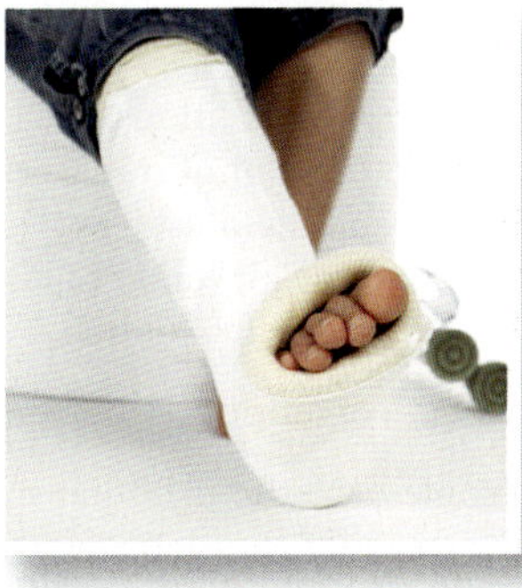

Task 3

Many illnesses have the same or very similar names in English and German, for example mumps, asthma, meningitis or conjunctivitis. Others have different names.

The box contains the names of four common childhood illnesses, and below it are descriptions of the illnesses. In pairs, match the illness to the symptoms described.

flu – measles – whooping cough – chicken pox

a. A fever may be present, followed by a rash which appears on the body and head and then spreads to the limbs. The rash begins as red spots but develops into itchy blisters.
b. Children may have a low fever and a mild cough at the start, but this develops into a violent, rapid cough. Children cough again and again until no air is left in their lungs, leading to a characteristic sound. Coughing will last for several weeks.
c. Symptoms include fever, a cough, sneezing, a runny nose, an aching body, a sore throat, a headache and exhaustion. Vomiting and diarrhoea can also occur.
d. This can start with fever, a cough and a runny nose. A red blotchy rash begins on the face between the third and seventh day of illness, and spreads to the rest of the body.

Task 4

With a partner, discuss the phrases *life-limiting condition* and *life-threatening condition*. What do you think the difference in meaning could be?

Sometimes children aren't going to get better

Joanna Giles works in a children's hospice in Chester as a nursery nurse. This is an interview about her work.

Could you tell us about the hospice and the people who work there?

The hospice provides support and treatment for local children who have life-limiting and life-threatening conditions. This can be in the hospice, but what a lot of people don't realise is that we also do a lot of our work in the children's homes. The team here is made up of doctors, nurses and therapists, as well as family support workers, bereavement counsellors, psychologists and social workers plus me and two other nursery nurses. A lot of our support is for the families of the ill children. We have sessions of sibling support, for example.

Tell us something about the children you work with.

People have the idea that most of the children we work with have cancer, but the reality is different. Of course we work with children with illnesses such as cancer, conditions which are life-threatening and which can be treated, although the treatment may not work. However, we also work with many children who have conditions in which early death is inevitable, where there may be long periods of intensive treatment aimed at prolonging life. An example would be cystic fibrosis. As well as this, we work with children who have progressive conditions with no curative treatment options. These are illnesses such as muscular dystrophy, where treatment is palliative and may often extend over many years.

Could you tell us a little bit about your daily routine?

The children here are just like other children, they like to play games and have fun. It's really important that the children the hospice cares for achieve as much as possible. Many of the children have special needs such as hearing or sight impairment, and others have limited mobility and/or learning disabilities. We have special equipment to meet the children's needs, and of course we provide the toys, books and crafts that you find in all nurseries. We try to vary the activities and we have as many outings as possible, sometimes we go to the park or to the zoo. People think that children's hospices are sad places, but most of the time I find this a happy place with a strong ethos of friendliness and support.

What qualities does a good hospice worker need?

You need good communication and listening skills. Of course qualifications and training are important, but having the right kind of personality is even more so. You need to be a caring person who has insight into what the families are going through. Flexibility is very important, as well as being able to work well within a team.

Comprehension

Task 5

Listen to the interview twice and then answer these questions.

a. Where do the hospice workers do their work?
b. Name three of the jobs from among those in the team who work at the hospice.
c. What is a common misconception that people have about children in a hospice?
d. What kinds of special needs do the children in the hospice often have?
e. Name three of the qualities which Joanna says that a hospice worker needs.

Task 6

Make sentences to explain words to do with hospitals. Use one word or phrase from each of the three boxes. The first one has been done as an example.

~~nurse~~ – ambulance – patient – X-ray – physiotherapist

~~person~~	takes sick people to hospital
machine	is sick or ill
person	~~cares for sick people~~
vehicle	treats people with mobility problems
person	takes a picture of the body showing the skeleton

e.g. A *nurse* is a *person* who *cares for sick people.*

Grammar

Identifying relative clauses

A relative clause is a part of a sentence. An identifying relative clause identifies a noun or a noun phrase. In other words it tells us *which* or *which type of* person or thing is meant.

e.g. A man works next door. He is an occupational therapist.
Which man is an occupational therapist?
The man **who works next door** is an occupational therapist.

Pronouns

For *people*, we use the pronouns ***who*** or ***that:***

e.g. People work with young children. These people often love their jobs.
People **who work with young children** often love their jobs.

For *things,* we use the pronouns ***which*** or ***that:***

e.g. The nursery uses activities. These activities help children to learn their numbers.
The nursery uses activities **that help children to learn their numbers.**

Note: we can't ever use ***what***.

e.g. The problems **what** he is facing. (incorrect).
The problems **that/which** he is facing. (correct)

Identifying the object of who, that or which

Often the noun we want to identify is the object of **who, which** or **that**:

e.g. The book **that Alan read** was very popular with the children.
Alan = subject the book = object

In these cases, if we want to we can leave out **who, which** or **that** from the sentence.

e.g. The book **Alan read** was very popular with the children.

Prepositions in relative clauses

If the relative clause includes a preposition, this will normally be at the end of the clause.

e.g. Those are the children. I work with them.
Those are the children **(who) I work with**.

e.g. You have applied *for* a job. The job is in Birmingham.
Is the job **(which) you have applied for** in Birmingham?

Only in very formal written English (not spoken English), can the preposition go at the beginning of the clause. In this case, ***who, which*** or ***that*** can't be left out.

e.g. The **job for which I am applying** is the one working with disabled children.

Task 7

Write out these sentences again, leaving out *who, that* or *which* when it is possible.

a. The boy who missed this morning's session has special needs.
b. I'm working with a little girl who wants to be a doctor.
c. It was the worst job interview that I've ever had.
d. The key which opens this door is the one which is missing.
e. All the people who I met at the clinic were very friendly.

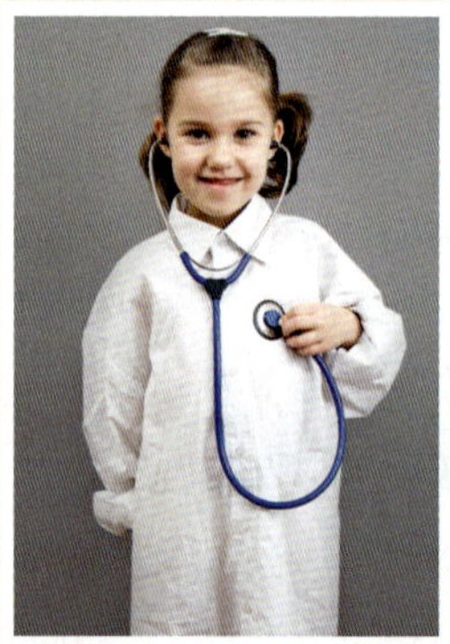

Relative clauses which give us extra information

The second type of relative clause gives us extra information about something. We already know which thing it is. We need to use commas to separate this clause from the sentence.

e.g. My school, **which is one of the best in the county**, is in Wakefield.

e.g. You can stay at the local hotel, **which is very comfortable.**

Pronouns

For *people*, we use the pronoun ***who***. We can't use ***that.***

e.g. The manager, **who is from Sweden**, is very supportive.

For *things*, we use the pronoun ***which***. We can't use ***that***.

e.g. Marian told me about the training course, **which she enjoyed very much**.

We cannot leave out *who* or *which* in any of these sentences.

Prepositions

As with identifying relative clauses, these usually go at the end of the clause.
e.g. She showed me the garden, **which had plenty of room for children to play in.**

Compare the two types of relative clause	
The man **who lives upstairs** is a teacher.	John, **who lives in London**, is a teacher.
This tells us which man is being talked about.	Even without the clause, we know who we are talking about – John.
• We don't use commas. • We can use **who/that or which/that.** • We can leave out **who/that/which** when it's with the object.	• We use commas to separate the clause. • We can only use **who** or **which.** • We can't leave out **who** or **which.**

Task 8

Read the information below and complete the sentences, using a relative clause. Decide which type of clause you need to use. The first one has been done already.

a. There is a woman living upstairs. She's French.
The woman who lives upstairs is French.
b. Olu was looking for some paints yesterday. She has found them now.
Olu has found ...
c. Jane has a sister. She showed me a photograph of her. She is a lawyer.
Jane showed me ...
d. Martin applied for several jobs last month. He's been offered one of them.
Martin has been offered ...
e. There was an electrical problem. It crashed all the computers. It has now been fixed.
The electrical problem ...
f. Daisy is one of my closest friends. I've known her for ten years.
Daisy ...

Module 3: Traumatised children

Everyone knows there's an international refugee crisis. But there is a vital issue that's in danger of being missed – the terrible psychological damage that's being done to millions of children. Such harm is less obvious than physical wounds, but most European countries haven't had to deal with childhood trauma on this scale since the end of the Second World War.

There are now 8 million of these children, according to UNICEF, and they constitute nearly half the world's refugees. It's hard to understand such huge numbers, but they are made up of countless heart-breaking individual stories. Earlier this year Stephen Cowan, a council leader from west London, visited the temporary camp in Calais, hoping to be able to bring a number of unaccompanied child refugees to England. On a mild autumn day, he saw a young Afghan boy who was shivering and sweating as though he had a fever. "Is he ill?" asked the councillor. The interpreter shook his head. "No," he said, "he's been in the camp for two months and it's driven him mad."

This anecdote will disturb anyone who knows about the importance of stable attachments for healthy childhood development. Babies recognise faces at a very early stage, and the negative effects of disrupting relationships with trusted adults – anxiety, insecurity, self-harm, aggression – have been well documented since British psychoanalyst John Bowlby's research on children, following the second world war.

In the care system, where resources are already limited, social workers try very hard to prevent refugee children from being shifted from one carer to another. We know a great deal about the impact on children of being separated from parents, even in places that aren't war zones. But unaccompanied child refugees are among the most vulnerable people on earth, and falling into the hands of traffickers is just one of the risks they face.

In Afghanistan, some families can afford to pay for one child to make the dangerous journey to Europe, often sending a teenage son to travel on his own. Syrian refugees may start out in family groups, but crossing the sea from Turkey or Libya is so hazardous that some children are rescued only after seeing parents or siblings drown. Syria and Afghanistan account for half of the child refugees under the protection of the UN refugee agency, demonstrating the destabilising impact of conflict even on those who survive without physical injuries. They are more or less guaranteed to suffer post-traumatic stress disorder, something that's hard to treat in over-crowded refugee camps.

Country after country is trying to shift the problem onto someone else, ignoring obligations under international treaties and conventions. They are also storing up trouble for the future. Boys (who according to some estimates outnumber girls nine to one among child refugees) and girls react differently to horrific childhood events. Boys are more likely to become aggressive, fail at school and get involved in petty crime. In the worst-case scenario, they may be vulnerable to radicalisation by extremists.

Organisations dedicated to helping displaced people have been overwhelmed by demand and are struggling to provide for basic needs, such as shelter and medicines. We in Europe haven't yet understood that we have a generation of severely traumatised children in our societies.

Resources are very limited, but the consequences of ignoring the problem are too terrible to imagine. For all our sakes we need to identify these children and try to teach them that the world is not always as evil or frightening as it must seem to them.

Adapted from: Smith, Joan: Europe is failing to help a generation of traumatised children, in: The Guardian Online, 27 December 2016, www.theguardian.com/commentisfree/2016/dec/27/europe-traumatised-children-child-refugees-mental-health, accessed 27 August 2017.

Task 1

Complete the following text using the terms below.

psychological damage – temporary camp – unaccompanied – stable attachments
social workers – traffickers – siblings – post traumatic stress disorder – outnumber
radicalisation

Child refugees suffer terrible ...(1)... when they arrive often ...(2)... - alone and without their parents or ...(3)... who they may last have seen drowning in the sea during a dangerous crossing. They often find themselves living in a ...(4)... waiting to make the journey to another country such as England. ...(5)... do their best to ensure that the children are not moved from one carer to another because they are aware that ...(6)... are vital to the healthy development of children. Lone children are very vulnerable to ...(7)...who sell them into slavery and prostitution. Refugee children who are forced to live under terrible conditions will almost certainly suffer ...(8)..., a condition most usually associated with soldiers who have had to endure battle conditions in war zones for too long. Male refugee children ...(9)... female children nine to one may in the worst cases be subject to ...(10)... which may lead them to committing acts of terrorism.

Comprehension

Task 2

Answer the following questions on the above text.

a. Why was the Afghan boy mentioned in the text shivering and sweating, according to the quoted source?
b. Name the four negative effects on babies and young children of disrupted relationships with trusted adults.
c. Which two countries account for half the total number of child refugees?
d. Why do nearly all child refugees suffer from post-traumatic stress disorder?
e. Why do relief organisations find it so difficult to deal with the problem of refugee children?
f. What have European citizens not yet properly understood?

Activity

Task 3

In groups of three or four, discuss the following questions:

- Do you believe European citizens and governments have a moral obligation to provide financial support and shelter to refugees? Explain your reasoning with the help of some examples.

- What do you think needs to be done to help social workers and relief organisations to provide child refugees with the material and psychological support they need?
- What do you think will be the effects in the future of ignoring the presence of millions of traumatised children in European societies?

Task 4

Write three sentences to describe the ways in which the experience of child refugees today is different to that of child refugees in Germany after World War II, and three to describe how it is similar. Use the internet or another source to research your answer.

Example: Child refugees today often don't know the language or culture of the countries they arrive in, whereas many of the refugees fleeing to parts of Germany after World War II were themselves displaced Germans.

Grammar

Reporting with passive verbs

When we want to report something we can use one of two special structures with a verb in the passive. These are often used in news reports.

e.g. **It is reported that** many nurseries in the UK are losing funding due to government cuts.
or: Many nurseries in the UK **are reported to be** losing funding due to government cuts.

Other verbs we often use in this structure are: *said, thought, believed, considered, known, expected, alleged, understood.*

e.g. It is **expected** that the nursery will close soon.
or: The nursery is **expected** to close soon.

Task 4

Rewrite these sentences using the alternative passive reporting structure.

a. It is thought that many childcare workers are now unemployed.
b. A crowd of people is reported to be outside the court building already.
c. A young man is alleged to have stolen the car from outside the shop.
d. It is considered to be one of the best schools in the city.
e. The social worker is known to have a very high caseload of children.

Activity

Task 5

Role-play the following situation with a partner.

Student A: You are a social worker dealing with a traumatised Afghan fourteen year old male refugee in a camp in Calais. He has travelled alone from his home country with other unaccompanied children and wants to complete his journey by reaching London. You need to explain to him the dangers involved in this plan and that you are trying to arrange a foster family to look after him.

Student B: You are a fourteen year old Afghan refugee. You have travelled from home all the way to Calais. You speak English well because you had a good teacher in your school. You want to finish the last part of your journey so you can find work in England picking fruit or working in the fields, as you did in Afghanistan. You feel that success is just a few kilometres away and you want to send money home to your family. You feel you don't need a family to take care of you. You are fourteen and in Afghanistan would be considered a young man and not a child.

Comprehension

Task 6

UNICEF (United Nations International Children's Emergency Fund) is an organisation that was set up after World War II to provide relief, emergency and support services to children affected by war, natural disaster, famine, poverty, crime and violence. The following extract is a timeline adapted from their website which outlines important dates and milestones in their history. The dates have been removed and the order of the milestone events mixed up. In pairs, complete the gap text below with the correct dates.

1946 – 1959 – 1965 – 1979 – 1982 – 1989 – 1990 – 1996 – 2001

- **Food to Europe**
  After World War II, European children faced famine and disease. UNICEF was created in December ...(1)... by the United Nations to provide food, clothing and healthcare to them.
- **Nobel Peace Prize**
  UNICEF was awarded the ...(2)... Nobel Peace Prize "for the promotion of brotherhood among nations."
- **International Year of the Child**
  ...(3)... was marked by celebrations around the world, where people and organisations reaffirmed their commitment to children's rights.

- **Children and conflict**
  War's effect on children received serious attention in the *Machel Report: The Impact of Armed Conflict on Children*, a study supported by UNICEF. The report was published in ...(4)... .
- **Declaration of the Rights of the Child**
  The UN General Assembly adopted the Declaration of the Rights of the Child in ...(5)..., which defined children's rights to protection, education, health care, shelter and good nutrition.
- **Convention on the Rights of the Child**
  The Convention was adopted by the UN General Assembly in ...(6)... It entered into force in September 1990. It became the most widely- and rapidly-accepted human rights treaty in history.
- **Say Yes for Children campaign launched**
  In ...(7)... the Global Movement for Children began mobilizing every citizen of every nation to change the world with children. The Say Yes for Children campaign built on this momentum, with millions of children and adults around the world pledging their support for critical actions to improve children's lives.
- **Child Survival and Development Revolution**
  In ...(8)... UNICEF launched a drive to save the lives of millions of children each year. The 'revolution' was based on four simple, low-cost techniques: growth monitoring, oral rehydration therapy, breastfeeding and immunisation.
- **World Summit for Children**
  An unprecedented summit held in ...(9)... of Heads of State and Government at the United Nations in New York City set 10-year goals for children's health, nutrition and education.

Adapted from: UNICEF: Our history, www.unicef.org/about/who/index_history.html, updated 04 April 2003, accessed 23 July 2018.

UNIT 10: Ethnic diversity

Module 1: The changing face of society

Integration and multiculturalism in Germany

Before the advent of air travel and mass communication, it was the norm to live in ethnically homogeneous communities. The inhabitants of a village or a city all shared the same traditions and customs, and they spoke the same language. Everyone lived their lives according to the same rules. The presence of outsiders was rare, and the native inhabitants thought nothing of tolerating those who were different, as they were foreigners.

Today we live in societies which embrace people of different social, cultural and ethnic backgrounds. Most metropolitan areas in Europe have large populations of ethnic minorities from Asia, Africa and the Middle East, as well as many people from other European nations.

The question of integration is still hotly debated in Germany. Are Germany's diverse ethnic communities properly integrated in German society? Do these communities assimilate in the dominant culture, or do these people live in "parallel societies"? Can a society such as Germany's be regarded as multicultural – one in which people feel united rather than divided by their differences? In this unit, we will explore ethnic diversity and what it means to belong to a minority group.

Task 1

Where do you think the people in the following pictures (page 148) come from? Give reasons for your answers. Now, listen to the four people who describe their lives in their home or host countries. Match the descriptions you hear to the pictures. The transcription of the audio can be found on page 202.

Task 2

Answer the following questions on the text above.

a. Why might Can not be considered German despite his German citizenship? Why might Can not be accepted as Turkish when he is in Turkey?
b. Selma is relieved that no one seems to object to her wearing a head scarf. Why do you think she anticipated this to be a problem in the United States?
c. Why might Germans think Amelia is German? What does this tell us about how people perceive and define foreignness?
d. What aspects of living in Germany made Katherine feel alienated?

Task 3

Reflect on the following questions with a partner. Then discuss your ideas with the rest of the class.

a. Katherine complains that she felt like an outsider while she was living in Germany. What steps could she have taken to feel more comfortable in her host culture?
b. Some ethnic minorities are reluctant to integrate themselves into German society. Do you think these communities are reluctant to assimilate by choice, or is it because there's a resistance on the part of Germans to accept them?

Grammar

Adverbs of frequency

Adverbs of frequency tell us how often an action is performed or an event occurs.
Some of the most common frequency adverbs are: *always, never, usually, often, sometimes, occasionally, rarely* and *seldom.* Phrases like *every month* or *once a day* are also frequency adverbs.

Example: Selma **always** wears her headscarf in public, but I have **often** seen her without it when I have visited her at home, as she **usually** takes it off.

Note the position of the adverbs in the example. We prefer to place frequency adverbs between **the subject** and the **main verb:**

Selma *always* wears her headscarf in public.

Or between the **auxiliary verb** and **main verb:**

I **have *often* seen** her without it.

Some frequency adverbs can also be placed at the beginning of a sentence, before the subject:

Sometimes/Occasionally I visit Selma at home.

This is a matter of preference, depending what the speaker wants to emphasise in the sentence. Note though, that *always* and *never* are never used at the beginning of sentences.

Task 4

Using the adverbs of frequency listed above, describe the frequency with which you do the following activities, giving a reason why.

I often watch foreign films because I am interested in how people from different cultures view the world.

How frequently do you:

a. get the chance to speak a foreign language?
b. visit other countries?
c. go to a Chinese or Indian restaurant?
d. attend a multicultural festival?
e. donate money to a charitable cause?
f. make friends with someone from a different country?

The changing face of the UK

Britain is a multicultural country. On the streets of every town in Britain you will encounter all kinds of people from a wide variety of different cultures. The great majority of these people are British but they all look and dress differently because Britain is a multiracial society. Britain has this in common with that other great melting pot culture, the United States. One of the interesting features of British society is that while Britons share a common national identity, their manners, attitudes and style of speech are often influenced by aspects of their ethnic background. A Sikh will speak with a London accent and support his local football team, but will continue to wear a turban and listen to the traditional music of his community.

Cultural crossover is a common phenomenon in Britain and as can be seen by the development of such musical genres as Bangra, which is a blend of Punjabi folk music and Western pop. The group *Cornershop* had a hit with their song "Brimful of Asha" which fused Western rhythms and Indian melodies with electronic dance beats. The song is about an Indian singer and mixes Punjabi and English lyrics. Its commercial success and appeal to music lovers of all ethnicities can be seen as a metaphor for the way in which British society has succeeded in embracing diversity and creating a unified, inclusive and constantly evolving identity from this multi-ethnic mix. Whether your background is Anglo-Saxon or Punjabi, it is nowadays just as British to enjoy a Mutton Vindaloo as it is to tuck in to a plate of fish and chips. Indian customs and cuisine have become very much a part of the British way of life.

Britain has always been a multiethnic society. The Romans, Normans, Vikings and Saxons invaded the island and settled it earlier in its history. The Irish began immigrating in large numbers to Britain from the mid-nineteenth century on. During the 1950s and 1960s people from former British colonies and other places came to Britain seeking a better life.

Despite all of this however, it would be wrong to assume that Britain is – or ever was – a paradise of racial harmony. Casual racism was very prevalent up to the 1970s when even a people as similar to the British as the Irish were openly discriminated against in areas such as employment and housing. Even today, race riots occasionally break out. On the whole though, Britain has managed quite well to assimilate its diverse peoples into a common sense of cultural identity. The road to a tolerant multicultural society has however proven to be a long, slow and sometimes painful one.

Activity

Task 5

With a partner, use Internet sources to research the current demographic compositions of Britain and Germany. Compare the demographic statistics and note some of the countries' differences. How do you account for these differences?

Task 6

In recent decades, Germany has become a multicultural society and home to many diverse ethnic communities. Do you think these communities are integrated into mainstream German society, or exist separately alongside of it? Write an essay of about 250 words, outlining your ideas and opinions. Use examples to help support and illustrate your arguments.

The changing face of Germany

An interview with Dilek Yalniz, a 29-year-old woman who was born and raised in Berlin.

Tell me a little bit about you and your background.

Dilek: I was born in Berlin and my parents come from Adana, Turkey. My mother came to Berlin when she was 14 because her parents were guest workers in Berlin. They sent for her when they decided to stay in Berlin.

What was your childhood like, particularly the time you spent in preschool?

Dilek: I started preschool when I was three years old. I remember liking all of my teachers. The children were all from mixed backgrounds, Turkish, Arab – but all of the teachers were German and spoke only German. At home, we spoke only Turkish. It was a good combination. In preschool we celebrated German holidays – Christmas, Easter, and I wanted to do the same at home. I remember correcting my mother's German when she didn't pronounce something correctly. We kids had more contact with Germans and the German language, and so it was natural for us to correct her.

Did you have any bad experiences in preschool?

Dilek: I remember only one negative experience during my preschool years. My preschool had to close for some reason and we had to go to another one for two months. It was lunch time and we were going to eat a vegetable casserole. I asked one of the adults whether there was pork in it and she said "no", and so I ate the lunch. Afterwards I asked again if there had been pork in it. She said there had been and asked me whether it had been that bad. I thought it was cruel of her to trick me like this.

Do you think there is such a thing as a typical Berlin family?

Dilek: I don't think so. Maybe mine is a typical Turkish family in Berlin. It's typical for a Turkish child in Germany to grow up between two cultures. It isn't easy. I was only influenced by my family's values and customs up to a certain age. Then I was introduced to German culture through my experience of attending kindergarten and later school. I have tried to take the most positive things from both cultures and feel I manage with this mixture very well. I don't think of my family as a typical Berlin family, but as typical of a family that lives in two different cultures, with its children developing in both.

How do other people react to you?

Dilek: People generally regard me as German. I feel most comfortable in Berlin as I was born and raised here. My family is here. For me, Turkey is a place to visit on holiday. I do have a special connection to Turkey, though. I can identify with Turkey but I don't want to live there. I feel secure and safe here in Berlin, whereas in Turkey, I feel emotions on a level which I don't experience in Germany.

Comprehension

Task 7

Answer the following questions.

a. Where does Dilek come from?
b. What might have motivated the woman Dilek mentions to trick her into eating pork?
c. What does Dilek feel is typical of her family?
d. Why does Dilek regard her exposure to two cultures as a positive experience?
e. Explain the differences in the way Dilek relates to Germany and Turkey respectively.

Task 8

a. Together with a partner make a list of what you consider to be the similarities and differences between German and Turkish cultures.

b. Dilek talks about taking the best from each culture and developing a complex sense of identity through blending the values, customs and outlooks of both. Think of some clear examples in which the experience of being raised in two cultures can be both enriching and problematic. Share your ideas in an open discussion with the rest of the group.

Module 2: Racism and stereotyping

Ethnic stereotypes – why do they matter?

Sabine Beyer runs training courses on equality and diversity awareness for social workers and early years' practitioners in Mannheim. Here, she talks about the damage that can be done by stereotyping people due to their ethnicity.

What is an ethnic stereotype?

Sabine: It's a generalised representation of an ethnic group, based on what are *perceived* to be typical characteristics of members of the group.
These generalisations are often not based on facts, but on myths or *skewed* perceptions. An example might be the stereotype that white people don't have rhythm and can't dance very well.

Are there other types of stereotypes as well as those to do with ethnicity?

Sabine: Stereotypes exist in all cultures and in all aspects of life. For example we see a man or a woman wearing a smart suit and make *assumptions* about him or her. It can be argued that stereotypes are useful – even necessary – tools to help us sort the constant flow of new data in our day-to-day lives. However, once race or ethnicity is involved, stereotypes have the potential to do great harm.

Are they ever harmless?

Sabine: There is an argument that when stereotypes are applied by one group to another group with more or less equal status in the world (for example between the British and the French) they are harmless. However, even in these situations stereotypes are based on ignorance and they mean that we ignore differences between individuals and assume things which are often not true. Because stereotypes – in common with any forms of *prejudice* – are fixed beliefs, someone who believes in them is less open to recognising the truth when it presents itself.

When do stereotypes become racist?

Sabine: Stereotypes become most dangerous when they are applied by a majority group in a society towards a minority group within that same society. This is especially true if the positions of power are held by people from the majority group. Then, stereotypes become *interwoven* with, and often *indistinguishable* from, racism. An example might be a white British person believing that a young black man was probably involved with crime or drugs. Another example could be a white German person thinking that a young German man of Turkish origin probably couldn't speak good German.

If people have only limited social contact with another group, they are more likely to have negative perceptions of them. This can grow into an "us and them"-mentality where the minority group is blamed for society's problems, even if in reality those problems stem from somewhere else.

Comprehension

Task 1

Find a word in italics in the text which can replace the words in italics in the following sentences.

a. The differences between this book and the other one are *imperceptible.*
b. It's normal to make *guesses* about things when we don't have all the information.
c. Her original ideas were now *intertwined* with those of her mentor.
d. People sometimes *see* what they expect to *see*, rather than what is actually there.
e. The man was said to have a strong *bias* against Muslims, which is also known as Islamophobia.
f. His views are completely *distorted* on the matter, ever since he was the victim of a robbery.

Task 2

In groups of three to four, discuss the following questions.

a. What stereotypes do you know about the Germans, French, British and Italians?
b. What can we do to combat racism, stereotyping and discrimination? Think of three concrete actions that could be taken in your workplace or college.

Scottish city nurseries launch first anti-racism programme

[...]
Glasgow has become the first local authority in Scotland to introduce a dedicated anti-racism curriculum in its nurseries. Staff will be taught how to tackle incidents, explain differences in skin colour and help children develop the skills to handle attacks.

Research shows racist attitudes can be picked up by children as young as two. A similar programme in 170 city primary schools in 2005 led to a slight drop in the number of racist incidents. Other Scots local authorities have adopted the primary pack and the new early years programme has already attracted interest from several councils.

Kubriya Binjamin's daughter Ambreen, three, goes to Kinning Park Nursery, where around 60 % of pupils are Asian. Born in Glasgow, the 29-year-old mum-of-three said, "I think there is still a lot of work to be done but it's much better now. There are so many different communities in Glasgow which has helped."

As well as large Asian communities, Glasgow is home to more than 5,000 asylum seekers from countries such as Iraq and 7,000 people from the EU accession countries including Poland. Council executive spokesman for education Gordon Matheson said: "This pack is about addressing race issues in an age specific way so children grow up celebrating diversity."

Adapted from: Friends launch anti-racism first in city nurseries, in: Evening Times, 6 February 2008, www.eveningtimes.co.uk/news/12799824.Friends_launch_anti-racism_first__in_city_nurseries/, accessed 17 September 2018.

Comprehension

Task 3

In pairs, think of alternative ways to express these phrases from the text in English.

tackle incidents – handle attacks – attract interest – address issues – pick up attitudes

Grammar

Reported speech

We use *reported* or *indirect speech* when we want to express what other people say, think or believe.

Form	Examples
In order to write reported speech we change the verbs from the present to the simple past.	The 29-year-old mum-of-three said, "I **think** there **is** still a lot of work to be done but it is much better now." *The 29-year-old mum-of-three said that she **thought** there **was** still a lot of work to be done but that it **was** much better now.*
can => could will => would	Paul said, "I **don't think** that I **can** do it." *Paul said that he **didn't think** that he **could** do it.* Jaz said, "My colleague **will** see you soon." *Jaz said that her colleague **would** see you soon.*
In compound tenses, the auxiliary is the one which changes.	Mia said, "Peter **has given up** his job." *Mia said that Peter **had given up** his job.*
If the verb is already in the simple past, we can either leave it the same, or change it to the past perfect.	Jim said, **"**I **woke up** early yesterday." *Jim said that he **woke up** early yesterday.* *Or: Jim said that he **had woken up** early yesterday.*
You can also leave out "that".	*Mia said Peter had given up his job.* *Jim said he woke up early yesterday.*

Task 4

Rewrite the sentences below using reported speech.

a. Amy said, "My boss wants to organise a party for Eid, but she doesn't have the staff."
b. Lidia said, "Our team has made great progress towards combating racism."
c. Ade said, "You'll need to work within the anti-discrimination policy."
d. Devon said, "I've been living in Britain since the 1950s, when my family came from Jamaica."
e. Joanna said, "Paco and Julio normally speak Spanish together, but today they're speaking English for the benefit of the visitors."

Language

Presenting your argument

Preparation
- Make sure that you have a clear structure to your argument. Think of it as though you're writing an essay. Include an introduction, a middle part and a conclusion.
- Get as many facts as possible to back up your argument. What you're looking for is evidence such as statistics from a reputable source. Ideally cross-reference your facts from different sources.
- You can use some opinion too, but remember you need to be convincing and to persuade others to agree with you, so be ready to back up your opinions with facts.

During a debate
- Listen. You won't convince anyone if you don't listen to the other person or team. React to what they say and comment on it, to show that you are listening and taking their points on board.
- Stay calm. Don't get too emotional. Present your arguments in a clear controlled voice, and keep your body language under control, for example, don't wave your arms around.

Activity

Task 5

In groups of four, prepare for a debate.

In recent years there has been an influx into Berlin of people from the USA, the UK, Spain, France and Italy.

Group A: You feel that this benefits the city and makes it a more vibrant place, and you believe that it will also bring more much-needed jobs to the German capital.

Group B: You feel that the foreigners have driven gentrification and forced rents and other prices up, so that local people can no longer afford to live in the areas where their families live.

Module 3: Growing up bilingual

What is bilingualism?

In countries such as Germany and Britain, where it is common for just one language to be used in the home, parents and educational professionals often feel it is better for children to learn just one language as they are growing up. But experts disagree over the issue of whether it is confusing or enriching for young children to be exposed to more than one language. Some linguists feel that learning more than one language delays language development, but many believe that children have no difficulty acquiring any number of languages from a very young age.

In societies such as Singapore, bilingualism is the norm and multilingualism is not uncommon. Speaking more than one language is a necessary competence as Singaporean society is made up of people from a wide variety of ethnic communities, all of whom speak different native languages. There, multilingualism is a required social skill that enables people to communicate with one another across different cultures, thus helping to preserve social harmony. Parents in such a culture expect their children to pick up the languages they need, and aren't concerned about issues of delayed development.

It is sometimes the case that a child's first language is the second or third language of his parents. Children always adopt the dominant language of the society they live in as their native tongue, regardless of the languages their parents speak to them at home. Amir lives in Berlin with a French father and an Iranian mother. French is the language used at home when the family sits down to eat or goes on a Sunday outing, but mother and son speak exclusively Farsi to one another when alone together. Amir, however, speaks German as his native language. Although he speaks the languages of both his parents very proficiently, German is the language through which he perceives and constructs the world. This is because German is clearly the dominant language in his environment and therefore, the one Amir uses most.

Even if a child grows up in a home in which two languages are spoken, this does not mean that the child will learn to speak both languages of equal fluency. Jennifer lives in Cologne with her German mother and American father. Her mum speaks only German to her, while her dad has always made a point of talking to her in English. Jennifer, however, usually responds to her father's questions in German and tends to use English only when she wants something from him, like pocket money or an ice cream. When she speaks English, she makes all the characteristic errors of German native speakers. She uses "false friends", German sentence constructions, German tense usage and direct translations of German expressions. Instead of saying, for example, "what time is it", she will say "how late is it", "gloves" are "handshoes", and verbs are sometimes placed at the end rather than at the beginning of sentences. This is because Jennifer is working from within the structures of her first language to acquire her knowledge of the second.

Comprehension

Task 1

Find words and expressions in the text that match the definitions below.

a. people who study how languages work and are used
b. the ability to speak two languages to a high degree of fluency
c. the capacity to speak a number of languages to a high degree of fluency
d. your mother tongue, the language in which you feel most at home

e. typical mistakes
f. the language spoken in Iran
g. an adjective which describes your ability to do something extremely well, such as playing the piano or speaking a language
h. a small sum of cash that children receive from their parents every week or month
i. a word that seems similar to another word in a different language, but which has a different meaning, e.g. the German word "brav" and the English word "brave"

Task 2

Answer the following questions on the text in your own words.

a. What issue do linguists disagree over concerning the language learning of children?
b. Why is the ability to speak more than one language the norm in Singapore?
c. What is one of the benefits of multilingualism to a multiethnic society?
d. Why does Jennifer speak English like a German learner, even though her father is a native speaker of English and talks to her in his own language every day?

Task 3

With a partner discuss whether children should learn more than one language from a young age. Do you think foreign parents should speak the dominant language of the community rather than their own native language to their children? Discuss your views and ideas with a partner, then share your conclusions with the rest of the group.

Grammar

The past perfect simple

The past perfect is formed using *had* + the past participle of the verb:

I/you/he/she/it/you/we/they *had spoken.*

The past perfect is used to refer to completed actions which have occurred before another event in the past:

Simple past: When I arrived at the room, the meeting *began*.
(I arrived at the room, and then the meeting began. I was on time.)

Past perfect: When I arrived at the room, the meeting *had* already *started.*
(The meeting began before I arrived at the room. I was late.)

Task 4

Complete the following sentences using *because* + past perfect and *so* + past perfect.

When I left the school, there was no one there ... (lock up) / (everybody / leave).

- *... so I locked up.* (subsequent event, simple past)
- *... because everyone had left.* (previous event, past perfect)

a. The playroom was in a mess (I/clean up/it)/(the children/it/not tidy up).
b. James couldn't speak French (he/decide to learn/it) / (he/not have/it/at school).
c. Jack was in a great mood (he/got the job)/(he/celebrate/with his friends).
d. I performed a play with the children (I/write one)/(they all/dress up).
e. Henry could speak Spanish (live/in Spain)/(teach it/at the preschool).

Case study

Paul is five years old. His father is English and his mother German. They moved to Berkshire, England, three months ago and Paul has been attending the local preschool since they arrived. He's a clever child who's doing his best to integrate and to get along with the other children. Paul can communicate in English but seems to prefer speaking in German. Paul's carer thinks that these problems have to do with his language skills and has referred him for testing.

Background information was gathered from Paul's carer and parents. His carer says that Paul does not always follow instructions, is often reluctant to participate in activities, and usually takes more time to complete tasks than the other children. He enjoys interacting with the other children, but often switches from English to German when playing.

Following language testing, Paul's language abilities were assessed as being equal to those of native English speaking children of his age in the area of concept words. Concept words are terms that relate to language area such as texture, social awareness, time and sequence (the order in which events occur). Paul's level of competence in these categories can be explained by the fact that this is the kind of language taught at school, but not usually reinforced at home by parents.

Comprehension

Task 5

Match the words and expressions below with their equivalents in the text.

a. to be sent for medical treatment or testing by a doctor or psychologist
b. to be unwilling to do something
c. to take part
d. to play, talk, communicate with other people
e. to exchange, swap or move from one thing to another
f. terms that relate to abstract rather than concrete ideas
g. the way something, like a piece of fabric, feels
h. to make stronger, or to teach something repeatedly until it is fully understood

Discussion

Task 6

Imagine you and your partner are preschool teachers. Discuss the case of Paul and think of things you could do to help him communicate more effectively.
Should you talk to his parents and find out more about his family background and home life? What else could be done? Write down your ideas.

Task 7

Write a short progress report on the ideas you developed in Task 6. In your report explain the language, communication and social issues facing Paul, and include some recommendations on what you think should be done to address these issues.

UNIT 11:
Social learning and behaviour

Module 1: The importance of play

Task 1

Before you listen to the following text, look at these words and find their meanings.

a. reward	1. to be occupied or involved in an activity
b. gratification	2. the act of imitating or imagining something real
c. o resist	3. something received in return for good behaviour
d. temptation	4. to deal with (a problem) effectively
e. to distract	5. natural or inherent, e.g. an ability
f. correlation	6. describing something that has not been changed or altered in any way
g. self-regulation	7. a desire to do something, particularly something unwise
h. to cope with	8. to divert someone's attention
i. to engage in	9. the interdependence or relationship between two variables or outcomes
j. innate	10. pleasure or satisfaction derived through fulfilling a desire or task
k. make-believe	11. to withstand an action
l. unadulterated	12. the ability to control one's own behaviour

The marshmallow experiment

In the late 1960s a man named Walter Mischel, a father of three young girls, discovered that his four-year-old had suddenly developed the ability to wait to receive a promised treat – a sweet reward. Before the age of four, she didn't know how to cope with desires that weren't immediately fulfilled. Mischel discovered that this was generally true for most four-year-olds, but some children were better at controlling themselves than others.

In 1968 Mischel started a longitudinal experiment at Stanford University that became known as the marshmallow experiment. A group of children aged four to six were invited to participate in the study. They were left alone one at a time in a small bare room, only containing a desk and a chair. On the table was a treat – a marshmallow or an Oreo cookie, and a bell. The children were made an offer: they could either eat the treat right away, or if they were willing to wait until the adult returned to the room, they would be rewarded with a second treat. If the child rang the bell, the adult would return, but the child would not get a second treat.

Most children were able to resist the temptation for several minutes; only about thirty per cent of the children successfully delayed gratification until the adult returned – a quarter of an hour later. Video footage of these children during the experiment shows that the ones who were successful used creative strategies to resist eating the treat. Some would turn themselves away from the treat, while others would talk or sing to themselves. Mischel called this skill the "strategic allocation of attention". Instead of focusing on the "hot stimulus", patient children can distract themselves to avoid thinking about the object they desire.

Over the next forty years after the initial experiment was conducted, Mischel maintained regular contact to the participants, requesting that they, their parents and teachers complete questionnaires that would provide valuable information about their social and emotional development. When Mischel and his research team began analysing the results, they realised that there was a correlation between the outcome of the experiment and later patterns of social behaviour. The participants who surrendered and ate the treat straight away were more likely to have behavioural problems; they weren't as successful at school, and often had difficulties maintaining relationships. Later studies confirmed that they even had higher body mass indexes as adults, and were more likely to have problems with drugs. Mischel and his colleagues concluded that self-regulation is, in fact, a better predictor of academic performance and success than IQs. The marshmallow experiment, Mischel argues, was not about measuring will power or self-control; it was about the cognitive skills needed to think strategically and to develop ways of coping with stressful situations.

How do children develop self-regulation? Is it an innate ability, or is it a skill children can learn to develop? According to Laura Berk of Illinois State University, children can develop self-regulation skills through make-believe play. When children play make-believe, they are engaged in private speech; they talk to themselves, mapping out what they are doing as they do it. They lay out rules for themselves in private speech, and this helps them learn how to regulate their behaviour. This is how adults manage their emotions and regulate their self-control, too.

Berk stresses the importance of giving children enough *Spielraum* – the time and space to engage in imaginative play. The child's play should not be disrupted or regulated by well-meaning adults. Supervised or organised activities are, in fact, counter-productive, as they do not allow children to negotiate the terms of their play by themselves. Unadulterated imaginative play is indeed the most valuable tool for a child's social and emotional development.

Comprehension

Task 2

Are the following statements true or false? Correct the sentences so that they are true.

a. Most three-year-olds can delay gratification.
b. The marshmallow experiment assessed the cognitive skills children need to develop strategies for coping with stressful situations and regulating their own behaviour.
c. There was no apparent correlation between the outcome of the experiment and the participants' success in school and later life.
d. Self-regulation is an intuitive skill that cannot be learned.
e. Make-believe play stimulates private speech, which is an important tool for developing self-regulation.

Task 3

Answer the following questions based on your understanding of the story.

a. What was the most significant discovery of the marshmallow experiment?
b. What is the correlation between the outcome of the experiment and the children's social and emotional development?
c. Why is imaginative play so important?

Task 4

a. **What are the benefits of play? Discuss with a partner whether the following descriptions are accurate:**

Play can occupy children while their parents work.
Play can divert a child's attention away from learning.
Play can teach children cooperation and consideration.
Play can improve children's motor skills.

b. **Can you name any other benefits of play? Share your ideas with the group.**

Task 5

Look at the developmental milestones and match them to the three children according to their age abilities.

Lilly, 1

Samantha, 3

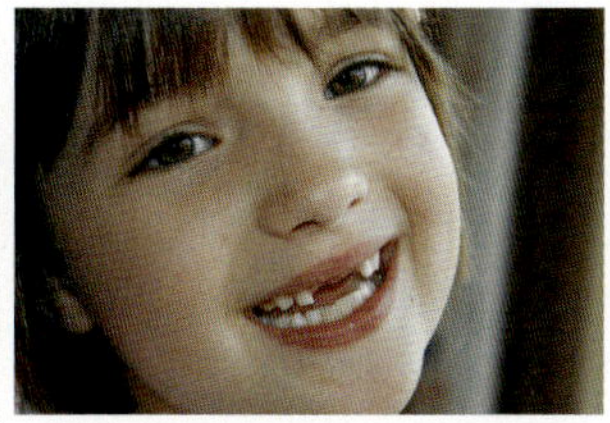

Megan, 5

a. plays simple games requiring memory
b. likes to hide and seek objects
c. forms first friendships
d. plays independently on the playground
e. prefers playing with a parent
f. likes to play make-believe
g. understands the object of games and rules
h. prefers playing with same-sex peers

Task 6

What kind of play or games did you most enjoy as a child and why? Write a paragraph no less than 150 words.

Language

Phrasal verbs

Phrasal verbs are two-part verbs: a verb that is followed by an adverbial particle or a preposition that has a slightly different meaning than the verb by itself. For example, the verb *grow* means to increase in size or amount. When *grow* is followed by an adverb, the verb phrase means something else.

Parents help their children ***grow up*** *to become responsible adults.*
Babies ***grow out of*** *their clothing quickly.*

The phrasal verb can also have an idiomatic meaning that is very different from the meaning of the verb by itself.

They were best friends as children, but ***grew apart*** *as they got older.*

Some phrasal verbs are not followed by objects; they are intransitive: *What time do you* ***get up*** *in the morning?* Intransitive phrasal verbs are always inseparable.

Other phrasal verbs are transitive: *The children* ***put away*** *their toys.*
Some of these phrasal verbs are separable, i.e. the adverb particles can go either before or after the noun objects: *The nanny helped the children* ***put*** *their toys* ***away****.*
Or: *The nanny helped the children* ***put away*** *their toys.*

Other transitive verbs are inseparable: *We asked a babysitter to **look after** the children.*
Not: *We asked a babysitter to look the children after.*

When the object is long noun phrase, we prefer to put the phrasal verb after the particle:

*We **put** our trip to the zoo **off** until next week.* (This sounds awkward.)
*We **put off** our trip to the zoo until next week.* (This sounds better.)

When the phrasal verb is followed by a pronoun object rather than a noun, the adverb participle goes after the pronoun object:

*We **put the toys away**.* Or: *We **put them away**.*
Also: *We **put away the toys**.* But not: *We put away them.*

Task 7

Complete each of the sentences using an appropriate phrasal verb from the box.

get along – name after – pick up – put off – put on – run out – set up
take after – throw up – turn off

a. Our son's name is Benjamin. He was ...(1)...
b. He is nothing like his mother. He ...(2)...
c. Ben has made a lot of new friends since he's been at the nursery. He ...(3)...
d. In fact, Ben likes nursery school so much he begins to cry when his mother ...(4)...
e. "Can he dress himself yet?" "He can take off his jacket and shoes, but he refuses to ...(5)... ."
f. Ben was ill today. After breakfast he ...(6)...
g. We wanted to do an art project for Easter today, but we...(7)...
h. We teach the children to conserve energy. They should remember to ... (8)...
i. Because of the poor weather, our trip to the zoo has been ...(9)...
j. The children like to play house. So, in one corner of the room, we ...(10)...

Playworking

Penny Wilson is a professional playworker at Play Association Tower Hamlets (PATH) based in the East End of London. PATH is a non-profit organisation, which supports campaigns and advocates for children's play in urban and impoverished communities.

Play is a serious business – and a lack of play opportunities for children is becoming a form of deprivation, say play organisations. All too often the subject of play has been trivialised, says Wilson. Play is an instinctive and essential part of childhood, she says, which is becoming more and more under pressure, with evidence that a lack of spontaneous play leaves a long-term social legacy.

"Play allows children to work out their emotions. When you're playing you're finding out about who you are," she says. "Play isn't about fun. Even with very small children, you can see there is a symbolism to their play, there's a meaning to it."

There are ambitious middle class parents who over-schedule their children's lives – so there is no time left for children to play their own imaginative games. Outdoor play in the streets and parks has become much more limited – with anxious parents afraid about safety.

"Children's worlds are shrinking," Wilson says. The design of modern cities has left fewer spaces for play. She shows some bleak pictures of modern housing developments with only the most token of play equipment. These play spaces, which can become threatening hang-outs, can even become places that children avoid. "Play deprivation" is a problem that is also being addressed in the United States – and Ms Wilson has been hired to advise on projects in New York, Chicago and Washington which are "trying to reintroduce the concept of play".

"I'm really frightened about that generation of children who are growing up without having played," she says. But how can play be under threat when every shopping centre has a barn-sized toy shop – and children's bedrooms are creaking with toys and gadgets? "There's a direct correlation, because with many of the toys we buy, the toys do the playing, not the child. Play shouldn't be based on ownership," she says. This consumerist approach has taken away the initiative from children, Wilson adds.

But there is also now a growing awareness of the importance of independent play. As an academic discipline, playwork can be studied to PhD level – and organisations are working to create more playable spaces. The Play Association Tower Hamlets has worked on estates to try to create areas where children can play safely, not just in designated playgrounds. The Glamis Adventure Playground in Shadwell, which has won the London Adventure Playground of the Year, is a multi-coloured play area, surrounded by grey flats and traffic rumbling through east London. Whatever the worries of the streets outside, in this protected space children up to the age of 15 can run around and make up their own games, using the climbing frames, walkways and quirky equipment, including a landlocked boat. For inner-city children whose parents are afraid to let them play outside, this is a chance for healthy outdoor play. If play is a serious aspect of children's health and well-being, then we need to take seriously the spaces available for them, says Ms Wilson.

Adapted from: Coughlan, Sean: Generation of 'play deprivation', in: BBC News UK, 25 September 2007, http://news.bbc.co.uk/2/hi/uk_news/education/7007378.stm, accessed 21 September 2017.

Comprehension

Task 8

Answer the following questions about the text in your own words.

a. What is play deprivation?
b. Why does Penny Wilson consider play "serious business"?
c. Why are children not playing as much today as they used to?
d. What does Penny Wilson do as a playworker?

Activity

Task 9

Look for an internet video showing an adventure playground in the United Kingdom. Try to describe the concept in your own words and explain how it is different than a traditional playground. Discuss your answers as a group.

Module 2: Finding friendship

Task 1

Do you remember your first friend? How did you meet and why did you become friends? Write a short paragraph about your first friend and the development of that friendship. Then find a partner and talk about your experiences.

Finding a friend

Making friends is one of the most important steps in a child's social and emotional development. Friendships are important for our emotional health because they reassure us that we are a valued companion. They help us develop empathy, mutual trust and the ability to resolve conflicts. And as a child grows and acquires further skills, the role friendships play in an adolescent's life will evolve too.

As a child's communication and emotional skills begin to emerge, their play is mostly independent or parallel. Toddlers may play alone or alongside their peers, but they don't begin to play interactively and cooperatively with other children until they understand things like sharing, taking turns, following rules and negotiation. These skills are developed at around age four through the ability to see things from another child's point of view. This interactive play is key in helping them develop further communication skills and engage in collaborative situations. Young children are not selective or discriminating in their choice of friends. They will interact with any other child regardless of their ethnicity or gender, but often rely on an adult to initiate the contact.

By the time a child enters school, friendship is defined by reciprocity and fairness. A child expects equal amounts of giving and taking in a relationship. They will learn how to compromise with each other and resolve their own conflicts.

Older children and teenagers are concerned with loyalty, gender and fitting into the group. They seek affirmation of their acceptance in a group and this is often expressed by their dress and recreational interests. They try to figure out acceptable social behavior and norms, and what makes a person popular. Adolescents usually interact regularly with one peer group of the same sex and may feel betrayed if a friend chooses to spend time with someone outside the peer group.

Friendships allow children to discover who they are and their social role by experimenting with behavior, dress and language. They also help adolescents become independent individuals who accept responsibility for self and others.

Comprehension

Task 2

Answer the following questions about the text.

a. What skills do children develop around age four?
b. Why are friendships crucial for a child's social development?

Task 3

Sometimes friends don't get along. They may have a row and say or do nasty things to each other. It may not be easy or possible to resolve the conflict. Interview a classmate you know well and ask her about an altercation she had with a close friend. Why did it occur? How did the dispute make her feel? Could they settle the conflict amicably? Write down your interview partner's answers, then summarise the interview in your own words.

Activity

Task 4

Many films focus on different kinds of friendships. Watch a film or choose one you remember well about a friendship and describe what made that friendship so special. How do the characters develop and what do they gain from the friendship? Discuss your ideas in the group.

Task 5

Social media platforms are changing the way we make and maintain friendships. Some people argue that social media is an ideal way to socialise, share personal experiences and stay in touch with friends. Others think, however, that the lack of personal interaction can cause friendships to become less meaningful. Write an essay stating your opinion about how social media affects the way we make and maintain friendships.

Module 3: Does gender matter?

Task 1

Make a list of skills you think women are better at performing than men. Do the same for men. Discuss your ideas as a group, and try to explain your reasons for believing in these differences.

Is the gender difference a delusion? Or, should we be teaching boys and girls differently?

The widespread belief that the differences between men's and women's abilities are innate is now being contested by a growing number of scientists. "Neurosexism", as they call it, has had major implications on the education and social upbringing of boys and girls, these researchers suggest. When parents believe their sons have poorer chances of acquiring verbal skills, and their daughters will probably never excel at mathematics, they will never attempt to help their children challenge and overcome their intellectual deficits.

According to Cordelia Fine, author of *Delusions of Gender*, there are no significant neurological differences between the sexes that can explain certain strengths and weaknesses in ability. Contrary to popular belief, our gender or genetic predisposition has no decisive impact on our intellect.

Lise Eliot of Chicago Medical School confirms the recent findings; she says the hard-wired differences between the male and female brain is a myth. Eliot claims the behavioural and intellectual differences are not inherited, but rather learned. As we grow older our behaviour becomes increasingly gender-oriented because we assume the social roles in our gendered culture. Girls' and boys' behaviour is the result of what we expect it to be. Boys develop better spatial skills not because of an inherent superiority, but because they are encouraged to perform well in sports that require throwing and catching. Similarly, girls are perceived as more emotional and communicative than boys, and so parents and teachers focus on their attention

on language skills. While Eliot does not deny that there are differences between boys and girls, these differences, she says, are far smaller than the stereotypes we propagate.

Parents and educators find these recent findings hard to believe. They observe considerable differences in boys' and girls' behaviour and learning aptitudes every day. Reception teacher, Steve Mynard, feels that teachers need to treat boys and girls differently in order to give them equal opportunities in school. Practitioners, Mynard asserts, need to understand the developmental differences and plan a curriculum that will take these gender differences into consideration. The Early Years Foundation Stage (EYFS) framework recognises gender differences and endorses providing girls and boys gender-specific opportunities. Taking their activity preferences and different learning styles into account is, paradoxically, viewed as the non-discriminatory approach to teaching.

Comprehension

Task 2

Find the words in the text that can replace the words in italics in the following sentences. Use a thesaurus to help you.

a. The question whether the gender differences in children's behaviour are a result of nature or nurture is an issue that has been *disputed* among educators for years.
b. Because of neurosexism, researchers claim, boys and girls do not *try* to develop certain skills to their greatest potential.
c. The differences in performance of certain skills are no longer attributed to *naturally inherent abilities* in men and women.
d. The outcome of the experiment had no *significant* correlation with the participants' social development later in life.
e. Most of the traits that make us unique individuals have actually been *passed on* to us by our parents and grandparents.
f. Society expects boys to *do* well in athletics, and girls in languages.
g. Most educators contend that girls and boys do have different gender-specific *abilities.*
h. The league for Early Years professionals *recommends* encouraging gender-oriented activities for boys and girls.

Task 3

Answer the following questions about the text in your own words.

a. What was the popular belief about the differences in men's and women's intellectual abilities up until most recently?
b. What have scientists recently discovered to discredit this former belief?
c. How do researchers explain why there are such differences in the way men and women behave?
d. Why are the recent findings so hard for educators to believe?

What are little boys made of?
"Snips and snails, and puppy dogs tails
That's what little boys are made of!"
What are little girls made of?
"Sugar and spice and all things nice
That's what little girls are made of!"

– Mother Goose Nursery Rhyme –

Grammar

Gerund or infinitive

Non-native speakers of English usually find it difficult knowing whether to use the infinitive or gerund verb form (the -ing form) after the main verb. Infinitives and gerunds are verb forms that can be used to replace a noun as the object in a sentence. Some main verbs are followed by infinitive verbs, while others are followed by gerunds.

*I like **working** with children.* (gerund)
*I like **to work** with children.* (infinitive)

Sometimes both forms are possible without a difference in the meaning of the sentence.
The verb *like* can be followed by both forms; there's no difference in the meaning. Other verbs, however, can be followed by either a gerund or infinitive, but not without a slight difference in meaning. Compare the following sentences:

*Maria didn't remember **to pack** her toothbrush.*
*Maria didn't remember **packing** her toothbrush.*

Do you recognise the difference in meaning?
The first sentence means: *Maria forgot to pack her toothbrush.*
The second sentence means: *Maria forgot whether she had packed her toothbrush or not.*

Unfortunately there is no patent way of knowing when to use the gerund or the infinitive. It is easiest to learn them gradually through practise.

Here are some of the common verbs that are followed by a gerund:

admit – appreciate – complete – consider – delay – deny – discuss – enjoy – involve
look after – look forward to – mention – postpone – recall – recommend risk – suggest –
take care of

These are some of the verbs that are followed by infinitives:

agree – appear – arrange – care – decide – expect – learn – neglect – need – offer – plan
prepare – pretend – promise – refuse – seem – wait – want

The -ing form is used when the main verb is followed by the preposition *to*. Examples of these verbs are: *look forward to, object to, be used to.*

*We **aren't used to walking** this far.*

It should be noted that some auxiliary verbs contain the preposition *to* (e.g. have to, used to) but this should not be confused with the infinitive *to*. In this example the infinitive form of *play* is used without the *to*, i.e. **used to** + **play** (not: used + to play).

*We **used to play** in the woods behind the barn.*

Only infinitives are used after indirect objects (a noun or pronoun) following main verbs.

*We **expect the children to put** away the toys when they're done with them.*

We usually use a gerund, not an infinitive, when the verb comes after a preposition.

*Look both ways **before crossing** the street.*
*We're thinking **about redecorating** the rooms.*

Task 4

Complete the sentences by putting the verb in the brackets in the gerund or infinitive form.

a. We look forward to (meet) the new children in September.
b. The children must learn (do) things by themselves.
c. Alex was proud of himself for (take) off his shoes.
d. We cannot risk (lose) one of the children in the crowd.
e. Nina and Felicia are pretending (be) princesses.
f. Just as we got outside, it started (rain).
g. Each boy denied (hit) the other.
h. We have to (purchase) new equipment for the nursery.
i. A playworker's job is to encourage children (play) and (use) their imaginations.
j. We can't prevent them from (do) what they want to do.

Sweden's gender-neutral preschools produce kids who are more likely to succeed

Inside a handful of public kindergartens in Sweden, toys are never divided into traditional gender camps. Dolls and baby strollers mingle freely with cars and wooden blocks. In posters, dump trucks haul around beaded jewelry, a bionic robot wears a tutu, and it's not a female or male Barbie who does the dishes—that's left to a skeleton.

These are Sweden's gender-neutral kindergartens, administered by Lotta Rajalin, who shared photos of the toyscapes and posters described above in a recent TEDx Talk. She also explained that at her schools, children can dabble in all kinds of activities, and are encouraged to explore their full range of emotions. Girls are not expected to suppress anger, and boys are not pressured to swallow their tears. All students are welcome to be as messy or tidy, rowdy, or passive as suits them.

"What we do in our schools, we [don't] put labels on the children. We don't say, 'Frida, she's so beautiful, cute and helpful,' and 'Mohammed is so wild and tough.'" Rajalin tells the audience.

Teachers are also trained to avoid talking about boys or girls, and instead speak of people, kids, humans and friends. "Hen", a still rarely used gender-neutral pronoun that first came into use in the 1960s, but only made the official dictionary two years ago, has replaced han (he) and hon (she).

Such efforts are probably paying off. In a small study published in Journal of Experimental Child Psychology, researchers at Uppsala University in Sweden report that children who attended one gender-neutral preschool were more likely to play with unfamiliar children of the opposite gender, and less likely to be influenced by culturally enforced gender stereotypes, compared to children enrolled at other pre-schools. Tests showed that the kids from the gender-neutral school were as likely as other children to group people by gender, but didn't attach traditional associations to the concepts of "male" or "female" children to the same degree. During a matching task, for instance, they were less likely to make choices in line with cultural norms when shown images of boys or girls and jeans or dresses.

"Together the results suggest that although gender-neutral pedagogy on its own may not reduce children's tendency to use gender to categorise people, it reduces their tendency to gender-stereotype and gender-segregate, which could widen the opportunities available to them," Ben Kenward, a researcher in psychology at Uppsala University and Oxford Brookes University. [...]

Plenty of research has explored the ways gender assumptions in the classroom are equally harmful to boys and girls. In the study, for instance, the authors point out that just as boys, not girls, are usually encouraged to play with blocks, which develops spatial skills, girls are expected to comply with an adult's direction, a trait that's connected to better academic performance. Psychologists have also determined that when a teacher or student believes most boys can't sit still long enough to read, or might not have the self-discipline required to thrive in a structured setting, it appears to negatively impact boys' grades. [...]

Gender-neutral kindergartens are rare, even in the country rated as the fourth-most gender-equal society in the world. [...] In 1998, an amendment to Sweden's education act required that public schools at all levels begin promoting gender-neutral policies and teaching styles. Rajalin has since taken the lead in pioneering norm-conscious policies for her kindergartens, "but they are not the only preschools that are moving this way," Kenward says. "All Swedish preschools are pretty right-on from the perspective of most other countries."

Comprehension

Task 5

Complete the sentences based on your understanding of the text.

a. The gender-neutral preschools in Sweden encourage ...(1)...
b. The teachers at gender-neutral preschools use language that ...(2)...
c. The toys in gender-neutral preschools ...(3)...
d. The teaching staff at want boys and girls ...(4)...
e. Lotta Rajalin explains that ...(5)...
f. Research suggests that ...(6)...
g. Swedish schools promote ...(7)...

Activity

Task 6

In a debate two teams will consider the question: Is a gender-neutral upbringing and education favourable or detrimental for a child's social development? The affirmative team will argue that gender-neutral education is favourable, while the negative team will argue it is detrimental. Each team presents two constructive speeches and two rebuttal speeches. At the end of the debate, take a class vote to see whether more students endorse gender-neutral upbringing and education or oppose it.

UNIT 12:
Emergencies in daily life

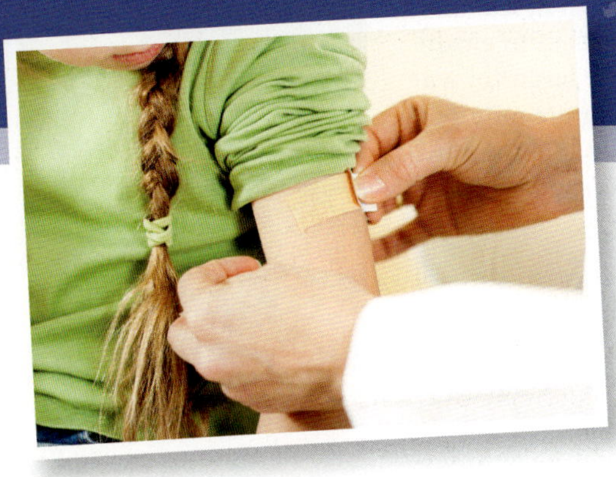

Module 1: Health and safety issues in the preschool

Preschool danger zones

As in the home or the workplace, the preschool environment presents potential dangers to the health and safety of children. Preschoolers are at an age where their sense of danger has not yet fully developed. They don't always exercise the degree of caution they should when faced with possible hazards in their environment. There are many areas in their immediate surroundings where the rambunctious preschooler needs to be protected from accident and injury, such as the bathroom, the classroom, the traffic on the way to and from school and the playground. In this unit we will explore typical dangers for the preschooler as well as examining ways in which these dangers can be reduced or eliminated altogether.

Areas of danger

The preschool classroom presents threats to the safety of children. Obvious dangers include damaged chairs which cannot bear the weight of the child, desks with broken edges and sharp corners, and badly-designed or broken toys and playthings. Poorly-designed furniture as well as improperly secured mats and rugs can also cause accidents. Windows that cannot be closed properly or that can be fully opened by a child also pose safety risks.

The health of children may also be endangered by poorly ventilated rooms, or by malfunctioning heaters and thermostats that fail to maintain the temperature at the right level. The presence of lead in the water supply of older buildings can also impair the health of children.

Rooms should be properly equipped with functioning fire alarms and smoke detectors, and fire exits kept clear at all times. Entrances and exits to the building should be properly watched and monitored to ensure that younger children cannot leave the building, and that unauthorised persons cannot enter.

In city preschools especially, traffic presents an immediate threat to safety whenever the children are taken outside on an outing. The volume and speed of traffic can be underestimated, not only by children but by their adult carers as well. A preschool may be located in an area where the pedestrian crossings are few in number, and impatient or impulsive children could be tempted to cross the street in a dangerous place, rather than take the time to walk to the pedestrian crossing at the end of the street.

Drowning is one of the most common causes of death in children of preschool age. Young children can drown in less than 15 cm of water, and particular care must be taken to ensure that buckets of water for mopping the floor, or basins of water for washing up are never left unattended, or are promptly emptied after use. It is also important to ensure that the hard, tiled floors of bathrooms are never left wet, as slippery floors can cause falls that may result in serious injury.

As in the home, the kindergarten kitchen poses all sorts of hazards to the unwary child. Sharp knives left lying on countertops, kettles containing boiling water and ovens with red hot hobs and heating elements all present serious threats to the safety of the child. Electrical sockets also pose a danger to curious children, who may electrocute themselves by inserting metal objects, such as knives or skewers, into the outlet.

The playground is another area which presents obvious risk of injury to children. Defective, damaged, poorly-designed or inadequately secured equipment can cause bad accidents. Swings need to be properly anchored into the ground, slides provided with guardrails, and bars on climbing frames spaced close enough together to ensure that small children don't fall through or get stuck between them. Protective surfacing such as rubber mats or mulch should also be generously placed around play equipment to help spare falling children serious injury.

Comprehension

Task 1

Find words and terms in the text above which match the definitions below.

a. device designed to regulate the temperature in a room
b. to damage or harm
c. to closely watch, observe, keep track of or supervise
d. people who do not have the required permission to enter restricted areas
e. a field trip or visit to somewhere outside the preschool, such as the zoo or a museum
f. the amount, mass or number of something
g. death caused by asphyxiation due to the inhalation of water
h. to be fixed or secured into the ground
i. barriers designed to lower or eliminate the risk of falling
j. soft material such as rubber matting or organic material intended to protect against injuries

Task 2

Collocations are commonly used verb-noun combinations. In the above text there are a number of collocations used, which express the idea of being exposed to risk.

Examples:
Unemptied buckets can *pose a risk* of drowning to small children.
Busy streets can *expose* children *to the risk* of being hit by a car.
Unprotected playground equipment can *present a danger* of falling.

Verb	Noun
to expose to	risk, danger
to present	a risk, a threat, a danger, a hazard
to pose	a risk, a threat, a danger, a hazard

Make a list of the types of dangerous situations presented by the following areas in and around the preschool: the bathroom, the kitchen, the classroom, the playground and the streets outside the preschool.
Then, using the collocations above, describe the kinds of risk which these situations potentially present.

Preschool safety checklist

It's important that preschool teachers and teachers' assistants are aware of all the potential dangers that the preschool environment presents. Making out a checklist is an effective means of identifying hazards with regard to developing a health and safety plan that will help prevent accidents from happening.

Toys used in the classroom should meet the health and safety requirements set out by the relevant government body or local authority. Toys should be made from safe, high quality materials and be manufactured to a high standard. Teachers should ensure that the toys are free from harmful chemicals and do not contain parts that break off or can be detached easily. Playthings such as dinner and tea sets should be disinfected after use to prevent the transmission of disease, as children may put the plastic cutlery into their mouths. It is also important to remember to store toys safely. Heavy boxes should not be placed on shelves that can be reached by children who may pull these heavy objects down upon themselves. Children should also be instructed and encouraged to use toys safely and appropriately. Building blocks, for example, should not be used to stand upon, nor thrown at other children. In games involving water, children should be discouraged from pouring water onto the floor, as wet floors present the risk of slipping.

Caregivers also need to be conscious of the dangers posed by the electricity supply. Exposed sockets should be secured using readily and cheaply available protective covers. Electrical cords should not be left exposed as they present both a tripping hazard as well as exposing children to the danger of electrocution. Cords should be mounted on walls, out of reach of the tallest child in the group and secured against skirting boards or placed beneath the floor boards of the room.

Cleaning supplies present a serious risk of poisoning and should always be securely locked away when not in use. Smoke and fire alarms should be regularly checked and properly maintained. Fire extinguishers need to be frequently tested and certified for use by fire inspectors. A fire drill should be drawn up, taught to the children and regularly practised. This can be done in a fun way as a learning activity to encourage the children to learn what procedures to follow in case of fire. Children should also be taught the emergency numbers of fire and ambulance services in case, for example, their caregiver should have an accident and lose consciousness.

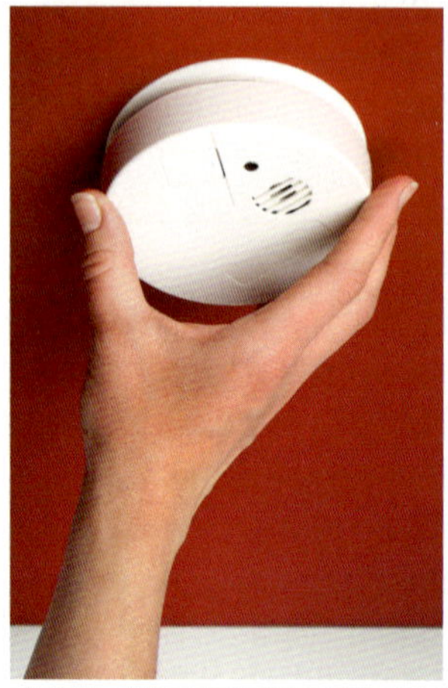

The most important precaution of all though is to ensure that the children are adequately supervised in an environment that has been made as safe for them as possible. Children should never be left alone, even for short periods of time, without supervision. Supervision does not have to be obtrusive or invasive. Children can be given the freedom they need to play independently with one another while still being discreetly supervised by a caregiver.

Task 3

Find words in the text which match the following definitions.

a. to make sure
b. to clean or chemically treat an object to rid it of germs
c. the communication or contraction of illness
d. knives, forks, spoons and other eating utensils
e. suitably, to do something in the right way
f. to receive an electric shock

Task 4

With a partner draw up a list of all the possible dangers children are potentially exposed to in the preschool environment. Then complete the checklist below on a separate sheet of paper with recommendations on how to counter these dangers. Some examples have been included.

Area	Risk	Countermeasure
Street	Fast moving traffic	Have local authority install speed bumps to slow cars down
	Distant pedestrian crossing	
Kitchen	Tables with sharp edges	Apply soft padding to the edges
Classroom		
Electricity	Exposed electrical cords	Place cords beneath floor boards

Area	Risk	Countermeasure
Playground	Hard ground	
Bathroom		
Fire Safety	Fire exits not clearly marked	

Grammar

Conditional III

The conditional III is used to talk about imaginary events in the past, i.e. events that did not take place but which might have affected the present situation if they had occurred.

Read the following sentences about a past action and the result of that action.

Jennifer did not prepare well for the interview for the position of preschool director. She did not get the job.

This is what actually occurred. But we can also imagine a different past situation, which might have produced a different outcome:

*If Jennifer **had prepared** well for the interview, she **would have got** the job.*

In the conditional III, the **past perfect** is used in the if-clause and the **past tense** of "would" in the remainder of the sentence:

if-clause	would-clause
Past perfect: **had (not) + past participle** (third form of verb)	Past tense of would: **would (not) have + past participle** (third form of verb)
If **we had dried** the kitchen floor properly, …	… Anna **would not have slipped** and **fallen.**

Task 5

Look at the following past situations and their results and express them as conditional III statements, i.e. say what would have happened if the situation had been different.

Example:
Jackie climbed onto the table. She fell off.
*If Jackie **had not climbed** onto the table, she **would not have fallen off**.*

a. Peter left the sharp bread knife on the table in the kitchen. Paul accidently cut himself with it.
b. Kevin stuck a fork into the electrical socket. He received an electric shock.
c. John forgot to lock the door to the kindergarten before he left. The cash box in the office was stolen.

d. Joshua didn't look both ways before he crossed the road. He was run over by a car and taken to hospital.
e. We installed a smoke detector in the kitchen. We heard the signal when the fire started last week.

Mixed conditionals

If we talk about a past action and its result in the present, we use mixed conditionals:

Past action: *John took a two month drama course.*
Present result: *Now he can do drama classes with the children.*
Mixed conditional: *If John* ***hadn't taken*** *the drama course, he* ***couldn't do*** *drama classes with the children.*

In mixed conditionals, the **past perfect** is used in the if-clause and the **present tense** of "would" in the remainder of the sentence.

if-clause	would-clause
Past perfect: **had (not)** + **past participle (third form of verb)**	Present tense of "would": **would (not)** + **infinitive** (first form of verb)
If Andrew ***had not installed*** *the protective matting in the playroom, …*	*… the children* ***would have*** *more accidents.*

Task 6

Express the following sentences as mixed conditional statements.

a. Jack received his passenger van licence last week. Now he can take the children out on drives.
b. Jim spent two years studying Farsi. Now he can talk to the Iranian children we have here in their native language.
c. We applied to the education board for more funding. This means we now have enough money to purchase new classroom equipment.

Task 7

Conditional review: Read the following sentences. Decide whether they are conditional I, II, or III or mixed conditionals, and complete them using the appropriate forms.

a. We (bring) the children to the museum today, if it (be) open on Mondays. I'll check on the internet and find out.
b. I (attend) the workshop at the weekend, if I (not have to) look after my sick relative.
c. If I (drive) to work yesterday instead of taking public transport, I (arrive) on time.
d. If I (not have) the experience of looking after so many younger brothers and sisters as I was growing up, I (not be) so good with children now.
e. I (apply) for a higher position in a year or two, when I (gain) more experience in this job.
f. Dagmar (repair) the chair in the classroom last week, if she (know) it was broken, and Max (not fall) through it.
g. I (set) up my own kindergarten, if I (have) the money, but the bank won't offer me a loan.

Module 2: Teaching children about safety

Helping children to learn about safety

One of the most effective ways of preventing accidents in the preschool is to make the children more aware of the potential dangers around them, as well as to teach them to behave and play safely with one another. Play activities can be used to encourage children to be more safety conscious. Children learn most easily and effectively through games, play and role-playing activities. Approaching the issue of safety in this way also presents the advantage of being able to teach children about danger and the risk of accident, without unduly frightening them. It is important to teach children about safety in a context that allows them to feel that they have control over their environment and can act to protect themselves and others from accident and injury.

Drafting a set of safety rules for the kindergarten provides the basis for the development of a comprehensive programme designed to prevent accidents. A good way of making children aware of the dangers present in the preschool environment is to take them into each room and ask them to imagine how they could hurt or injure themselves there. A list of their responses can be taken. For example, in the kitchen, Jennifer might mention how she once cut her hand on a knife that was left on the kitchen table at home. Max might reply that the same thing happened to him, and Paul might add that he once hit his head off the corner of the table in the kitchen and was bleeding from the cut. The caregiver can note down each of these remarks.

The children can then be brought back to the classroom and asked how these accidents could have been prevented. They may well respond with a variety of suggestions, such as: “We should always put the knives back in the drawer when we’re not using them”; or “We don’t need sharp knives, we shouldn’t have them in the kitchen”; or “Mum puts a plastic guard on the blade of our sharp knives so we don’t cut ourselves”. The caregiver can then take each of these suggestions in turn and discuss them with the group. She may ask the children questions such as “Can we always return knives straight to the drawer when we’re not using them? I was preparing breakfast this morning and was cutting tomatoes. Then I left the knife I was using on the chopping board while I made some tea, because I needed it again afterwards to cut the cheese. Should I always put it away immediately, as soon as I stop using it?”; or “But if we have no sharp knives in the kitchen, how can we cut up and chop food. Paul, you tried cutting a piece of bread yesterday with a butter knife. Did that work for you?”

Questions such as these may lead the children to the conclusion that there can be no such thing as a totally safe environment, where all potential dangers are put out of harm’s way.

The children may then start to think in terms of what they need to learn and how they need to behave in order to avoid injuring themselves and causing accidents in the kitchen. The teacher’s comments and questions can elicit responses from the children like: “We should make sure that the knife is left on a safe place on the table and warn other children that it is there until we are finished using it and ready to put it away”; or “We should always pick up the knife by the handle and never by the blade”; or “We should never point a knife at anyone”; or “Sometimes it’s more dangerous to use a knife that’s not sharp. When I tried to use the butter knife to cut the bread, the knife slipped and I hurt my finger”. Getting children to reflect on their own experience to find solutions to the problems they encounter in their environment encourages them to think independently and to develop a sense of responsibility for their own actions and behaviour. This process leads in turn to increasing the children's sense of control over their own environment and enables them to learn that they have the power to prevent accidents and make their surroundings safe for both themselves and others. Making children aware of their ability as well as their responsibility to take care of themselves and others is a meaningful and effective way of minimising the risk of accident. Asking questions that evoke responses to the issue of safety can also be instructive for caregivers who may not have considered some of the novel solutions that the imaginativeness and inventiveness of children can think up! Caregivers can also learn from this kind of interaction with children that a safety plan does not have to consist only of a list of dos and don'ts.

Comprehension

Task 1

Find the words and expressions that match the definitions below.

a. to be aware of risks and how to minimise or eliminate them
b. wide-ranging, inclusive, thorough
c. a wooden or plastic tablet used for cutting vegetables, meat or bread
d. to draw out answers from a person by asking them directed questions
e. to think about, e.g. an experience or event in order to learn from it
f. to suddenly meet with a person or a problem
g. a word which means one's immediate environment
h. an experience you can learn from can be described in this way
i. the ability to find novel solutions to problems or to create ingenious ideas

Task 2

With a partner discuss the following questions.

a. Is it always a good idea to involve young children in the drafting of a safety programme?
b. To what extent should children be permitted to determine the procedures and precautions the plan should contain?
c. In what sorts of situations would it be justifiable to simply issue children with instructions and impose prohibitions, without discussing the safety issues with them beforehand?

Dialogue between a child and a fireman about fire safety

Fireman Jack: Hello Jenny! Are you ready to learn about fire safety rules today?

Jenny: Yes, Jack. Fire safety is really important.

Jack: That's very true, Jenny. You know, it's really important to know what to do to get out of your school if there's a fire. So, Jenny, did you draw a map of the escape routes with your friends?

Jenny: (showing Jack her map): I drew all the exits in the school and how to get to them from my classroom.

Jack: That's great, Jenny. You know, smoke from a fire can make it hard to see where you're going, so you need to know your way out of the school. The main thing is to get out quickly and safely.

Jenny: The best way to get out of the school is through the front door, but we can use the back door as well, if we have to.

Jack: Very good, Jenny. It's important to know that there's more than one way to leave the building in case of fire. Now, let's talk about the safety rules you need to know if a fire breaks out in your school. First, check to see if there's heat or smoke coming through the cracks under and at the sides of the door.

Jenny: Yes! If you see smoke coming under the door, you should block the cracks with sheets, towels or clothing to stop the heat and smoke from getting in.

Jack: And if you think there might be a fire, but can't see any smoke?

Jenny: Then you should touch the door handle and if it's hot or very warm, don't open the door!

Jack: Yes! And if the door handle is cool, open the door very carefully. If you feel a wave of heat coming in, shut it again quickly. It probably means there's a fire outside.

Jenny: But if there's no heat from outside the door, then you can follow an escape route to the closest exit.

Jack: True, but let's imagine now that the door handle is hot, or that smoke and heat are coming through. What should you do then?

Jenny: Shout for help from the window, or call 911 on my phone, or both!

Jack: That's right. And another important thing is to never hide no matter how frightened you are. Adults and firemen will be looking for you and you'll want them to find you as soon as possible! Now let's pretend we're doing a fire drill to practice your escape.

Jenny: OK.

Jack: So, let's say you notice that the door handle is cool, but you notice a little smoke. What do you do?

Jenny: I open the door slowly to check for fire. And if there is smoke, I should take a towel or T-shirt, wet it if I can, and breathe through that.

Jack: Yes, and as you go you should stay as low to the ground as you can. Do you know why?

Jenny: Is it because smoke goes up and all the clean air is close to the floor?

Jack: Very good. And when you're out you should go to the meeting place your teacher told you about, and never go back inside for any reason.

Jenny: But what if Arnold, our pet hamster, is still in there? Shouldn't I try to go back for him?

Jack: No, Jenny, once you're out, you stay out and one of my fireman friends will rescue Arnold if he can. You know, it's also very important to do safety drills at school.

Jenny: Yes, at least twice a year, to stay in practice in case there's a real fire.

Jack: That's right, Jenny. Do you also know what to do if your clothes catch fire?

Jenny: Hmmm... there are three things aren't there? Stop, drop and roll. Rolling on the ground will help you put out the flames.

Jack: Yes, that's right. And remember the best way to deal with fires is to prevent them from happening in the first place. Never play with matches, lighters or fireplaces. A big fire can start from a small match and get quickly out of control. So, will you visit me again with your school friends soon, Jenny?

Jenny: Yes, Jack. We're coming on a class trip next month.

Jack: Well, I'm looking forward to seeing you all again.

Jenny: Thanks, Jack.

Activity

Task 3

Break into pairs. One of you will play the role of caregiver and the other the role of a child, as in the above dialogue. Choose an area of health and safety that the child should be made aware of and taught about, e.g. crossing a busy street; safety in the bathroom; safety in the playground.

Prepare the script together, rehearse it until you feel familiar with your role and can repeat the lines fluently. Then perform it in front of your fellow students. If you feel confident enough, try acting out your scene without referring to your script.

Elicit feedback from your audience and discuss your performance with them. You might talk about the following questions:

- Did the caregiver give useful and accurate advice?
- Was the information clearly communicated in a way the child could easily understand?
- Did the child demonstrate that she had understood the information correctly?
- Did the caregiver add important information to the child's responses or correct them where necessary?
- Was the information exchanged between caregiver and child a complete account of what should be done to avoid danger and maximise safety in the given situation

If necessary, change your script to take account of the feedback you've received and perform the sketch again.

Module 3: Dealing with emergencies

Accidents will happen!

No matter how much we try to avoid them, accidents do occur. In a preschool containing up to 30 or 40 children, accidents, cuts, falls and bruises are simply a part of the daily life. No safety programme, no matter how comprehensive, detailed or thoroughly applied can prevent all instances of accident or injury. Serious accidents are thankfully rare in a well-run preschool, but they do still occur, and caregivers have to be prepared to deal with them when they do. In this module we will be looking at what can be done when a child starts choking and how to place a child in the recovery position, as well as what is involved in filling out an incident report. In all cases of accident and injury an incident report will have to be completed, detailing the circumstances under which an accident happened. This is necessary in order to have a clear record of exactly what occurred, especially if medical personnel or emergency services need to be involved. It is also of course reassuring for parents to know that the preschool management and staff take the issue of safety seriously, and are prepared to deal responsibly with crises in accordance with established procedures when they occur.

Dealing with choking

One of the most distressing occurrences preschool staff have to deal with is when a child suddenly begins to choke. The sight of a child unable to catch its breath can be sufficient to induce panic or paralysis in a carer and it is important for this reason that staff are fully trained and ready to deal with this eventuality should they be confronted with it.

What to do when a child is choking

Babies and young children can choke on anything that can fit through a toilet roll. To prevent choking: keep small objects out of reach, cut up food into very small pieces and supervise children while they're eating, especially if they are under five years old.

Signs of choking:

Unable to speak or cry, clutching their throat, struggling to breathe.

How to help a choking child over one year:

If a child shows signs of choking, stay calm and ask them to cough to help remove the object. If they are unable to cough:

- Bend the child forward, supporting them on their chest with one hand. With the other hand, use the flat of your hand to give a sharp back blow between the shoulder blades.
- Check to see if the blockage has cleared before giving another blow – give up to 5 back blows checking each time to see if the blockage has cleared.

If the back blows haven't helped get an ambulance on the way.

- If the blockage hasn't cleared after five blows, the next stage is to do an abdominal thrust/Heimlich manoeuvre:

  Stand behind the child and place one hand in a fist under their rib cage. Use the other hand to pull up and under in a J shaped motion, to dislodge the obstruction.

2. Perform abdominal thrusts up to 5 times, checking each time to see if the obstruction has cleared. Anyone who has received abdominal thrusts must be seen by a doctor.
3. If the child is still choking, call 911 (or 999 in Britain and Ireland) and alternate five back blows and five abdominal thrusts until emergency help arrives. If at any point the child becomes unconscious, start CPR.

Adapted from: Choking – how to help your child, in: First Aid for Life, 19 October 2015, https://firstaidforlife.org.uk/choking-how-to-help-your-child/.

The recovery position

When a child loses consciousness because of heatstroke or in the aftermath of an epileptic fit, they should be placed in the recovery position. This is a position which allows the child to breathe freely, helps prevent injury should they experience a fit, and greatly reduces the risk of suffocation should they vomit.

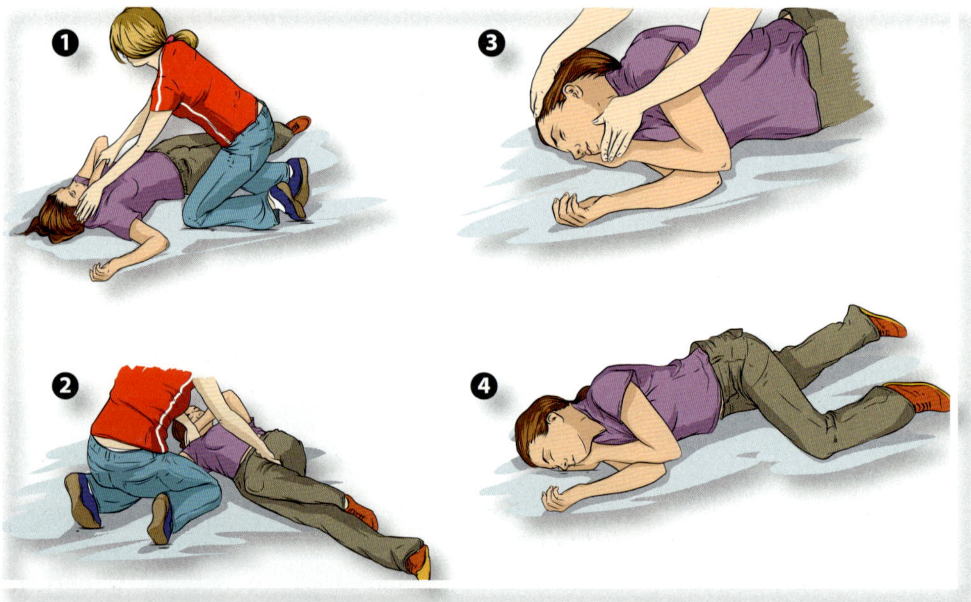

To place a person in the recovery position, follow these steps (see illustration):

1. With the person lying on their back, kneel on the floor at their side. Place the arm nearest you at a right angle to their body with their hand upwards, towards the head.
2. Tuck their other hand under the side of their head, so that the back of their hand is touching their cheek bend the knee farthest from you to a right angle.
3. Carefully roll the person onto their side by pulling on the bent knee. The top arm should be supporting the head and the bottom arm will stop you from rolling them too far.
4. Open their airway by gently tilting their head back and lifting their chin, and check that nothing is blocking their airway. Stay with the person and monitor their condition until help arrives.

Adapted from: Recovery position – First aid, www.nhs.uk/conditions/first-aid/recovery-position/, 08 January 2016, accessed 23 July 2018.

Comprehension

Task 1

Find words or expressions in the text that match the definitions below.

a. a document which details the circumstances of an accident
b. a word which means "occurrence"/"happening"
c. the palm (of the hand)
d. to strike someone, e.g. to free their airway of a blockage
e. either of two large, flat, triangular bones located in the top left and right corners of the back
f. sharp movements of the hand into the upper stomach area, as used in the procedure to prevent choking
g. a tightly clenched hand
h. to free or release an object from the position in which it is stuck
i. the object or cause of a blockage in the airway
j. the three-letter abbreviation for "cardio pulmonary resuscitation"

Activity

Task 2

Break into pairs. Using the information above, as well as other sources such as videos and images from the internet, prepare a short presentation demonstrating *on a doll or pillow* how to perform either the anti-choking procedure, or how to place someone in the recovery position to an audience of carers who need to learn these techniques as part of their training to work in a kindergarten.

Please note that performing this procedure on a person could result in serious injury.

Your presentation should consist of:

- A general introduction outlining the importance of learning these techniques and the situations in which you may be required to use them.
- The main part in which you demonstrate in clear steps how the technique is carried out.
- A conclusion in which you summarise the most important points to note.

If you are familiar with Microsoft PowerPoint or Apple Keynote, prepare a slideshow to help illustrate and support the points you wish to make.

Task 3

If a child has suffered a serious accident in your kindergarten, you will need to call its parents to inform them of what has happened. It is important in such situations to remain calm and communicate as clearly, reassuringly and sympathetically as possible. It is essential to be open and honest about what has happened and to answer questions as directly and as comprehensively as possible.

With a partner perform a telephone role-play based on the following scenario (page 186). One of you will play the parent and the other the carer making the call.

Robert, a five-year-old, slipped on the kitchen floor and cut his forehead. You and another member of staff managed to stop the bleeding and put a bandage on the wound, which was not too deep. As Robert fell unconscious you immediately called an ambulance and he was taken to hospital. The ambulance arrived within five minutes of your call and Robert had already stated to regain consciousness before it arrived. The paramedic examined the wound and told you it would need some stitches, but reassured you that the cut was not serious. He also said that Robert would probably suffer some mild concussion and would probably need to rest at home for a few days. Your colleague accompanied Robert in the ambulance to the hospital, the Quentin Blake Hospital, in Dublin Street.

Incident Report Forms

When an accident involving a serious injury occurs, an incident report detailing the circumstances of the accident and the nature of the injuries incurred must be filled out.

Sample Incident Report

Incident report – Elysium Kindergarten	
Name of child: Michael Wright	**Date of birth:** 2 February 2014
Details of incident **Time/Date:** 10:15/30 March 2018 **Type (accident, illness etc.):** Accident resulting in injury **Location** (playground, classroom etc.): Playground	
Details of incident: Michael was playing in the playground with the other children during the break. He was climbing up the ladder to the top of the slide when he lost his footing and fell to the ground, a distance of about two metres. He fell badly on his arm and cried out in pain. Kindergarten staff immediately called for an ambulance. The other children were brought back to the kindergarten. Two members of staff remained with Michael, covered him with a blanket and comforted him while waiting for the ambulance, which arrived shortly afterwards. **Injuries incurred/Nature of illness:** Michael suffered a broken forearm and some scratches and bruising to the face as a result of the fall. **Medical treatment/services:** Staff called emergency services at 10:15, as soon as the accident occurred, and an ambulance arrived within 10 minutes, shortly before 10:25. Michael was examined and treated by paramedics where he lay, before being taken to the emergency room in the Quentin Blake Children's Hospital in Dublin Street.	
Parent/Relative/Other contacted: **Name:** Sylvia Wright (Mother)	 **Time/Date:** 10:30/30 March 2018
Witnesses: **Name(s):** Karen Fiedler, Jackie Baggot (Kindergarten staff members). **Note:** Karen travelled in the ambulance with Michael to the hospital and remained there with him until his mother arrived.	
Signature: ***J. Baggot***	**Time/Date:** 30 March 2018
Recommendations for future prevention: Place rubber foot grips on the rungs of the slide's ladder and extend protective matting around the area of the slide.	

Task 4

Together with your partner from Task 3, write an incident report modelled on the sample report above, which describes the details of the accident suffered by Robert in Task 3 above. When completed, read out your report to the rest of the class.

UNIT 13:
Conflict management

Module 1: Resolving conflict

Are children the best people to resolve their own conflicts?

Norma Hunter works in the Behaviour Support Unit of a primary school in Manchester. Here, she talks about what causes conflict among young children, and how the children themselves can often find a solution to the problem.

Why do children fall out?

Conflict is a part of life for people of all ages and of course young children are not immune. Finding ways to resolve conflict is a very important part of a child's development. In the UK, part of the national curriculum is known as SEAL (Social and Emotional Aspects of Learning) and its second theme is called Getting On and Falling Out. Conflict in preschool education tends to arise over such issues as sharing toys, taking turns, personal space, who the children play with and who they don't, and sometimes due to not understanding fully what is happening. Young children are very focused on what they want, not on what the children around them want.

What does a teacher or an educator need to do?

Don't ignore it or avoid it. Step in fast enough to avoid children getting hurt, but don't rush into imposing a solution of your own. Keep calm, if you get angry it will definitely make things worse. Avoid responding with a threat or an ultimatum. If that's the only model of conflict resolution the children learn, it won't be helpful for their development. Use differentiated responses which are appropriate for the individual children involved.

Children want adults to be clear and concrete. Vague concepts of "kindness" and "niceness" don't mean much to a three-year-old. Caring about others and empathy have to be modelled and coached, rather than just telling a child "let's all be friends."

What is the best way to resolve the disputes?

In most cases, the children can come up with the solutions themselves if the adult facilitates this in the right way. For a start, wait until they've calmed down. Acknowledge and accept their emotions, don't tell them "you shouldn't be angry or upset." To them, the emotion is very real and important, so give them a little time to be angry or upset. After they've calmed down ask them "What's the problem? What happened exactly?" Listen, and repeat it back so that it's very clear for everybody. For example "You wanted the book which Charlene had. You took it from her. Charlene wanted to keep the book." Then ask what ideas the children have as to how the problem can be solved. You'd be surprised how often and how well children can come up with good ideas for resolution of the conflict.

Comprehension

Task 1

Decide if these statements about the text are true or false.

a. Young children are focused on the needs of other children around them.
b. Teachers and educators should react fast and try to find a solution as quickly as possible.
c. It can be useful to respond by making a threat.
d. Teachers and educators should use different responses depending on their knowledge of each child.
e. It's a good idea to tell the children to stop crying because there is really no reason for them to be upset.

Task 2

Replace the word or phrase in italics in these sentences with a synonym from the text.

a. The children usually *alternate with each other* in using the slide.
b. I think that the manager *dictates* the ethos and objectives of the kindergarten without consulting parents and staff.
c. We generally make sure that we *make a distinction* between the needs of all our children.
d. Maya is our administrative assistant. She really *assists the progress* of our group.
e. You have to make sure that you *recognise* everybody's contribution.

Activity

Task 3

Role-play the following situation in pairs.

Student A
You are the mother or father of a boy who has been involved in a fight at his nursery. Your son bit and hit another child in a conflict over a toy. You believe strongly in letting children find their own solutions to conflict, and in letting the children express what they are feeling rather

than telling them what to do or not do. You don't like to tell your son that the one or other the type of behaviour is "wrong."

Student B

You are the grandparent of (and main carer for) a child who has been involved in conflict at her nursery. She has been hit and bitten by another child. You are not convinced by the theory of letting children resolve their own disputes. You think that children need boundaries and clear rules about what is acceptable behaviour and what is not, and they look to adults for this information. You think that sometimes it is important to tell a child that a type of behaviour is unacceptable.

Task 4

In groups of four, brainstorm to come up with a list of all the skills which children could develop from finding solutions to conflicts themselves.

Grammar

Review of tenses

Task 5

Decide which of the sentences in the following pairs is correct.

a. I am living in Dresden since I was ten.
b. I have lived in Dresden since I was ten.

c. She was speaking to her brother on the phone when the doorbell rang.
d. She spoke to her brother on the phone when the doorbell was ringing.

e. The doctor told us that he had already sent the tests away to the laboratory.
f. The doctor told us that he already sent the tests away to the laboratory.

g. We normally work until 5 p.m. but this week we finish at 4.30.
h. We normally work until 5 p.m. but this week we are finishing at 4.30.

i. May is in hospital for a planned operation, I'm going to visit her tomorrow.
j. May is in hospital for a planned operation, I will visit her tomorrow.

Task 6

In pairs, rewrite the following sentences, using the words in brackets and other words which you need to think of. Don't change the form of the word in brackets.

a. Understanding every word isn't the most important thing.
It ...(matter)... if you don't understand every word.

b. Oh no, it's still raining.
Oh no, ...(yet)...
c. I knocked on your classroom door yesterday – why didn't you answer?
What ...(doing)... yesterday?
d. John arrived there. The game of football was over.
The game ...(already)... when John arrived.
e. I can hear Peter and Lawrence talking, but what language is that?
What is that language ...(which)...?

Task 7

Identify all the tenses used in the sentences in Task 6, and say why you used each one.

Module 2: Conflicts between children and parents and caregivers

Is positive reinforcement of children manipulation? Should you use praise and rewards to get children to cooperate?

Working with young children, toddlers especially, can be very frustrating. Trying to *coax* a toddler into doing things you'd like him to do requires a lot of patience. Both parents and caregivers readily admit being hesitant about how to respond to a child who cannot – or does not want to – cooperate. Although we all may disagree with applying certain methods of punishment, such as spanking or forcible isolation ("time out"), we may differ on the usefulness of doling out rewards and *praise* for positive behaviour. Because young children haven't learned yet to distinguish between good and bad behaviour, admonishment for not cooperating doesn't seem to be as appropriate or effective as positive reinforcement is for cooperative behaviour. But can too much positive reinforcement be a form of manipulation? Could it even have a *detrimental* effect on a child's social development?

Verbal rewards are used to reinforce desirable behaviour patterns; they're intended to get children to comply with our requests or instructions. Although it can be effective in conditioning a child to behave appropriately, it is doubtful whether a child will learn to recognise why that type of behaviour is necessary and appreciated in particular situations.

The more a child is rewarded for doing something well, the less interested the child becomes in the activity itself; instead, the child will only focus on receiving the reward. A study conducted by Joan Grusec (1992) at the University of Toronto uncovered that children who were frequently praised for being *generous* with others became progressively less generous; they were, in fact, less interested in sharing or helping than those children who were not praised for the same behaviour. The acts of generosity were no longer seen as something valuable in their own right, but rather merely as a means of getting a reaction from an adult.

Similar studies reveal that children who are praised for doing a creative task well are less likely to be just as competent at the next creative task. Researchers suggest that praise puts children under pressure to produce praiseworthy work. The more a child anticipates praise, the less likely he or she is to take the risks that are necessary to be creative.

Children need unconditional love and support. By overindulging a child with praise for positive behaviour, we are teaching the child to believe that our affection for the child *is* conditional. But what is the most effective alternative to using positive reinforcement in order to *discourage* misbehaviour? If a child is doing something it shouldn't be, rather than threatening or bribing, you should ask the child how his problem behaviour can be corrected. Allowing the child to participate in the decision-making process conveys the message that you take his ideas and feelings seriously. And children who are treated with more respect will in turn show more respect for others.

Rather than simply saying, "Good job!" for doing a good deed, recognise the child's accomplishment with an evaluation-free statement like, "You did it!" If the child has done something generous, drawing his attention to the positive effect of his action will reinforce its purpose. Instead of showing him that he has made you proud, he sees reason to be proud of himself. Encouraging children to do tasks successfully and to behave well is not about spoon-feeding them positive reinforcement, but more importantly about recognizing the worthiness of their tasks and deeds.

Comprehension

Task 1

Find one word in the following sentences that is used incorrectly. Correct the sentences by replacing the word with one of the appropriate words in italics from the text.

a. Many parents use bribery as a reliable method of conveying a child into doing something favourable.
b. A child is more likely to be genuinely selfish if he is made aware of the virtue of his generosity.
c. Some experts say that too much positive reinforcement has a desirable effect on a child's social development.
d. One way to encourage misbehaviour is to show a child more respect for his ideas and feelings.
e. Children who are constantly bribed for doing good deeds do not learn to recognise the worthiness of their deeds.

Task 2

Answer the following questions in your own words based on your understanding of the text.

a. Why are verbal rewards not effective in teaching children appropriate behaviour?
b. What message does frequent praise convey to children?
c. What are more effective alternatives to positive reinforcement?

Task 3

Read the scenario descriptions below and discuss with a partner the mistakes the teachers make in resolving the conflicts. How could the conflicts be resolved more effectively?

a. After the children had all worked hard to put away the toys at the end of the day, Emil (2 ½) dumped out a bin of building blocks and proceeded to play with them. The nursery school teacher scolded Emil and made him clean up the blocks all by himself. All of the children but Emil were sent outside to the playground.
b. Max (4) chose to ignore his nursery teacher's requests to stop playing and to go inside. His teacher said that if he did not stop playing immediately, he would not receive a snack when they went inside.
c. Sarah (3) needed help taking off her jacket and shoes. Her childminder told her that she should be able to do that at her age, adding "only babies need help getting undressed."
d. Two five-year-old girls in Ms Slade's reception class have a row about who gets to take care of the baby doll. The girls play tug-of-war on the doll, shouting at each other "It's mine!" until Ms Slade comes over. She tells the girls that if they couldn't agree, neither of them would get the baby doll to play with. She takes the doll away and hands it to a younger bystander.

Talking to parents

A childcare professional must have good communication skills, especially when working with parents. It can be challenging for a practitioner to raise concerns and sensitive issues with a parent. This requires good listening skills, empathy and tact on the part of a childcare professional. Mutual respect and trust are the keys to establishing a good working relationship with parents and this can be achieved through clear communication.

As a childcare provider, you must assume that all parents want to hear good news about their child. They want to be proud and hopeful of their child, and want to have the feeling that they are good parents. So, it's important that you carefully select your words and try not to be blaming or judgmental. If a parent challenges your opinion, resist the temptation to become defensive. Instead, acknowledge their viewpoint and concerns. Tell them that you value their opinion.

Here are some techniques for positive communication with parents:

Parents like to hear positive qualities about their child, so before you express criticism, find a positive attribute about the child you can praise.

"Adam is particularly good at ..., but he does have difficulty with ..."

Instead of saying, "your child will never be able to ...," you should say, "your child may have trouble with ..."

> "It's a funny thing about mothers and fathers. Even when their own child is the most disgusting little blister you could ever imagine, they still think that he or she is wonderful."
>
> Roald Dahl, *Matilda*

When a parent comes to collect their child at the end of the day, you should not wait for a family member to initiate conversation. Instead, you should freely comment on the child's experiences that day. If you are asked how a child's day was, avoid just saying "fine." Instead, give a parent a clear picture of the day's events using adjectives to help describe the child's experiences.

When you have something difficult to say, it's a good idea to introduce your intent with a phrase like,

- I think you should know ...
- I thought you'd like to know ...
- I think it's important for you to know that ...
- I'd like to talk to you about ... When would be a good time to talk?

Show a parent you are sincerely concerned:
"I am a little worried about Adam. He stopped what he was doing and started crying several times throughout the day."

Don't make assumptions about causes of a child's behaviour. Instead, allow parents to maintain control over the conversation by asking them for a possible explanation for their child's behaviour.

"I've noticed that ... Do you have any idea what the cause of this could be?"

And finally, avoid blameful questions like, "Why can't you bring Adam to nursery on time?" Instead be polite when you make requests:

- It would be very helpful if you could bring Adam to nursery a little earlier.
- I'd like to ask you to ...
- Could I ask you to ...
- We'd greatly appreciate it if ...

Task 4

Read the following comments and try to rephrase them using more diplomatic language.

a. If you cared about Emily, you wouldn't allow her to do that.
b. Unlike the other children his age, Jamal isn't capable of using a pair of scissors.
c. Michael's behaviour is very disappointing.
d. I doubt Charlotte will be ready to enter school by autumn.
e. It's obvious that Dean isn't getting enough attention at home.

Activity

Task 5

Choose one of the statements in Task 4 and create a dialogue which demonstrates positive communication between a childcare professional and a parent. Role-play your dialogue together with a partner in front of the class.

Module 3: Is disciplining necessary?

Listening

Listen to three young adults speak about their upbringings. How much do you understand by listening? Take notes as you listen. Then, try to answer the questions below. Try to do this exercise without reading the transcript.

How my parents raised me

Elizabeth, 35

My parents were strict, especially my father. I wouldn't necessarily say that they were authoritarian, but they certainly were authoritative. My father set limits and enforced rules with a very resolute voice and used physical disciplining if necessary. Although I might not have realised it at the time, my parents – both educators – were responsive and nurturing, and my sister and I lacked for nothing. My parents recognised the value of a good education and instilled in us the importance of diligence and achievement. Everything that could possibly distract us from our studies and jeopardise our prospects was not tolerated. There were rules we found hard to understand; in fact, it seemed there was no rationale to them at all. We were not allowed to get our ears pierced, wear make-up, apply nail polish or date boys until we turned 16. For two girls in puberty, these rules seemed both harsh and archaic to us in the 1970s and 80s. The older I got though, the better I got at finding ways to get around these nonsensical rules my parents laid down for us. Although I respected my parents' authority, I had also developed a strong self-esteem and confidence. I had to test my limits for myself. Now, I would say that I am a successful person because my parents taught me respect and self-respect, discipline and self-discipline.

Sibel, 40

I grew up in a traditional Muslim family with four siblings. My parents emigrated to Germany from Turkey in 1978 and my brothers and I were born shortly afterwards. I am the middle child; I have three brothers and one younger sister. My sister and I were raised to obey my father and our brothers. Although my mother was responsible for my upbringing and education, she had no authority in our home. When I turned 10, my mother said that I would have to wear a headscarf to protect my female integrity. This was the custom in our family, and it never occurred to me to question the validity of this Islamic "sacrament". My father was very domineering – authoritarian. He did not allow me to leave the house, to play with my friends, or to go to the cinema without being chaperoned by my brothers. I grew up in fear. My father would often beat me, my sister and my mother, and he permitted my brothers to beat us, too. It was all about power and control, not about discipline. My father wanted me to become a devout Muslim woman who would obey and serve her husband. I feared the consequences of not becoming this woman, but I could not respect my father for being such a cruel and brutal person either. So, I have always had to live my life in secret, hiding my talents and passions from my family. Even today in the company of my friends, I feel uncomfortable unveiling my true colours. I only wish my family could be proud of me for who I really am. I feel alone without a family I can trust.

James, 25

My parents were hippies. They believed in raising me and my brother as equal counterparts to themselves. We were a democratic family, and my parents never imposed rules upon us that we disagreed with or couldn't understand. My brother and I never really lived by rules. We

did what we wanted when we wanted to – and we still do! My parents firmly believed that life itself would teach us all the lessons we needed. They never preached or scolded, but they would explain the consequences of our actions when we made poor decisions. For a child, having anti-authoritarian or permissive parents is great: no bedtime, no television limits, no curfew. However, the downside of this kind of upbringing was that I got bad grades in school; my parents said that it was my responsibility to do my homework, which I routinely neglected to do. Instead I would hang out with my mates and get into mischief. Now as an adult, I find it difficult to set limits for myself, and I find it hard to decide what is necessary and important for me to do. I jump around from one job to the next. If I'm honest with myself, I lack discipline and diligence, and I lack self-control. My parents undoubtedly love me, and I believe they were convinced they were being the best parents they could be.

Comprehension

Task 1

Are the following statements true or false?

a. Elizabeth says her father would occasionally smack her as a young child for being disobedient.
b. Sibel is the eldest of five children.
c. James's parents are teachers.
d. Elizabeth's parents taught her to be a hard worker.
e. Sibel was allowed to go to the cinema by herself.
f. James was allowed to stay up as long as he wanted.
g. Elizabeth accepted her parents' rules, but didn't always follow them.
h. Sibel grew up in a religious family.
i. James says he is successful today because he had to learn to be responsible for himself at a young age.

Task 2

Discuss the following question with a partner. Then, share your ideas with the group.

a. Which three types of child-rearing methods were mentioned by the speakers?
b. How do you think these peoples' upbringings have affected their personal development?
c. Which person do you think is most well-adjusted? Least well-adjusted? Explain.
d. Which child-rearing method would you endorse?

Grammar

We use the simple present tense to talk about permanent situations, temporary continuing events, or things that happen on a regular basis. However, when we want to talk about things that occurred routinely in the past, we use the modal verbs would or used to + infinitive. See the examples from the text:

*My father **would** often **beat** me …*
*I **would have to wear** a headscarf …*

Task 3

Can you find any other examples in the text?

Task 4

Rewrite the following sentences using *would* + infinitive or *used to* + infinitive to show that these events happened routinely in the past.

a. My parents always let me make my own decisions.
b. I was scared of the dark.
c. I went to bed whenever I wanted to.
d. She sucked her thumb until she was ten.
e. My parents always went out on Saturday evenings while I stayed home with the babysitter.

The parenting gap: why French mothers prefer to use the firm smack of authority

In her book French Children Don't Throw Food, American mother-of-three Pamela Druckerman, who lives in Paris, asks how the French manage to raise children who, unlike many of their US or British counterparts, sleep through the night at two months, are not picky eaters, do not throw tantrums in the supermarket and go to bed without making a fuss.

In France a child is rarely considered an equal, but a small human being ready to be formatted, partly by its parents, but mostly by the state education system. It has to be *encadré*, kept within a clearly and often rigidly defined framework that places disciplines such as manners and mathematics above creativity and expression.
A French child who has a tantrum is unlikely to be cut any slack on the grounds that it is expressing itself, is quite likely to be smacked and, if the tantrums continue, packed off to see a child psychologist. The "terrible twos" is not a recognised phenomenon in France.

Druckerman makes a great deal of how French children are taught to be better behaved in public and social situations. Passengers on the Eurostar can often identify a child's nationality without hearing them speak. You can more or less bet the one running up and down the carriage screaming his head off will not be French.

Bénédicte Lohe-Le Blanc, 38, a teacher originally from Brittany, and her husband Vincent, 39, live with their three children, Sten, 11, Yaelle, nine, and Kenan, six, in west London. She believes British parents are lax with their children.

"I was at an English friend's house and her six-year-old son was thumping the piano as we were trying to speak. His mother said 'yes that's lovely, but not so loud'. He just carried on. I said to myself, if this were France, the child would have been hauled off to another part of the room and made to stop. British parental culture is very relaxed, while we terrorise our children."

Lohe-Le Blanc is convinced this is a backlash from the laissez-faire attitudes that prevailed in France after the May 1968 student riots that brought a form of the swinging 60s to French society. "In the wake of May 68 we were more relaxed and we rejected authority. But my generation saw the damage that lack of limits did to children and how it ultimately caused them problems, so we went back to being authoritarian."

She added: "We consider our children to be small people, but they are not equal to an adult. They need authority, they need rules and they need to be kept in line. A child is a child and has his place. In France we see authority as a form of affection and believe that a child blossoms because of, not in spite of, that authority. The bottom line is my child can have his own opinion, but it's me who decides."

Adapted from: Willsher, Kim: The parenting gap: why French mothers prefer to use the firm smack of authority, in: The Guardian, 1 January 2012, www.theguardian.com/lifeandstyle/2012/jan/01/parenting-france-britain, accessed 25 April 25 2018.

Comprehension

Task 5

Find the appropriate vocabulary from the text to conclude the sentences.

a. A child who eats almost everything is not a ...(1)...
b. A child who is reluctant or rejects doing something puts up a ...(2)...
c. A child who cries and screams uncontrollably is having a ...(3)...
d. A parent who hits the child on its bottom is giving it a ...(4)...
e. Parents who are not strict are said to be ...(5)...
f. French parents believe that children need rules to be kept ...(6)...

Task 6

Answer the following questions in your own words based on your understanding of the text.

a. Describe the differences in young children's behaviour in England and France.
b. Explain why the British and French approaches to child-rearing are so different.
c. How does the German child-rearing approach compare to those of the British and French?

Grammar

Compound prepositions

When we want to show that something has happened as a result of something else, we use the compound prepositions *due to*, *owing to*, *on account of* or *because of* before noun phrases, but not preceding independent clauses, i.e.:

I cannot go to work today ***owing to*** *my son's illness.* (correct)
I cannot go to work today ***due to*** *my son is sick.* (Not correct, because ... *my son is sick* is an independent clause.)

Due to can be used after the verb *be*, but *owing to* cannot.

His absence today was ***due to*** *illness.* (correct)
His absence today was ***owing to*** *illness.* (incorrect)

We were unable to go on our excursion ***on account of*** *the poor weather.* (correct)
Because of *the poor weather, we were unable to go on our excursion.* (correct)

Task 7

Rewrite these two sentences as one sentence using one of the compound prepositions. Make any other necessary changes.

a. Many children are hospitalised each year. They are abused by family members.
b. Our kindergarten will be closed this summer. They will be expanding and modernising the building.
c. Most three-year-olds cannot write their names. They lack hand-eye coordination.
d. We cannot disclose personal information. We have a confidentiality policy.
e. We could not hire Ms Peters. She did not have the required qualifications.
f. Rebecca cannot have any food with nuts in it. She has a nut allergy.

Activity

Task 8

Have a cross-cultural classroom debate on discipline. Split into two teams. One team will support the French approach to child-rearing, while the other team will support the British parenting style. Before you open the debate discussion, each team should collect and prepare their arguments. Once both teams have presented their arguments, decide as a group which team was most persuasive.

Task 9

How did your parents raise you? Were they too strict, or not strict enough? Would you do anything differently as a parent? Write a short composition of no more than 200 words.

Listening transcriptions

Unit 1, Module 3

Finding a job

Sandra Hare
My name is Sandra Hare and I'm 55. I worked as a preschool teacher for 24 years and I loved every minute of it. Because working in preschool is very strenuous work that requires a lot of energy, I'm looking around for a new employment opportunity better suited to my age. You see, my husband died about a year ago and I'm caring for my elderly mother at home now. I just don't have the same amount of energy as I used to. But I'm not ready to retire yet; I don't want to sit at home. But I don't want to work full-time anymore either. And besides, I need an income. Whatever it is, working with children is an absolute must!

Geoffrey Madden
I'm Geoffrey Madden, 28 years old, with a degree in social work with a focus on education. I finished my college education three years ago and have been working until now in temporary positions. I'm looking for a permanent full-time position, preferably working with adolescents. My experience has been in local education authority settings and recreational facilities for troubled youths. I've thought about working in approved homes or with youths who are at risk. I grew up in a multi-cultural environment in London myself and can appreciate the difficulties teens of minority backgrounds have in society. Naturally my native language is English, but I understand a bit of Bengali, too.

Julia Martens
My name is Julia Martens and I'm 19 years old. I'm currently attending the local vocational college, studying Early Childhood Education. As I haven't finished my degree yet, I'm not exactly sure what kind of job I want. I love working with people, especially children – young children. When I was a child, I wanted to become a nurse. I spent a lot of time in hospital and the nurses who cared for me were my role models. I do have experience working as a summer camp counsellor, so I'm able to plan and facilitate group activities. In my free time I volunteer at the village fire brigade rescue squad. I'm qualified in First Aid and CPR.

Claire Peters
Claire Peters is my name. I'm 42 years young and a full-time mum of two children, eight and ten. I've been unemployed for ten years, since the birth of my oldest daughter. Now, that my kids are older and more independent, I feel it's time for me to go back to work. I'd like flexible part-time employment during the day in the field in which I got my training: Early Childhood Education. My first working experience after college was working with children with learning disabilities. I did that for about six years before I decided to have kids of my own. It would be nice to work with infants, although it's been a while since I comforted little babies!

Unit 7, Module 2

Teenage confessions

Emma, 17
I don't like looking at myself in the mirror. All I see is a fat, ugly girl looking back at me. I turn sideways and see the bulge below my waist. I see a huge bum and protruding hips and thighs. I hate my body.
It all started when I was about 13. I was fond of a lad at school at the time, and I thought if I looked really good, better than any of the other girls, he would finally notice me. I started dieting.

Genetically, I was never predestined to be thin. Because my mum is overweight and my father used to be overweight, my parents are very conscientious about what we eat. Whenever I would eat something high in calorie, like ice-cream or pizza, my mum would always make me feel guilty for it, as if I were committing a sin. I began to believe it myself.
In the beginning, dieting required a lot of self-discipline. It was frustrating at first, but when I finally lost my first stone, I was really proud of myself. Now, I measure my success according to my weight. Seeing the scale go down makes me feel really good about myself. I'm so scared of gaining weight. I don't want to be a failure and I'm completely fixed on not letting myself succumb to my weakness. There's always a little devil looking over my shoulder – a voice in my head that scolds me for eating something I shouldn't.
Whenever my schoolmates invite me to come over for a movie night or a party, I don't go because I don't want to be tempted by the food and drink. I try to think of all kinds of excuses to decline food. And when I am forced to eat, I feel like I am betraying myself and then I hate myself all over again.

Stephen, 18
As soon as I come home from school, I turn on my computer. On weekdays, I game for about five or six hours at a time. But on weekends I can spend up to 15 hours online. Once I get started, I just can't stop. I sit there in front of the screen and I'm in a totally different world, where time stands still. In the virtual world I can create new roles for myself and take on superhuman powers. Sometimes I get so involved in my role I forget to eat, drink and sleep; I lose track of time. When I game I forget all of my problems; it's like escaping reality for a few hours.
My parents are concerned that I'm shutting myself off from my friends. But I'm not! Online gaming is actually quite social. When you play online, you play with different people from all over the world. It's even easier to make friends online than in real life. You work together as a team; it gives you a sense of belonging as you work towards a common goal. Sometimes I organize game parties; I invite my friends over and we game together.
My parents think I'm an addict. I wouldn't say I'm addicted; there are plenty of people who watch telly for five and six hours a day. The game makes you want to keep playing; it's hard to let go because it's potentially never-ending. With each new quest or each new level, you always try to top yourself and your opponents. You always have to set yourself a new goal, and every time you reach that goal, you feel rewarded. That's what I live for. It's awesome.

Jane, 16
When Amy Winehouse died, it really shook me up. I really don't want to end up like her. I'm 16 and I weigh 16 stone and yet I can drink ... well – more than you might expect.
I go out with my friends to the pubs at the weekends. It's the only thing to do around here really. We're a big circle of friends, and we each pony up for a round of pints. So, by the end of the evening, we've all had at least six pints and are really wasted. Whoever drinks the most is like the paragon, so it becomes kind of competitive. We all have a good time together while we're there, but I usually don't remember anything by the morning. Sometimes I regret it, when I hear about the things I've said and done the next day. I've tried to imagine what my life would be like if I stopped drinking, but to tell you the truth, I wouldn't want to miss hanging out with my mates. They're like family to me.
My parents got divorced when I was 13. My father drank, and he would get pretty aggressive. My mum set him an ultimatum, but he just couldn't stay sober. I stayed with my mum, but we've had a rough time, the two of us. I want to make her proud of me, so I put myself under a lot of academic pressure. But it can be so overwhelming at times. I look forward to the weekends to relieve stress and numb the pain.

Unit 10, Module 1, Task 1

Can
I am 23, and I live in Berlin. I recently decided to become a German citizen and to give up my Turkish citizenship. This will make living in Germany easier even though most Germans don't consider me German. When I visit my extended family in Ankara, most people there think I am German. So, I'm not really Turkish, but not really German either.

Selma
I just moved to the United States because my husband got a good job in Boston in a big company. Most people here don't even seem to notice my headscarf. I am quite relieved about that!

Amelia
Most people assume I am German until they talk to me. Then they realize that I must be Scandinavian. I actually come from Denmark, but I spent most of my life in Australia – so I consider myself Australian. I was able to get a very good position in Germany because of the various languages I can speak. I've made a lot of new friends in Germany, and I enjoy living here. I plan on staying for at least the next five years.

Katherine
I have been living in Ottawa, the capital of Canada, for the past two years. I enjoy living here because most people take it for granted that I am Canadian. Everybody here has mixed roots, and most people think positively of the fact that mine are Lebanese. I grew up in Cambridge because both of my parents work at the university there. I also lived in Düsseldorf for a few months, but because of the language and cultural differences there, I felt like an outsider.

Vocabulary English – German

Unit 1
Working with children – working for institutions of childcare

after-school care club [ˌɑ:ftə ˈsku:l kɜə klʌb]	Hort
approved school (UK) [əˈpru:vd ˌsku:l]	Erziehungsheim
childminder [ˈtʃaɪld ˌmaɪndə]	Tagesmutter
child-rearing [ˈtʃaɪld ˌrɪərɪŋ]	Erziehung
coin [kɔɪn]	(ein Wort) erfinden, prägen
compulsory [kəmˈpʌlsəri]	verpflichtend
conducive [kənˈdju:sɪv]	dienlich, zu etw. beitragend
contemporaneously [kənˌtempəˈreɪniəsli]	gleichzeitig
CPR (cardiopulmonary resuscitation) [si: pi: ɑ: (ˌkɑ:diəʊˈpʌlmənəri rɪˌsʌsɪˈteɪʃən)]	die Herz-Lungen-Reanimation
crèche [kreʃ]	Kinderkrippe
discriminatory [dɪˈskrɪmɪnətri]	benachteiligend
early childhood practitioner [ˈɜ:li ˈtʃaɪldhʊd prækˈtɪʃənə]	Erzieher/-in
educator [ˈedʒu:keɪtə]	Pädagoge
equipment [ɪˈkwɪpmənt]	Anlage, Ausrüstung
found sth. [ˈfaʊnd ˌsʌmθɪŋ]	etw. gründen
infant [ˈɪnfənt]	Säugling
Makaton® [ˈmækətɒn]	eine Gebärdensprache
meagre [ˈmi:gə]	ärmlich, mager
merely [ˈmɪəli]	lediglich
monitor [ˈmɔnɪtə]	beaufsichtigen, überwachen
preferential treatment [ˌprefəˈrenʃəl ˈtri:tmənt]	bevorzugte Behandlung
prejudice [ˈpredʒədɪs]	Vorurteil, Befangenheit
provision [prəˈvɪʒən]	Bereitstellung, Beschaffung
reception [rɪˈsepʃən]	Vorschule
recreation facility [ˌri:kriˈeɪʃən fəˈsɪləti]	Freizeiteinrichtung
reform school (US) [rɪˈfɔ:m ˌsku:l]	Erziehungsheim
refuge [ˈrefju:dʒ]	Schutzort, Zuflucht
retire [rɪˈtaɪə]	in Ruhestand gehen
unsettling [ˌʌnˈsetlɪŋ]	beunruhigend
volunteer [ˌvɒlənˈtɪə]	ehrenamtlich tätig sein

Unit 2
Protecting children

abuse [əˈbju:s]	Missbrauch
at risk [æt ˈrɪsk]	gefährdet
authorised [ˈɔ:θəraɪzd]	ermächtigt
budgeting [ˈbʌdʒɪtɪŋ]	Haushaltsplanung
congenital [kənˈdʒenɪtəl]	angeboren
consent [kənˈsent]	Bewilligung
dietician [ˌdaɪəˈtɪʃən]	Ernährungswissenschaftler
disadvantaged [ˌdɪsədˈvɑ:ntɪʒd]	benachteiligt
disclose [dɪsˈkləʊz]	offenbaren

disruptive [dɪsˈrʌptɪv]	unterbrechend
distressed [dɪsˈtrest]	bekümmert
excerpt [ˈekss:pt]	Ausschnitt
foster [ˈfɒstə]	in Pflege haben, fördern
foster child/parents [ˈfɒstə ˌtʃaɪld / ˈpeərənts]	Pflegekind/-eltern
impact [ˈɪmpækt]	Auswirkung
impair [ɪmˈpeə]	beeinträchtigen
inappropriate [ˌɪnəˈprəʊpriət]	unangemessen
investigation [ɪnˌvestɪˈgeɪʃən]	Untersuchung
justified [ˈdʒʌstɪfaɪd]	berechtigt
lawfully [ˈlɔ:fʊli]	rechtmäßig
minutes [ˈmɪnɪts]	Protokoll
moderate [ˈmɒdərət]	gemäßigt
monitor [ˈmɒnɪtə]	überwachen
neglect [nɪˈglekt]	Nachlässigkeit
overcrowded [ˌəʊvəˈkraʊdɪd]	überbelegt
praise [preɪz]	loben
prediction [prɪˈdɪkʃən]	Voraussage
reassure [ri:əˈʃʊə]	beruhigen
record [rɪˈkɔ:d]	erfassen
refer [rɪˈfɜ:]	verweisen
session [ˈseʃən]	Sitzung
sharing [ˈʃeərɪŋ]	Austausch
significant [sɪgˈnɪfɪkənt]	bedeutend
slight [slaɪt]	gering
speech therapy [ˈspi:tʃ ˌθerəpi]	Logopädie
supportive [səˈpɔ:tɪv]	unterstützend
vulnerable [ˈvʌlnərəbl]	verwundbar
welfare [ˈwelfeə]	Wohl

Unit 3
Social background

admissions policy [ədˈmɪʃənz ˈpɒlɪsi]	Zulassungsverfahren
afford sth. [əˈfɔ:d ˌsʌmθɪŋ]	sich etw. leisten
asylum seeker [əˈsaɪləm ˈsi:kə]	Asylsuchende/-r
attend school [əˌtend ˈsku:l]	die Schule besuchen
chief executive [ˈtʃi:f ɪgˈzekjətɪv]	Geschäftsleiter/-in
cite [saɪt]	zitieren
conspicuous [kənˈspɪkjuəs]	auffällig
day care facility [ˈdeɪ ˌkeə fəˈsɪləti]	Kindertagesbetreuung, Kindertagesstätte
depict sth. [dɪˈpɪkt ˌsʌmθɪŋ]	bildlich darstellen
devastating [ˈdevəsteɪtɪŋ]	verheerend
disappointment [ˌdɪsəˈpɔɪntmənt]	Enttäuschung
emphasise [ˈemfəsaɪz]	betonen
excuse notes [ɪkˈskju:s ˌnəʊts]	Entschuldigung (Schule)
hardship [ˈhɑ:dʃɪp]	Beschwernis
inner city [ˌɪnə ˈsɪti]	Innenstadt
intervene [ɪntəˈvi:n]	eingreifen
job vacancies [ˈdʒɒb ˌveɪkənsiz]	freie Arbeitsstellen
lack (of something) [læk]	Mangel
language proficiency [ˈlæŋwɪdʒ prəˈfɪʃənsi]	Sprachkompetenz

launch a business ['lɔːntʃ ə 'bɪznɪs]	ein Geschäft eröffnen
legal entitlement ['liːgəl ɪn'taɪtəlmənt]	Rechtsanspruch
means [miːnz]	Geldmittel
merge [mɜːdʒ]	fusionieren
nursery ['nɜːsəri]	Kindertagesstätte, Kindergarten, Kinderladen
overhaul [ˌəʊvə'hɔːl]	überholen, ausbessern
perceived [pə'siːvd]	vermeintlich
political persecution [pə'lɪtɪkəl ˌpɜːsɪ'kjuːʃən]	politische Verfolgung
poverty line ['pɒvəti ˌlaɪn]	Armutsgrenze
poverty trap ['pɒvəti ˌtræp]	Armutsfalle
prohibitively expensive [prəʊ'hɪbətɪvli ɪk'spensɪv]	unbezahlbar, unverschämt teuer
refurbish [ˌriː'fɜːbɪʃ]	renovieren
rudimentary [ˌruːdɪ'mentəri]	elementar
self-esteem [ˌselfɪ'stiːm]	Selbstwertgefühl
shortage of ['ʃɔːtɪdʒ ɒf]	Mangel an
shortfall ['ʃɔːtfɔːl]	Fehlmenge, Defizit
single-raising mother ['sɪŋgl ˌreɪzɪŋ 'mʌðə]	alleinerziehende Mutter
social housing [ˌsəʊʃəl 'haʊzɪŋ]	Sozialwohnung
social mobility ['səʊʃəl məʊ'bɪləti]	soziale Mobilität (zwischen den Schichten)
sue [suː], [sjuː]	verklagen
temporary accommodation ['tempərəri əˌkɒmə'deɪʃən]	provisorische Unterkunft
unemployment benefit [ˌʌnɪmplɔɪmənt 'benəfɪt]	Arbeitslosengeld
unification [ˌjuːnɪfɪ'keɪʃən]	Vereinigung
urgent ['ɜːdʒənt]	dringend
vocational college [vəʊ'keɪʃənəl 'kɒlɪdʒ]	berufsbildende Schule
voluntary worker ['vɒləntəri 'wɜːkə]	freiwillige/-r Mitarbeiter/-in
vulnerable ['vʌlnərəbl]	schutzbedürftig, verletzlich
wealthy ['welθi]	reich, wohlhabend
workforce ['wɜːkfɔːs]	Arbeiterschaft

Unit 4
Living in a family

accountant [ə'kaʊntənt]	Buchhalter/-in
amicable ['æmɪkəbl]	friedlich
artificial insemination [ˌɑːtɪ'fɪʃəl ɪnˌsemɪ'neɪʃən]	künstliche Befruchtung
average ['ævərɪdʒ]	Durchschnitt
avoid [ə'vɔɪd]	vermeiden
be bullied [bi 'bʊlid]	eingeschüchtert werden
be made up of sth. [bi meɪd 'ʌp əf sʌmθɪŋ]	aus etw. bestehen
be raised [bi 'reɪzd]	aufgezogen werden
be teased [bi 'tiːzd]	gehänselt werden
benefit ['benəfɪt]	jmd. zugute kommen
biological parents [ˌbaɪə'lɒdʒɪkəl 'peərənts]	leibliche Eltern
blend [blend]	(ver-)mischen
breadwinner ['bredwɪnə]	Ernährer
childless family ['tʃaɪldləs 'fæməli]	kinderlose Familie
commitment [kə'mɪtmənt]	Verpflichtung
consider [kən'sɪdə]	bedenken, erwägen
consist of [kən'sɪst ɒf]	bestehen aus, aus etw. gebildet sein

contraception [ˌkɒntrəˈsepʃən] — Verhütung
divorce [dɪˈvɔːs] — Scheidung, sich scheiden lassen
elope with sb. [ɪˈləʊp wɪð sʌmbədi] — mit jmd. durchbrennen
explore [ɪkˈsplɔː] — erforschen, untersuchen
extend [ɪkˈstend] — erweitern, verlängern
fulfil [fʊlˈfɪl] — verwirklichen
goal [gəʊl] — Ziel
honeymoon [ˈhʌnimuːn] — Flitterwochen
immediate family [ɪˈmiːdiət ˈfæməli] — engste Angehörige
impairment [ɪmˈpeəmənt] — Beeinträchtigung, Schwächung
interaction [ˌɪntərˈækʃən] — Interaktion, Wechselwirkung
judgement [ˈdʒʌdʒmənt] — Beurteilung, Urteil
LGBT family [el dʒiːbiːtiː ˈfæməli] — Regenbogenfamilie
lone mother [ləʊn ˈmʌðə] — alleinerziehende Mutter
maintain sth. [meɪnˈteɪn ˌsʌmθɪŋ] — etw. beibehalten, aufrechterhalten, instand halten
pass away [pɑːs əˈweɪ] — sterben, entschlafen
patch [pætʃ] — Flicken
patchwork [ˈpætʃwɜːk] — Flickenteppich, Flickwerk
ponder sth. [ˈpɒndə sʌmθɪŋ] — etw. durchdenken
previously [ˈpriːviəsli] — vorher
procedure [prəˈsiːdʒə] — Ablauf
prosperous [ˈprɒspərəs] — wohlhabend, florierend
provide [prəʊˈvaɪd] — bereitstellen
rear [rɪə] — jmd. großziehen
related [rɪˈleɪtɪd] — verwandt
reside [rɪˈzaɪd] — seinen Wohnsitz haben
same-sex parents [ˌseɪmseks ˈpeərənts] — gleichgeschlechtliche Eltern
significant [sɪgˈnɪfɪkənt] — bedeutend, beachtlich
single parents [ˌsɪŋgl ˈpeərənts] — alleinerziehende Eltern
sperm donor [ˈspɜːm ˌdəʊnə] — Samenspender
spread out [ˌspred ˈaʊt] — sich ausbreiten
stepchildren [ˈstepˌtʃɪldrən] — Stiefkinder
step-parents [ˈstep ˌpeərənts] — Stiefeltern
stigmatise [ˈstɪgmətaɪz] — brandmarken
support [səˈpɔːt] — Unterstützung
surrogate mother [ˌsʌrəgɪt ˈmʌðə] — Leihmutter
unconditional [ˌʌnkənˈdɪʃənəl] — bedingungslos
value [ˈvæljuː] — Wert

Unit 5
Stages of development

ability [əˈbɪləti] — Fähigkeit, Kompetenz
achieve [əˈtʃiːv] — erreichen
allow [əˈlaʊ] — erlauben
burden with sth. [ˈbɜːdən wɪð sʌmθɪŋ] — mit etw. belasten
confidence [ˈkɒnfɪdəns] — (Selbst-)Vertrauen
context [ˈkɒntekst] — Zusammenhang
develop [dɪˈveləp] — entwickeln, kultivieren
differ from sth. [ˈdɪfə frɒm sʌmθɪŋ] — von etw. abweichen, sich unterscheiden

direct surroundings [ˌdɪrekt səˈraʊndɪŋz]; [ˌdaɪ-]	unmittelbare Umgebung, Umwelt
enable [ɪnˈeɪbl]	ermöglichen
extend into sth. [ɪkˈstend ˌɪntu sʌmθɪŋ]	in etw. hineinreichen
facilitate [fəˈsɪlɪteɪt]	erleichtern
fidelity [fɪˈdeləti]	Treue
(guilt) feelings [(gɪlt) ˈfiːlɪŋz]	(Schuld-)Gefühle
holistic [həʊˈlɪstɪk]	ganzheitlich
immediate environment [ɪˈmiːdiət ɪnˈvaɪərənmənt]	unmittelbare Umgebung, Umwelt
independence [ɪndɪˈpendəns]	Unabhängigkeit
inevitable [ɪnˈevɪtəbl]	unvermeidbar
inhibition [ɪnhɪˈbɪʃən]	Hemmung
interfere [ɪntəˈfɪə]	einmischen
intervene [ɪntəˈviːn]	eingreifen, intervenieren
maturity [məˈtjʊərəti]	Reife
observe [əbˈzɜːv]	beobachten
observation [ˌɒbzəˈveɪʃən]	Beobachtung
perform a task [pəˈfɔːm ə tɑːsk]	eine Aufgabe ausführen
permission [pəˈmɪʃən]	Erlaubnis
permit [pəˈmɪt]	erlauben
persevere [ˌpɜːsɪˈvɪə]	durchhalten, sich beharrlich bemühen
promote [prəˈməʊt]	fördern
purpose [ˈpɜːpəs]	der Zweck
self-esteem [ˈself ɪˈstiːm]	die Selbstachtung
self-inhibiting [ˈself ɪnˈhɪbɪtɪŋ]	selbsthemmend

Unit 6
Working with children under three

acquisition [ˌækwɪˈzɪʃən]	Erwerb
anxiety [æŋˈzaɪəti]	Sorge
appreciate [əˈpriːʃieɪt]	anerkennen, verstehen
apron [ˈeɪprən]	Schürze
assertion [əˈsɜːʃən]	Erklärung, Behauptung
attribute to sth. [əˈtrɪbjuːt tu ˈsʌmθɪŋ]	auf etw. zurückführen
benchmark [ˈbentʃmɑːk]	Maßstab
competency/competence [ˈkɒmpɪtənsi / ˈkɒmpɪtəns]	Fähigkeit, Kompetenz
comply with sth. [kəmˈplaɪ wɪð sʌmθɪŋ]	etw. befolgen
continuity [ˌkɒntɪˈnjuːəti]	durchhalten, Kontinuität
convenient [kənˈviːːniənt]	praktisch, gelegen
convey [kənˈveɪ]	vermitteln, zum Ausdruck bringen
cot [kɒt]	Kinderbettchen, Feldbett
crawl [krɔːl]	krabbeln
crib [krɪb]	Kinderbett
disobedience [ˌdɪsəʊˈbiːdiəns]	Ungehorsam
dispense [dɪˈspens]	austeilen
disturbed [dɪˈstɜːbd]	verhaltensgestört
emergence [ɪˈmɜːdʒəns]	Entstehung, auch: Auftauchen
enhance [ɪnˈhɑːns]	verbessern
equipment [ɪˈkwɪpmənt]	Ausstattung
evident [ˈevɪdənt]	ersichtlich

expectation [ˌekspekˈteɪʃən]	Erwartung
exposure [ɪkˈspəʊʒə]	Kontakt
facility [fəˈsɪləti]	Einrichtung
flannel [ˈflænəl]	Waschlappen
germs [dʒɜːmz]	Keime, Bazillen
grapple with sth. [ˈgræpl wɪð sʌmθɪŋ]	sich mit etw. auseinandersetzen
grasp [grɑːsp]	verstehen, begreifen
immune system [ɪˈmjuːn ˌsɪstəm]	Immunsystem
implicitly [ɪmˈplɪsɪtli]	indirekt
(be) in charge of [(bi) ɪn tʃɑːdʒ ɒf]	für etw. verantwortlich (sein)
inappropriate [ˌɪnəˈprəʊpriət]	ungeeignet
keen [kiːn]	stark
marginal [ˈmɑːdʒɪnəl]	gering
medium [ˈmiːdiəm]	Medium
multiplicity [ˌmʌltɪˈplɪsəti]	Vielzahl
nappy [ˈnæpi]	Windel
negotiation skills [nɪˌgəʊʃiˈeɪʃən ˌskɪlz]	Verhandlungsgeschick
observe [əbˈzɜːv]	beachten
pacify [ˈpæsɪfaɪ]	beruhigen
perception [pəˈsepʃən]	Wahrnehmung
potty [ˈpɒti]	Töpfchen
provision [prəˈvɪʒən]	Bereitstellung, Beschaffung
relieve [rɪˈliːv]	lindern, abbauen
reluctant [rɪˈlʌktənt]	zögernd, unwillig
retain [rɪˈteɪn]	beibehalten
salary [ˈsæləri]	Einkommen
soiled [ˈsɔɪld]	verschmutzt
sound [saʊnd]	heil, stabil
subsidised [ˈsʌbsɪdaɪzd]	subventioniert
susceptible [səˈseptəbl]	anfällig
transition [trænˈzɪʃən]	Übergang
validate [ˈvælɪdeɪt]	etw. bestätigen
waste [weɪst]	Abfall

Unit 7
Growing up

adolescent [ˌædəˈlesənt]	Jugendliche/-r
amygdala [əˈmɪgdələ]	Amygdala (Teil des menschlichen Gehirns)
be fixed on sth. [bi ˈfɪkst ɒn sʌmθɪŋ]	eingenommen sein von etw.
bulge [bʌldʒ]	Wölbung, Rundung
bullying [ˈbʊliɪŋ]	Mobbing
bum [bʌm]	Hintern, Po
conduct [ˈkɒndʌkt]	Verhalten
deluge [ˈdeljuːdʒ]	überschwemmen
device [dɪˈvaɪs]	Gerät
disadvantaged [ˌdɪsədˈvɑːntɪdʒd]	benachteiligt
distorted [dɪˈstɔːtɪd]	verzerrt
dote on sb. [ˈdəʊt ɒn sʌmbədi]	jmd. verhätscheln
eagerness [ˈiːgənəs]	Eifer, Ungeduld
encumbrance [ɪnˈkʌmbrəns]	Belastung
erratic [ɪˈrætɪk]	sprunghaft, launisch

erupt [ɪˈrʌpt]	ausbrechen
exhibit [ɪgˈzɪbɪt]	aufzeigen
facial expression [ˈfeɪʃəl ɪkˈspreʃən]	Gesichtsausdruck
futile [ˈfjuːtaɪl]	aussichtslos
hover [ˈhɒvə]	über etwas schweben
humiliation [hjuːˌmɪliˈeɪʃən]	Erniedrigung
inappropriate [ˌɪnəˈprəʊpriət]	unangebracht
inevitable [ɪˈnevɪtəbl]	unabwendbar
mature [məˈtjʊə]	reifen, sich entwickeln
mood swings [muːd swɪŋz]	Stimmungsschwankungen
numb [nʌm]	betäuben
obstacles [ˈɒbstəklz]	Hürden, Hindernisse
offset sth. [ˌɒfˈset sʌmθɪŋ]	etwas ausgleichen
offspring [ˈɒfsprɪŋ]	Nachwuchs
pamper sb. [ˈpæmpə sʌmbədi]	jmd. verwöhnen
paragon [ˈpærəgən]	Vorbild
placid [ˈplæsɪd]	gelassen, seelenruhig
predestined [ˌpriːˈdestɪnd]	prädestiniert
premises [ˈpremɪsɪz]	Räumlichkeiten
prenatal [ˌpriːˈneɪtəl]	vorgeburtlich, pränatal
preoccupation [priːˌɒkjəˈpeɪʃən]	Beschäftigung, Vertieftsein
protruding [prəˈtruːdɪŋ]	hinausragend
quarrel [ˈkwɒrəl]	Streit
self-reliant [ˌselfrɪˈlaɪənt]	selbstständig
sober [ˈsəʊbə]	nüchtern
social cues [ˈsəʊʃəl kjuːz]	Signale durch Gesten und Körpersprache
spiteful [ˈspaɪtfʊl]	gemein, gehässig
spread rumours [ˌspred ˈruːməz]	Gerüchte verbreiten
stone (plural: stone) [stəʊn]	6,35 kg (brit. Gewichtseinheit)
stoop to sth. [ˈstuːp tu sʌmθɪŋ]	sich zu etw. herablassen
succumb to sb./sth. [səˈkʌm tu sʌmbədi / sʌmθɪŋ]	jmd./et w. erliegen
surveillance [səˈveɪləns]	Überwachung
thrills [θrɪlz]	Kicks, Angstlust
undermine [ˌʌndəˈmaɪn]	untergraben
unduly [ʌnˈdjuːli]	unangemessenerweise
vicariously [vɪˈkeəriəsli]	indirekt
vulnerable [ˈvʌlnərəbl]	verwundbar, gefährdet

Unit 8
Food and health

accuse [əˈkjuːz]	anklagen
airwaves [ˈeəweɪvz]	Ätherwellen
anxious [ˈæŋkʃəs]	besorgt
appeal to [əˈpiːl tu]	gefallen
benefits [ˈbenəfɪts]	Vorteile
body mass index [ˈbɒdi mæs ˈɪndeks]	Körpergewichtsindex
collapse [kəˈlæps]	einstürzen
concise [kənˈsaɪs]	knapp und präzise
consistently [kənˈsɪstəntli]	beständig
crack [kræk]	Riss

decline [dɪˈklaɪn] – senken
deprive [dɪˈpraɪv] – aberkennen, entziehen
determining [dɪˈtɜːmɪnɪŋ] – bestimmend
digest [daɪˈdʒest] – verdauen
disorder [dɪˈsɔːdə] – Erkrankung
disruption [dɪsˈrʌpʃən] – Unterbrechung
equivalent [ɪˈkwɪvələnt] – gleichwertig
impact [ɪmˈpækt] – Auswirkungen haben
initiate [ɪˈnɪʃieɪt] – einleiten
nutrition [njuːˈtrɪʃən] – Essen, Nahrung
nutritional advisor [njuːˈtrɪʃənəl ədˈvaɪzə] – Ernährungsberater
obesity [əʊˈbiːsəti] – Fettleibigkeit
plug [plʌg] – verstopfen
pulse [pʌls] – Hülsenfrucht
ratings [ˈreɪtɪŋz] – Einschaltquoten
reliance [rɪˈlaɪəns] – Vertrauen
tough [tʌf] – hart
tricky [ˈtrɪki] – verzwickt
unsuitable [ʌnˈsjuːtəbl] – ungeeignet

Unit 9
Disability and illness

alleged [əˈledʒd] – angeblich
attachment [əˈtætʃmənt] – Verbundenheit
attitude [ˈætɪtjuːd] – Gesinnung
barking [ˈbɑːkɪŋ] – bellend
bereavement [bɪˈriːvmənt] – Todesfall
blotchy [ˈblɒtʃi] – fleckig
Braille [breɪl] – Blindenschrift
breastfeeding [ˈbrestfiːdɪŋ] – Stillen
conduct [kənˈdʌkt] – durchführen
dexterity [deksˈterəti] – Geschicklichkeit
diarrhoea [ˌdaɪəˈrɪə] – Durchfall
facilities [fəˈsɪlətiz] – Anlageteile
famine [ˈfæmɪn] – Hungersnot
feeble [ˈfiːbl] – schwach
framework [ˈfreɪmwɜːk] – Bezugssystem
geared to [gɪəd tu] – abgestimmt auf
ground-breaking [ˈgraʊndˌbreɪkɪŋ] – bahnbrechend
grounds [graʊndz] – Gelände, Gründe
human rights [ˌhjuːmən ˈraɪts] – Menschenrechte
humiliating [hjuːˈmɪlieɪtɪŋ] – demütigend
incapacity [ˌɪnkəˈpæsəti] – Unfähigkeit
inevitable [ɪˈnevɪtəbl] – unvermeidlich
jumbled [ˈdʒʌmbld] – durcheinander
limb [lɪm] – Glied
mainstream [ˈmeɪnstriːm] – einbinden
measles [ˈmiːzlz] – Masern
moral obligation [ˈmɒrəl ˌɒblɪˈgeɪʃən] – moralische Verpflichtung
natural disaster [ˈnætʃərəl dɪˈzɒːstə] – Naturkatastrophe
numeracy [ˈnjuːmərəsi] – Rechenkenntnis

nutrition [njuːˈtrɪʃən]	Ernährung
objectives [əbˈdʒektɪvz]	Ziele
occupational therapist [ˌɒkjəˈpeɪʃənəl ˈθerəpɪst]	Ergotherapeut/-in
occupational therapy [ˌɒkjəˈpeɪʃənəl ˈθerəpi]	Ergotherapie
outnumber [ˌaʊtˈnʌmbə]	(zahlenmäßig) übertreffen
post-traumatic stress disorder ˌpəʊsttrɔ :ˌmætɪkˈstresdɪˌsɔːdə	posttraumatische Belastungsstörung
prolong [prəʊˈlɒŋ]	verlängern
protection [prəˈtekʃən]	Schutz
raspy [ˈrɑːspi]	kratzend
reaffirm [ˌriːəˈfɜːm]	beteuern
refugee [ˌrefjʊˈdʒiː]	Flüchtling
rubella/German measles [ruːˈbelə / ˈdʒɜːmən ˈmiːzlz]	Röteln
segregated [ˈsegrɪgeɪtɪd]	getrennt
shelter [ˈʃeltə]	Obdach, Schutz
siblings [ˈsɪblɪŋz]	Geschwister
special needs [ˈspeʃəl niːdz]	besondere Förderung
tailored [ˈteɪləd]	angepasst
testimony [ˈtestɪməni]	Zeugnis
threatening [ˈθretnɪŋ]	bedrohlich
trafficker [ˈtræfɪkə]	Schleuser
transformation [ˌtrænsfəˈmeɪʃən]	Verwandlung
transition [trænˈzɪʃən]	Übergang
Treasury [ˈtreʒəri]	Finanzministerium
violence [ˈvaɪələns]	Gewalt
ward [wɔːd]	Station
whooping cough [ˈhuːpɪŋkɒf]	Keuchhusten

Unit 10
Ethnic diversity

acquire sth. [əˈkwaɪə sʌmθɪŋ]	etw. erwerben
adopt [əˈdɒpt]	annehmen
advent [ədˈvent]	Beginn
alienated [ˈeɪliəneɪtɪd]	befremdet, entfremdet
appeal [əˈpiːl]	Anreiz
assumption [əˈsʌmpʃən]	Annahme, Vermutung
citizenship [ˈsɪtɪzənʃɪp]	Bürgerschaft, Staatsangehörigkeit
dedicated [ˈdedɪkeɪtɪd]	zweckbestimmt
delayed [dɪˈleɪd]	verspätet
distorted [dɪˈstɔːtɪd]	verzerrt
effective [ɪˈfektɪv]	wirksam
embrace [ɪmˈbreɪs]	einbeziehen
encounter [ɪnˈkaʊntə]	antreffen
enrich [ɪnˈrɪtʃ]	bereichern
homogeneous [ˌhɒməˈdʒiːniəs]	gleichartig
imperceptible [ˌɪmpəˈseptəbl]	unmerklich
in the midst of [ɪn ðə mɪdst ɒf]	inmitten von, unter
indigenous [ɪnˈdɪdʒənəs]	einheimisch
indistinguishable [ˌɪndɪˈstɪŋgwɪʃəbl]	ununterscheidbar

influx ['ɪnflʌks] — Zustrom
inhabitants [ɪn'hæbɪtənts] — Einwohnerschaft
instructions [ɪn'strʌkʃənz] — Anweisungen
intertwine [ˌɪntə'twaɪn] — ineinandergreifen
interweave [ˌɪntə'wiːv] — verweben
issue ['ɪʃuː] — Frage, Thema, Angelegenheit
perceive [pə'siːv] — wahrnehmen
reluctant [rɪ'lʌktənt] — unwillig
representation [ˌreprɪzen'teɪʃən] — Darstellung, Vertretung
reputable ['repjətəbl] — achtbar
tackle ['tækl] — anpacken
vibrant ['vaɪbrənt] — lebhaft

Unit 11
Social learning and behaviour

ambitious [æm'bɪʃəs] — ehrgeizig
aptitude ['æptɪtjuːd] — Fähigkeit
bleak [bliːk] — düster, trostlos
blur [blɜː] — verwischen
clay [kleɪ] — Knete
contest [kən'test] — bestreiten
cope with sth. [kəʊp wɪð sʌmθɪŋ] — mit etw. fertigwerden
deliberately [dɪ'lɪbərətli] — absichtlich
deprivation [ˌdeprɪ'veɪʃən] — Entzug, Mangel
designated ['dezɪgneɪtɪd] — vorgesehen
detrimental [ˌdetrɪ'mentəl] — schädlich, nachteilig
distract sb. [dɪ'strækt sʌmbədi] — jmd. ablenken
endorse [ɪn'dɔːs] — befürworten
engage in sth. [ɪn'geɪdʒ ɪn sʌmθɪŋ] — sich mit etw. beschäftigen
fuss [fʌs] — Aufhebens
gadgets ['gædʒɪts] — technische Spielerei
gratification [ˌgrætɪfɪ'keɪʃən] — Belohnung
implication [ˌɪmplɪ'keɪʃən] — Auswirkung, Konsequenz
innate [ɪ'neɪt] — angeboren
make-believe ['meɪk bɪˌliːv] — Fantasie
predisposition [ˌpriːdɪspə'zɪʃən] — Veranlagung
rebuttal [rɪ'bʌtəl] — Widerlegung
resist [rɪ'zɪst] — widerstehen
reward [rɪ'wɔːd] — Belohnung
self-regulation [ˌself regjə'leɪʃən] — Selbstregulierung
spatial skills ['speɪʃəl skɪlz] — räumliche Wahrnehmung
temptation [temp'teɪʃən] — Verlockung
unadulterated [ˌʌnə'dʌltəreɪtɪd] — ungetrübt, unverfälscht

Unit 12
Emergencies in daily life

accident ['æksɪdənt] — Unfall
ambulance ['æmbjələns] — Krankenwagen
anchored ['æŋkəd] — befestigt
bear the weight [beə ðə weɪt] — das Gewicht tragen
blade [bleɪd] — Klinge
bruise [bruːz] — blauer Fleck

cardiopulmonary resuscitation [ˌkɑːdiəʊˈpʌlmənəri rɪˌsʌsɪˈteɪʃən] – Herz-Lungen-Reanimation
cause [kɔːz] – Ursache
checklist [ˈtʃeklɪst] – Überprüfungsliste
choke on sth. [tʃəʊk ɒn sʌmθɪŋ] – sich an etw. verschlucken
climbing frame [ˈklaɪmɪŋ ˌfreɪm] – Klettergerüst
comprehensive [ˌkɒmprɪˈhensɪv] – umfassend
emergency room [ɪˈmɜːdʒənsi ˌrʊm] – Notaufnahme
exercise caution [ˈeksəsaɪz ˈkɔːʃən] – Vorsicht walten lassen
fire drill [ˈfaɪə ˌdrɪl] – Feuerübung
guardrail [ˈgɑːdreɪl] – Absturzsicherung
harmful [ˈhɑːmfʊl] – gesundheitsschädlich
health and safety [helθ ənd ˈseɪfti] – Sicherheit und Gesundheitsschutz
heatstroke [ˈhiːtstrəʊk] – Hitzschlag
imaginativeness [ɪˈmædʒɪnətɪvnəs] – Ideenreichtum, Phantasiereichtum
impair one's health [ɪmˈpeə wʌnz helθ] – seiner Gesundheit schaden
incident report [ˈɪnsɪdənt rɪˈpɔːt] – Vorgangsbericht
injury [ˈɪndʒəri] – Verletzung
lose one's footing [luːz wʌnz ˈfʊtɪŋ] – Halt verlieren
paramedic [ˌpærəˈmedɪk] – Rettungssanitäter
pedestrian crossing [pɪˈdestriən ˈkrɒsɪŋ] – Fußgängerübergang
playthings [ˈpleɪθɪŋz] – Spielzeuge
poisoning [ˈpɔɪzənɪŋ] – Vergiftung
poorly ventilated room [ˈpʊəli ˈventɪleɪtɪd rʊm] – schlecht gelüfteter Raum
position [pəˈzɪʃən] – Stellung
prompt [prɒmt] – anregen
public transport [ˈpʌblɪk ˈtrænspɔːt] – öffentlicher Personennahverkehr
reassuring [ˌriːəˈʃʊərɪŋ] – beruhigend
requirements [rɪˈkwaɪəmənts] – Anforderungen
scope [skəʊp] – Spielraum
skirting board [ˈskɜːtɪŋbɔːd] – Scheuerleiste, Sockelleiste
smoke detector [ˈsməʊk dɪˌtektə] – Rauchmelder
suffocation [ˌsʌfəˈkeɪʃən] – Erstickung
supervise [ˈsjuːpəvaɪz] – beaufsichtigen, kontrollieren, überwachen

Unit 13
Conflict management

admonishment [ədˈmɒnɪʃmənt] – Ermahnung
anticipate [ænˈtɪsɪpeɪt] – erwarten
archaic [ɑːˈkeɪɪk] – altertümlich
blameful [ˈbleɪmfʊl] – tadelnswert
bribe [braɪb] – bestechen
coax sb. to do sth. [kəʊks sʌmbədi tu duː sʌmθɪŋ] – jmd. etw. entlocken; jmd. dazu bringen, etw. zu tun
cut sb. some slack [kʌt sʌmbədi sʌm slæk] – Nachsicht mit jmd. haben
diligence [ˈdɪlɪdʒəns] – Fleiß
discourage [dɪˈskʌrɪdʒ] – entmutigen
domineering [ˌdɒmɪˈnɪərɪŋ] – herrisch
forcible isolation [ˈfɔːsəbl ˌaɪsəˈleɪʃən] – Time-out-Technik
fuss [fʌs] – Lärm/Aufhebens machen
generosity [ˌdʒenəˈrɒsəti] – Großzügigkeit

lax [læks]	locker, lasch
mischief [ˈmɪstʃɪf]; [-tʃiːf]	Übermut, Unheil
permissive [pəˈmɪsɪv]	freizügig, erlaubend
praise [preɪz]	Lob
prospects [ˈprɒspekts]	Erfolgsaussichten
resolute [ˈrezəluːt]	entschieden, resolut
scold [skəʊld]	ausschimpfen, schelten
smack [smæk]	Klaps geben
spank [spæŋk]	Klaps geben
tact [tækt]	Takt
verbal reward [ˈvɜːbəl rɪˈwɔːd]	Lob
well-adjusted [ˌweləˈdʒʌstɪd]	ausgeglichen

Bildquellenverzeichnis

Adobe Stock: S. 8 (danielabarreto), 16 (dglimages), 32 (Christin Lola), 51.1 (Spencer), 58 (drubig-photo), 65 (WavebreakMediaMicro), 66 (Jaren Wicklund), 67 (xana_ukr), 71 (Monkey Business), 75 (dglimages), 92 (Pavla Zakova), 102 (matka_Wariatka), 109 (Creative Mood), 111 (Argus), 113 (pressmaster), 114 (Myst), 118.1 (ruslanshug), 118.2 (micmacpics), 118.3 (paul_brighton), 118.4 (Maksud), 118.5 (kreygscottphoto), 119.1 (istetiana), 119.2 (koss13), 120 (Olga Nayashkova), 121.1 (John Takai), 121.2 (MR), 123 (Alena Ozerova), 126.1 (Pavla Zakova), 126.2 (Africa Studio), 127 (eldarnurkovic), 128 (pep), 141 (Prazis Images), 142 (Roman Bodnarchuk), 143 (JEGAS RA), 144 (Giovanni Cancemi), 145 (Lefteris Papaulakis), 148.4 (Alen-D), 155 (alexandre zveiger), 156.1 (Monkey Business), 156.2 (iofoto), 160 (Daxiao Productions), 164 (gpointstudio), 167 (Lorelyn Medina), 170 (Dron), 174.1 (Cherry-Merry), 174.2 (Christian Schwier), 176 (fovito), 178 (Africa Studio), 181 (sanchairat), 183.1 (pixelaway), 183.2 (pixelaway), 193 (diego cervo), 194 (LangnerRT)

Children's Defense Fund & U.S. Census Bureau: S. 57.1

Fotolia Deutschland GmbH: S. 7 (wildworx), 9.1 (babimu), 9.2 (Steve Wright), 9.3 (Helmut Brands), 9.4 (Paul Maguire), 9.5 (Kasia Gryniewicz), 11 (micromonkey), 13 (KaYann), 14.1 (nyul), 14.2 (Pavel Losevsky), 19 (Neo Edmund), 36 (Kati Molin), 37 (artivista | werbeatelier), 39 (Yuri Arcurs), 40 (Hugh O'Neill), 41 (tarajane), 42 (anandkrish16), 45 (Gennadiy Poznyakov), 46 (Monart Design), 48 (pojoslaw), 49 (soupstock), 51.2 (Andriy Petrenko), 53 (Adam Gregor), 55.1 (contrastwerkstatt), 55.2 (contrastwerkstatt), 56 (emily2k), 60 (Elenathewise), 62 (mangostock), 63 (Yuri Arcurs), 69 (AGphotographer), 78 (matka_Wariatka), 81 (Grum_l), 82 (yanlev), 83 (Yuri Arcurs), 84 (frankoppermann), 85.1 (Ella), 85.2 (ChristArt), 86 (lunamarina), 88 (sparkmom), 90 (Markus Bormann), 91 (kentoh), 97 (Szasz-Fabian Erika), 98 (Tomas Sereda), 100 (Susan Stevenson), 103 (jeecis), 104 (Anita P Peppers), 106.1 (jjpixs), 106.2 (MAK), 107 (David Davis), 110 (mogwai), 132 (Jaren Wicklund), 133 (robert mobley), 136 (barneyboogles), 137 (kameel), 140 (st-fotograf), 147 (Franz Pfluegl), 148.1 (Gina Sanders), 148.2 (Yuri Arcurs), 148.3 (Christian Jung), 149 (rootsartz), 150 (Andres Rodriguez), 152 (bojorgensen), 153 (iQoncept), 158 (Monkey Business), 161 (Berna Şafoğlu), 163.1 (BlueOrange Studio), 163.2 (Brebca), 163.3 (Kathrin39), 165 (elisabetta figus), 168 (jeancliclac), 169 (Julie Hagan), 171 (auremar), 173 (Kzenon), 175 (matka_Wariatka), 179 (pegbes), 182 (fotodesign-jegg.de), 188 (somenski), 189 (somenski) 190 (Marek), 191 (OlgaLIS), 196 (Kwest), 197 (Felix Mizioznikov), 198 (Johan Larson), 199 (dedMazay)

Frances Kregler: S. 21, 22, 93, 95

iStockPhoto: S. 184 (lukaves)

Shutterstock: S. 57.2 (Yermek)

ullstein bild: S. 79 (The Granger Collection)

Oliver Wetterauer/Bildungsverlag EINS: S. 15, 43

Umschlagfoto: Adobe Stock (VadimGuzhva)

Wir arbeiten sehr sorgfältig daran, für den Abdruck aller Bilder die Rechteinhaberinnen und Rechteinhaber zu ermitteln. Sollte uns dies im Einzelfall nicht vollständig gelungen sein, werden berechtigte Ansprüche selbstverständlich im Rahmen der üblichen Vereinbarungen abgegolten.